DIRTY GOURMET
PLANT POWER

DIRTY GOURMET
PLANT
POWER

FOOD FOR YOUR OUTDOOR ADVENTURES

AIMEE TRUDEAU | EMILY NIELSON | MAI-YAN KWAN

SKIPSTONE

Published by Skipstone, an imprint of Mountaineers Books—an independent, nonprofit publisher
Skipstone and its colophon are registered trademarks of The Mountaineers organization.

Printed in China
26 25 24 23   1 2 3 4 5

Copyeditor: Kristi Hein
Design: Jen Grable
Cover photograph: *Mighty Meal Salad*
All photographs by the authors unless credited otherwise
Photographs on pages 5 (bottom), 10, 14, 26, 53, 58, 63, 111, 219, 247, and 317 © Daniel Pouliot
Photographs on pages 9 (middle), 12, 201, 318, and 319 © Virginia Trudeau

Library of Congress Control Number: 2022951854

Printed on FSC®-certified materials

ISBN (paperback): 978-1-68051-630-2
ISBN (ebook): 978-1-68051-631-9

FSC
www.fsc.org
MIX
Paper | Supporting
responsible forestry
FSC® C008047

Skipstone books may be purchased for corporate, educational, or other promotional sales, and our authors are available for a wide range of events. For information on special discounts or booking an author, contact our customer service at 800.553.4453 or mbooks@mountaineersbooks.org.

Skipstone
1001 SW Klickitat Way, Suite 201
Seattle, Washington 98134
206.223.6303
www.skipstonebooks.org
www.mountaineersbooks.org

LIVE LIFE. MAKE RIPPLES.

CONTENTS

The Guide

The Recipes

RECIPE INDEX

LUNCHES

MAINS

SIDE DISHES

INTRODUCTION
We're on an Adventure Together!

You are our audience. We see you out there, enjoying the outdoors, just as we hoped you would. We want to be a part of *your* outdoor experience, no matter where you are going or what you are doing.

The world has evolved a lot since our first book, *Dirty Gourmet: Food for Your Outdoor Adventures*, and we have too. We have new ideas to share, and we've developed a list of fabulous recipes that we hope will empower you to cook for your needs, your trip, your family, and your outdoor experience—whether that's among the trees, at the beach, or simply in your backyard. Our recipes are delicious and practical for virtually any outdoor setting.

The recipes in this book are 100-percent plant-based. That does not mean, however, that all of your outdoor meals must be 100-percent plant-based—ours aren't! We simply have found over time that, for a number of reasons, plant-based recipes work best for outdoor cooking. First, perishability is less of a concern for plant-based foods. Second, plant-

based eating is a natural common denominator, since everyone should eat fruits and vegetables. You cannot easily make multiple meals in the outdoors to accommodate individual needs, so making one meal that works for everyone is ideal. Finally, plants undeniably have a lower impact on the environment than animal products. Whether you are headed deep into the backcountry with no access to refrigeration or you have friends with specific dietary restrictions, plant-based recipes are most likely to see you through.

Most of all, we love the adaptability of plant-based recipes. If you've ever tried to reduce your animal protein consumption, you've undoubtedly struggled to adapt a meat-centric recipe, where you must remove ingredients to make something vegetarian. What we've done is reversed that process by starting with the foods that most people won't need—or want to—remove. *Adding* an ingredient to a recipe—or even to just an individual portion—is much simpler than removing it. So if a recipe in this

new collection doesn't meet your exact needs, just add to or adjust it until it does.

One of our fundamental values is caring for the natural world. It's important to us to teach you how to not only nourish yourselves but also protect and support our public lands. We hope we are leading our readers to be responsible stewards, helping to ensure that future outdoorists can continue to enjoy public landscapes just as they do today.

As always, go forth and remember to make food a true part of your outdoor adventures. Experiment with these recipes, collect stories, and please share them with us. This is a collaboration and an ongoing conversation! Let's continue to be resources for one another so we can keep growing as a food-loving outdoor community.

Happy trails!

THE GUIDE

Camp cooking involves a lot more than simply following a recipe. Once you leave the comfort and convenience of your home kitchen, specific considerations and techniques for outdoor cooking emerge. Fear not! Our combined years of camping and teaching cooking workshops is equal to a lifetime's worth of experience (and mistakes!), and this guide is a distillation of what we have learned. We will first discuss our favorite ingredients in the Plantry (or Plant-Based Pantry) section. Then we'll help you navigate factors that can affect your camp-kitchen setup, like weather and outfitting. Finally, we'll share helpful cooking techniques to set you up for success and satisfaction. If you *still* have questions after reading this guide, please ask us!

PLANTRY

So many people have become plant-curious over the past few years that demand has encouraged food manufacturers to come up with some pretty great new products. These are usually marketed for health and sustainability, but many are also ideal for your outdoor kitchen, thanks to their better shelf stability and reduced risk of cross-contamination (especially in a water-logged cooler). We know it can be a little intimidating and costly to experiment with a lot of new food products, so we are sharing our favorite plant-based ingredients. We hope to inspire you to try them out, and eventually, maybe even fold them into your everyday cooking routine!

VERSATILE PLANT-BASED INGREDIENTS

We aren't afraid to make use of meat or dairy substitutes when that will help us retain the appeal of a favorite recipe, but they aren't always practical or necessary, and obviously plant-based eating should rely heavily on actual plants. There are plenty of whole foods that have their place in perfectly balanced and healthy camping recipes. In fact, we usually find that making recipes more plant-based goes hand in hand with making them more camping-friendly. Here are some that we typically keep handy.

Quick-Cooking Beans

There is an incredible variety of beans in the world, but they don't all lend themselves well to camp cooking. We rely on the quick cookers for a boost of protein, allowing us to do without processed meat substitutes. Our favorites include lentils of all colors, mung beans, split peas, and some canned varieties like chickpeas and white beans.

Dehydrated and Freeze-Dried Products

Do-it-yourself or purchase? That's a common question when assembling ingredients for camp cooking. We've included instructions on how to dehydrate food yourself when possible (see "Dehydrating Food" in the Outdoor Cooking Techniques chapter), but for convenience you can also just buy dehydrated fruits and

vegetables. We don't recommend doing your own freeze-drying of foods: it's a specific process that cannot be easily done in a home context and that often alters the natural texture of the food. Freeze-dried foods can be an asset since they can add crunch to a recipe.

Here are some ingredients we commonly purchase rather than make ourselves:

- Shallot, onion, and garlic flakes or powders
- Lemon juice powder
- Tomato powder
- Dehydrated bean flakes
- Dried chiles
- Freeze-dried peas (better than dehydrated)
- Freeze-dried berries

Nut and Seed Butters

There are so many options now—many are even maple or chocolate flavored! We often have several types in our plantry, which is great for navigating specific nut or legume allergies. We like to use nut butters to add creaminess to cooked grains, salad dressings, and even soups. Many of these are interchangeable, just like plant milks, but they will definitely taste like the nut or seed they're made from. Raw cashew butter tends to be our go-to for simply adding creaminess without a lot of nut-specific flavor. If you'd like to try making your own nut butters, you'll find a few recipes in our earlier book, *Dirty Gourmet: Food for Your Outdoor Adventures*.

Oils

Most home sautéing starts with a drizzle of oil in a hot pan. This isn't different for outdoor cooking, but packing oil is admittedly a challenge and can get messy if not done well. To simplify things, we recommend using prepackaged oil packets, especially for backcountry camping. Olive oil and coconut oil are relatively easy to find in small packets.

Coconut oil is also easy to travel with since it's solid at room temperature and therefore less prone to leaking. Use unrefined coconut oil if you want that coconut flavor, and refined when you don't.

Neutral oils are specified in many of our recipes. These are oils that don't have a strong flavor, such as grapeseed, avocado, or vegetable oil.

Quick-Cooking Noodles

Good choices in this category include thin wheat noodles like ramen and lo mein, rice noodles, soba noodles, and short pasta shapes like penne, orzo, orecchiette, and shells.

Quick-Cooking Grains

Wheat choices include couscous and bulgur; quinoa is a complete protein. Rice can easily be found par-boiled for super quick cooking. White rice—jasmine, basmati—cooks faster than brown but is not as nutritious. Rolled oats and sometimes steel-cut oats also come in a quick-cooking version.

MEAT AND DAIRY SUBSTITUTES

Many plant-based ingredients used in this book are substitutions for typical meat or dairy ingredients. Although we always try to prioritize whole foods over processed, we accept that the myriad processed options make the transition easier and more flavorful in many cases. Some substitutions, like vegetarian sausage or plant-based butter, are close mimics; others, like tofu and cashew cream, have their own fla-vor or texture profiles. Substitutes contribute elements like protein content or creamy textures and create dishes that can stand on their own, regardless of how close or far they are from their meat- or dairy-based counterparts.

Plant-Based Meat Products

There are plant-based alternatives for virtually all types of meat. We've listed our favorite and most frequently used options below.

SAUSAGE: From breakfast patties to beer brats, the plant-based world has probably come the furthest with sausage. Sometimes we call for precooked sausage and sometimes we don't. The Beyond brand sausages look just like meat, complete with casing, and need to be cooked through. Field Roast and Tofurky both make precooked sausage.

GROUND BEEF: You can purchase fresh, frozen, and dehydrated veggie beef crumbles or—even more shocking—ground veggie beef powder. Much of this has been around for years; Beyond and Impossible are two brands leading the way on this front.

CHICKEN: Going by weight consumed annually, chicken is the most popular meat in the US, and it has a distinct texture that many people have a hard time giving up. It can be the trickiest to mimic, though plant-based substitutes are getting better every day. day. There are a few products we rely on heavily because they mimic the texture well.

- *Soy Curls:* These are dehydrated strips of soy that, if you're new to meat substitutes, look like they'll be your worst nightmare, but they are so lightweight and quick to rehydrate that they are a

Charred Tofu

wonderful option for backcountry cooking. We highly recommend them and think they taste great.

- *Seitan:* This is not always used as a true meat mimic—it is simply made from wheat gluten and has been a part of Buddhist cooking for centuries. But it works perfectly well in place of chicken in many sautéed dishes, as it gives you that chewy texture and browns and crisps nicely. This is also a soy-free option for those who have allergies or intolerances to the popular protein. Try our Seitan Adobo (page 188) for the best showcase of seitan masquerading as chicken.

PORK: Jackfruit is a very large fruit that can be found fresh or canned in brine. It breaks down into a nice shredded texture that works well in place of pulled pork in classic dishes like barbecue and carnitas. Another soy-free option, it is low in protein, so it's used to mimic the tex-ture, rather than provide the nutritional profile, of meat.

Soy for Soy's Sake

Many meat alternatives are soy-based, but soy was a commonly used plant protein long before the first veggie burger was created. It can be great just as it is, without trying to mimic something different.

TOFU: Finally we come to tofu. The most common, most widely used, most revered, and most scorned of plant proteins used in place of meat. Yes, we use plenty of tofu throughout our book—don't be put off! All three of us have been through a tofu-hating stage and came through it just fine. As with most new foods, you just need to learn how to prepare it. Our recipes should make it easy to love, as we have ensured depth of flavor and enjoyable texture. This is a high-protein food, so it works well as the centerpiece of many dishes.

HOW TO PRESS TOFU

Tofu can be pressed with any heavy, flat-bottomed implement, such as a cast iron skillet or a cutting board. Simply wrap the tofu in a clean dishtowel or paper towels and place the heavy item on top for about 15 minutes to remove most of the water. The water may drip, so make sure you do this over a surface that can catch the drips.

TEMPEH: This fermented soybean product is not as well known as tofu and can be tricky to fall in love with at first sight. Mai-Yan's Spicy and Sweet Tempeh Stir-Fry (page 181) will surely delight you no matter your experience with this extremely healthy ingredient, and we suspect you will be looking for many more ways to use it.

Plant-Based Dairy Products

As we've gone on our own journey to include more plant-based ingredients in our diets, we've saved the dairy adjustment for last—because we once thought, *Who can live without dairy and still be happy?!* Unfortunately, dairy is perishable and does not generally travel well on outdoor adventures. Use your camp cooking as an opportunity to try some dairy alternatives.

PLANT MILKS: These have been readily available for quite a while and are fairly common in our American culture these days. You can easily find oat, soy, and rice milk at almost any grocery outlet, and suppliers are coming out with other options focused on closer-to-dairy taste, higher nutrient content, and more sustainable farming practices. For most recipes these milks are interchangeable, so feel free to use what you're most familiar with. If a recipe requires a particular plant milk, we specify it. The most common ones we use are soy milk for its protein content, oat milk for its creaminess, and coconut milk when we aren't trying to mimic dairy flavor.

You will also see powdered versions of these milks called out in Backcountry Recipes. We've enjoyed having these on hand so much that we often use them in place of the liquid version even when weight and space aren't an issue. We always like to maximize space in our coolers for the important stuff (snacks and drinks!).

BUTTER: For a long time, the only vegan option was Earth Balance. It is still great, but definitely is more like margarine than butter. Now you can find actual cultured plant butters that give you the full buttery experience. Our favorite cultured butter is Miyoko's. If you're baking or want a really great butter flavor, that's our recommendation. If you're simply spreading it on toast, however, go with a plastic-tub style, which can handle the melty ice in the cooler better (we generally pack either butter style in a waterproof container to be on the safe side, though).

CHEESE: Like tofu, plant-based cheese can be a deal breaker for those trying to go vegan. Even

Butter with a Side of Vegetables

cheeses, our favorite brands include Violife, Chao, Follow Your Heart, and Miyoko's.

On top of all that, we like to use other ingredients that add creaminess or sharpness without using a cheese substitute. You'll love our Cashew Dream Sauce (page 288) as the base to pasta sauces or dips. You may find you can't live without having a large jar of our Nutty Parmesan (page 288) in both your home kitchen and your camp bin. Cashew butter makes for amazing cheesy grits in the backcountry. We will teach you the ways!

Baking Helpers and Egg Replacers

Baking without eggs can seem impossible, but there are several substitutes that make it surprisingly easy.

FLAX AND CHIA SEEDS: These seeds are tiny but pack a mighty punch of protein and fiber; they are also a great binder, so you can use them in place of eggs in baked goods without adding anything perishable or breakable to your ingredients. Most recipes that call for a "flax egg" suggest that you mix 1 tablespoon of ground flax meal with 3 tablespoons of water to create that egg and then add it to the batter. We realized that we could usually add the flax meal directly to the dry batter ingredients. This way you can pack in fewer containers and avoid dirtying another dish when it comes time to make it.

CHICKPEA FLOUR: We are super impressed with how chickpea flour can take the place of eggs in outdoor cooking. It is basically the whole batter for our French Toast (page 118) and the eggy topping in our savory Socca Tortilla (page 234).

the most committed vegans often struggle to enjoy vegan cheese and will often just skip it in a recipe. In all honesty, it is *not* the same as a beautiful high-quality cheese—yet. But the world is a-changin'! With so many more people trying out all the new vegan cheese varieties, good ones are rising to the top, which creates competition, and the cheeses are getting sooo much better! Even if you aren't into snacking on vegan cheese, there are quesos and soft spreads and shredded cheeses that add so much flavor to a dish, you won't even care that it is dairy-free. For off-the-shelf plant-based

UMAMI FLAVOR MAKERS

Umami is one of the more recently identified tastes (besides the familiar sweet, bitter, sour, and salty); it means "essence of deliciousness" in Japanese. This is an important flavor profile, and many of the following ingredients are included in our recipes.

MISO PASTE: This fermented soybean paste adds a lot of flavor to broths and sauces.

NUTRITIONAL YEAST: This dry, flaky product is one that you wouldn't consider buying unless you were looking for it specifically. It's not only very nutritious but also gives a sharp Parmesan quality to whatever it's used in (and we do use it in our Nutty Parmesan, page 288). We love it straight on popcorn or garlic bread, and it's a major ingredient in our homemade Bouillon Powder (page 286). Make sure you get the fortified version (most are) so you get a B-12 boost.

BOUILLON: Vegetable broth or stock is a wonderful base for soups and pastas, but it is not very practical to schlep outdoors. Luckily, there are many types of bouillon you can use, from cubes to pastes; we have created our own Bouillon Powder recipe that adds umami without adding weight or perishability.

MUSHROOMS: Mushrooms add umami and a meaty texture and flavor to dishes that don't necessarily rely heavily on meat substitutes. There are a variety of types, and they come fresh, dried, and powdered.

SURPRISE! THEY'RE PLANT-BASED

There are many ingredients that just happen to be plant-based and that you may have been using all along. Others might be less familiar, like nutritional yeast and tahini, but we hope you will give them a try. The most popular brands of these products are usually plant-based, but check ingredients to be sure.

- Crescent roll dough
- Biscuit dough
- Puff pastry
- Graham crackers
- Instant pudding mix

SURPRISE! THEY AREN'T PLANT-BASED

And then there are the foods that you'd never guess contain animal products, but frequently they do.

WORCESTERSHIRE: Traditional versions of this sauce usually include anchovies, so check the ingredients list or look for the word "plant-based" or "vegan" on the label.

MARSHMALLOWS: Marshmallows aren't naturally vegetarian, as they're made with gelatin, an animal product. Trader Joe's makes vegan marshmallows; so does the Dandies brand.

CHOCOLATE: Even some dark chocolate contains dairy as an ingredient, especially the mainstream grocery-store brands. But the chocolate that has a higher cocoa powder content will often be plant-based. Some newer brands have started making coconut- or oat-milk chocolate, and the bigger brands are catching on quickly.

SOURCING INGREDIENTS

The internet has changed the game of sourcing specialty ingredients for all types of cooking-related activities, and it has allowed us to get more in-depth with camp cooking. It also has allowed us to make plant-based recipes that would be impossible or at least not very tasty if we couldn't readily track down the best ingredient substitutes. Specialty flours, seeds, beans, powdered plant milks, and spices are all part of recipes you'll find in this book. Almost everything can be purchased online, often in bulk, saving on packaging waste, which makes it less important that you have great grocery stores in your town. If you do have a local natural or health foods store, though, they may have items even we have yet to discover, and it's always great to support shopping local.

Favorite Online Shops

- **Rancho Gordo**, for beans, grains, and the occasional novelty spice
- **King Arthur Baking Company**, for specialty flours, extracts
- **Bob's Red Mill**, for wheat gluten, grains
- **Diaspora Co.**, for spices
- **Renegade Foods**, for the very best plant-based salami
- **Harmony House** dehydrated foods, including bean flakes, vegetable samplers, and plant-based proteins
- **Honeyville Inc.**, for bulk dehydrated foods
- **Packit Gourmet** for specialty dehydrated and freeze-dried ingredients and condiment packets

It can take a bit of trial and error to figure out which brands and styles of meat and dairy substitutes work best for you, but your tastes will evolve over time as your experience grows. The more we learn, the more there is to be discovered, and we think that is the best part of any adventure.

Condiment Packets

We like to forage for and collect small, shelf-stable condiment packets for our outdoor pantry. Condiments add a lot of flavor to a meal but can be difficult to pack in a leakproof way. These travel-size formats are ideal for outdoor cooking to reduce volume and lower the risk of spills. Using up packets from your local fast-food restaurants, diners, delis, and takeout orders also helps to reduce waste. The following are some of our most coveted items. Happy foraging!

- Soy sauce
- Mustard
- Ketchup
- Hot sauce: Tapatío, Sriracha
- Jam
- Peanut butter
- Crushed red peppers
- Airline travel-size snacks: peanuts, crackers, cookies
- Barbecue sauce
- Salt and pepper

CAMP COOKING CONSIDERATIONS

As you prepare for your next adventure, keep in mind that practicality and planning are essential to having fun and enjoying great meals. We know some people are willing to schlep excessive supplies to the top of a mountain just so they can say they baked a cake at the summit. That sounds like a fun friend to have, but we don't want that friend to be you (or us!). You may be inspired to try out new recipes, but you need to be realistic about how much time and motivation you'll have to cook once you're out there.

KNOW BEFORE YOU GO

The terrain, climate, and transportation method of the outdoor adventures you go on will directly affect which recipes you can prepare and the gear you need to bring to execute them. Regardless of the adventure, there are common big-picture factors to consider before you leave the house.

Weather

At home and work, we generally operate in climate-controlled environments, but once we step out the door, Mother Nature is in charge. Camping in the cold will make you yearn for cozy soups, while hot-weather camping will make chilled salads more enjoyable. Plan for comfort by doing some quick research before you leave home:

- Check the forecast for temperature, wind, and precipitation. It's very uncomfortable to do anything outside with wind whipping all your things around and rain dripping into your eyes. Also, rough weather will significantly decrease your fuel efficiency, potentially halting all cooking ability. Aim to find a weatherproofed location to set up your camp kitchen.
- If you're planning way ahead, do some research to see what the historic weather patterns are in the period when you'll be

heading out, and also check the hourly and ten-day forecasts right before your departure date. Conditions can change quickly!

Altitude

It's important to know the altitude at which you'll be adventuring. Three thousand feet above sea level is generally considered high altitude. In such conditions, water and other liquids evaporate more quickly and boil at a lower temperature. The higher you go, the lower the boiling point will become. That means a meal that calls for 10 minutes of simmering will take longer than that to cook if camp is in the mountains versus at the beach. Longer cooking times mean more fuel use and more waiting time until you can eat. Plan accordingly:

- Pack extra ready-to-eat snacks and fuel, knowing it may take a while to prepare a hot meal.

- Choose recipes that are mostly powder-based or have ingredients that rehydrate almost instantly so cooking time isn't further lengthened by dense ingredients (like dried carrots or peas) that refuse to soften. You can add texture back into your meal with toppings.
- Resist the temptation to turn the heat all the way up, as water cannot exceed its boiling point and this will only cause the liquids to boil away faster and increase the risk of burning your food.
- Faster water evaporation also means faster dehydration of your body. Make sure to plan for enough drinking and cooking water throughout your trip.
- Temperatures are generally cooler as altitude increases, so you may want to modify your recipe and stove/fuel selections.
- Altitude impacts baking as well, but our Dutch oven recipes aren't very fussy, so

this shouldn't affect the recipes in this book.

Water

Is water available where you're going? You'll need water not only for cooking but also for hydration, hygiene, and cleaning dishes on multiday trips. In California, where drought is a worsening problem, this is often a serious concern—and there are many other places grappling with this situation. There are many desert locations and even established campgrounds where no water is available. Once more, a little advanced planning leads to the best results:

- Prioritize ready-made foods that require no cooking water, or choose recipes that need less water. For example, soup or pasta recipes require more water than something like a sandwich, like our Charred Tofu Breakfast Sandwiches (page 117), which is mostly about assembling ingredients.
- Choose recipes that use a small number of dishes for preparation and create as little cleanup as possible. You don't want to waste precious water cleaning sticky food out of the one pot you need to use for the rest of your trip.
- If there is water, is it potable? Most running water in developed countries is potable; but when you begin to expand your horizons, that may no longer be the case. Similarly, in a backcountry situation where your water source might be a lake or running stream, you'll need to be prepared to treat or filter your water before drinking it.

- For multiday backcountry or off-roading trips, stashing caches of water at strategic points is sometimes an option. This option requires serious forethought and planning.
- If your adventure mode allows it, you may be able to bring all the water you need for the trip right from the start. This isn't a huge concern if you have ample storage in a vehicle. If you are picnicking, bikepacking, or kayaking, each mode presents its own limitations, most commonly storage space and weight.

Space and Weight

Packing and carrying heavy, bulky items will literally and mentally weigh you down, and your anticipated adventure can quickly start to feel burdensome. If prepping the food feels like too much work, you may lose your enthusiasm or even abandon your plans. Going to the beach

or park, for example, can entail bringing all your drinking water, ready-made food, and the gear you'll need for comfort and shade. You *can* stuff your car with all these things, but then you'll likely have to walk some distance from your parking spot to your destination. Even a quarter mile can become an arduous journey when you're dragging a heavy cooler with chairs strapped to your back and little ones in tow. We've been those people!

Now picture a truly restricted situation, like trekking in the backcountry, where space and weight can become even more serious concerns—like health and safety, if you take heavy, perishable foods or you bring too many "wants" and can't fit in the essentials.

TIPS:

- Reduce weight and volume whenever possible. For example, for recipes that call for broth, use Bouillon Powder (page 286) instead, or premeasure your liquid broth rather than bringing the whole container.

- Figure out the maximum weight or volume that you're willing to manage and balance your priorities within those restrictions. For example, keeping your backpacking base weight (food, water, and fuel don't count here because they fluctuate throughout the trip) under twenty pounds or your camp cooking supplies limited to a single bin will help you determine what to leave behind.

Campfire/Grill Access

With wildfire season now running almost year-round, it's no longer safe to assume a night under the stars is going to come with a crackling campfire. Before you go, find out what the current regulations are for your destination and plan accordingly.

TIPS:

- If no campfire restrictions are in place, confirm whether fires must be in established campfire rings and whether there's a grate if you anticipate needing that to cook. For primitive camping situations, often fires are not allowed, or campers must bring a portable fire pit and pack the ashes out.
- Most areas have issues with invasive species and require that you burn only local firewood. That means you'll need to find and buy firewood close to your camp. Please respect these restrictions, as they're designed to protect the health of entire ecosystems.

Site Amenities

Many parks and established campgrounds provide picnic tables, but it's good to know whether your destination will have one. Other important amenities are shade and weather protection. This is especially pertinent when the weather is hot. Extensive sun exposure increases food perishability and hydration needs, so take proper precautions.

GEAR

One of the biggest factors for determining what recipes can be executed on a trip is the equipment you have on that trip. Here is a rundown of considerations you should take into account as you choose your camp kitchen setup.

Camp Stoves

Some sort of heat source is essential for any type of cooking you do at camp. There are many camp stove options on the market and entire websites dedicated to discussing the nitty gritty details of each. If it generates heat, you should be able to cook a meal with it. Here are some differences to consider:

Weight, Space, and Stability
Stoves range in size and weight from those that will easily fit into a small backpack snuggled into the pot to those bigger than a home grill.

Larger stoves—like you might use for a car-camping trip—usually have more than one burner, typically two. These stoves can accommodate large cookware, which means you can make more food. They are also more stable. If you are planning to cook multiple elements for a single meal or cook for more than a couple of people, you should consider a larger stove. This is also a good time to use a campfire or grill as part of your camp-kitchen arsenal, either to supplement your camp stove capacity or to cook an entire meal.

If you will be carrying all of your gear on your back, you'll need to think differently and confine your recipe choices to meals that work well with a smaller, lightweight stove. A smaller stove is also better if you're boating or biking some distance, or even if you just have a small car with limited carrying capacity. The best recipes to cook for this setup will be simple,

one-pot meals that can be rehydrated or heated simply without complicated techniques.

BTUs and Simmer Control

Most camp stove marketing specifications include BTU information, which stands for British Thermal Units. These measure energy: one BTU is equivalent to burning one match. The more BTUs, the higher the heat will be. For reference, a typical camp stove BTU range is 10,000 to 30,000 BTUs. By comparison, a campfire can be as hot as 100,000 BTUs.

However impressive these numbers are, they don't take into account simmer control, which is critical if you're going to be doing anything other than trying to boil water as fast as possible. When you can control and maintain a low flame, you can do more nuanced cooking, like simmering and sautéing, without burning your food.

Fuel Types

It should go without saying, but it's important to have the right cooking fuel for your particular stove, so you can get the sustenance you need on your adventure. The most common types of fuel used for camp cooking are:

- Propane
- Isobutane
- White gas
- Butane
- Wood
- Charcoal

Fuel and camp stoves go hand in hand; the stove you buy will specify which fuel type to use or vice versa. The main difference between fuel types is their performance in cold temperatures, with white gas being the better choice for chilly, high-altitude adventures.

If you aren't ready to make a camp stove purchase and aren't traveling far afield, you can use the classic outdoor cooking fuels: firewood and charcoal. Typically, these are used in campsite fire rings and charcoal grills.

Different types of fuel are more readily available in different countries, and most can't be transported by air. Be sure you'll be able to source the kind of fuel you need at your destination.

Cookware

We like to be as minimal as possible with our cookware, bringing only the items we truly need. We believe you don't need to run out and buy every piece of cookware on the market, but there are some benefits to owning a few camp-specific products, as they will likely provide benefits such as versatility, durability, and weight savings.

Pots and Pans

We can be very particular about pots and skillets, but we understand the practicality of trying to make one pot set work for all of your different adventures. For instance, you may really want to make our Citrus Poppy Seed Pancakes (page 220) on your next bike tour, but you don't have a nonstick skillet, so you pack an ultralight titanium one. You can make it work by modifying the techniques or ingredients used, even if it isn't perfect. It will be more difficult to keep the pancakes from sticking, so you should bring more oil and plan to watch the pancakes

more closely as you cook them. If your stove doesn't have flame adjustability and you notice burning, lifting the skillet up off of the flame is a quick way to "lower the heat."

Size is important. If your pot set is too small, you will find yourself having to cook recipes in rounds, which can get complicated and cumbersome. On the other hand, if your pot is too large, it might fall off a less-stable stove. We list the pot size that we used ourselves to make each recipe. It's best to pick the pot you have that's closest to those sizes.

What the cookware is made of also matters. The ratio of weight to heat distribution is the most important factor when choosing cookware. Interestingly, the lightest-weight cookware is usually the most finicky *and* the most expensive.

CAST IRON: This material (well seasoned) tends to be your best bet for nonstick, even-heating cookware that can stand the test of time and use. It does require some specific care, but that doesn't mean it's difficult. It is the heaviest option, so it's not practical for any type of trip with weight limitations, but it is the only workable option for campfire cooking and for baking. You'll need a Dutch oven for any camp baking, and virtually all are made of cast iron, for good reason. You may also want to invest in a cast iron skillet that can be used to cook on the grate of the campfire as well as your camp stovetop. We heavily rely on these even at home, so they often go straight from our stovetop to campfire grates. The other type of cast iron cookware you'll see featured in this book is the pie iron, a fun tool for making individual pockets of food.

TITANIUM: There are some very expensive titanium pot sets on the market that are a great option for a weight-restricted trip. These tend to be very thin, however, so they easily develop hot spots, especially when using a stove with limited simmer control. They are also usually quite small, with the expectation that you are cooking only one or two servings at a time. These sets are ideal for backcountry trips that require little more technique than boiling water.

NONSTICK: Many different types of materials are classified as nonstick: Anolon, hard-anodized, PFAS, Teflon, and so on. These are coatings of varying durability and, consequently, price. Though some are safer and more versatile than others, they all should be used over lower heat and will eventually wear down,

creating risk of physical contamination in your food. Plan to follow care instructions mindfully and avoid using these over heat sources that are difficult to regulate, such as your campfire.

STAINLESS STEEL: This type of cookware is not coated, so you'll have to deal with stuck-on food more frequently, but it is durable and long-lasting like cast iron. It also comes in many different sizes, so a compact pan can be a practical compromise for a backcountry trip where weight is less important.

ALUMINUM: This can be the least expensive type of cookware, and it tends to be lightweight. Again, that's good for a weight-restricted adventure but not as good for even cooking. Many aluminum skillets are also coated with a sealant, which will wear off over time.

Cooking Accessories

You put care into what you use at home, and the same should be true for your fundamental camp-kitchen accessories. Bring tools that you like to use and that work well. This seems obvious, but we admit we've been sucked into buying gadget versions of some kitchen tools, like the minuscule can opener that turned a simple task into a frustrating and time-consuming ordeal. The following no-nonsense list will dramatically improve your camp cooking experience and the outcome of your meals.

KNIVES: The number one rule is that your knives should be sharp! With a dull knife, not only are you increasing the risk of injury, but all your prep will take longer, which can cut into your fun time.

- *Pocket knife or multitool:* This one should come on all your adventures. When space and weight are limited, this becomes the go-to option to have on hand. It's best for simple preparation of small items. If you're cooking dinner for a family, it's not the ideal tool but will get the job done in a pinch. Try to store yours in a handy and consistent place; their small size makes it easy to lose them.

- *Chef's knife with sheath:* A chef's knife is one with a long and deep blade, unlike a skinny steak knife or small paring knife. With this all-purpose tool, you should be able to cut anything from a watermelon to a tomato. The sheath is critical for safety and for storing in your bin without damaging other items. Some knives come with a sheath, but if yours doesn't, you can easily improvise by wrapping the knife in a thick kitchen towel or piece of folded cardboard. Safety first!

CUTTING BOARDS: If you're car camping, do yourself a flavor and ditch the razor-thin plastic cutting boards. They're convenient, but you'll be mad when all the prep you just finished gets flung into the dirt by a little gust of wind. Don't say we didn't warn you.

TOOL MATERIALS: In general, plastic tools aren't durable and tend to melt. When they do eventually fail, we highly recommend replacing them with wood or metal tools. That being said, there are a few rules of thumb to follow:

- *For Cast Iron:* Metal cooking tools are essential for cast iron cooking because of the high cooking heat. Cast iron is tough, so you don't have to worry about scratching it.
- *For Nonstick:* Never use metal cooking tools on nonstick cookware. Scratching the nonstick coating will compromise your pots and pans and could pose long-term health risks if you ingest the coating.

Building Your Base Kit

These are the setups that we own and keep at the ready for any type of camping trip that comes up. They include more items than every recipe requires, so you can edit or customize them to your liking. See the sidebar for checklists for each kit.

On the Trail Base Kit

We keep these supplies in our backpacks and/or car rather than in a bin. Though you may not need some of these items (for example, a spork) for every trip, they are lightweight and versatile enough to have handy. You don't want to go too light in your base kit; we've made that mistake in the past and, in moments of desperation, we have eaten grain salad using grubby fingers or small fragments of chips, having left our spork at home.

Car Camping Base Kit

We prefer to use a clear bin for car camping supplies and take the whole bin with us when we travel. It holds all the essentials from the trail base kit list, plus a few other items that are necessities for our particular family (for

BASE KIT CHECKLISTS

Use these handy lists to make trip prep a little easier and faster. Feel free to adjust these to fit your menu and trip context as the checklists may include more items than you need.

ON THE TRAIL BASE KIT

- ☐ Bandana to use as a napkin, placemat, or sandwich wrapper
- ☐ Granola bar, energy gel, or snack mix, in case something happens to your meal (like you left it in the fridge)
- ☐ Pocket knife
- ☐ Small bag to be used for found trash, leftovers, peels, empty drink cans, and the like
- ☐ Spork

CAR CAMPING BASE KIT

- ☐ Items listed for "On the Trail" plus:
- ☐ Headlamp or flashlight
- ☐ Cooler
- ☐ Camp stove with appropriate fuel
- ☐ Matches/lighter, plus a backup
- ☐ Skillet and/or pot
- ☐ Aluminum foil
- ☐ Cooking spray
- ☐ Spatula
- ☐ Large spoon
- ☐ Long tongs
- ☐ Knife
- ☐ Cutting board
- ☐ Can opener
- ☐ Bottle/wine opener
- ☐ Coffee- or tea-making supplies
- ☐ Salt and pepper
- ☐ Mess kits (dishware and flatware, enough for all participants)
- ☐ Nonperishable emergency food, in case something happens to your meal (like it got a bit too "rustic" in the campfire)
- ☐ Paper towels or wet wipes
- ☐ Dishwashing tub or bucket
- ☐ Sponge and biodegradable soap
- ☐ Dishtowel
- ☐ Trash bags

CAMPFIRE BASE KIT

- ☐ 10-inch and 12-inch cast iron skillets
- ☐ 10-inch Dutch oven (recipes will simply call for a Dutch oven)
- ☐ Dutch oven lid lifter
- ☐ Aluminum foil
- ☐ Heatproof gloves
- ☐ Pie iron
- ☐ Hatchet
- ☐ Lighter or matches, plus a backup
- ☐ Firewood or charcoal
- ☐ Long tongs
- ☐ Extra water for dousing the fire

BACKCOUNTRY BASE KIT

- ☐ Water container, preferably with measurement markings
- ☐ Bear-proof container, where appropriate
- ☐ Small bag to be used for found trash, leftovers, peels, empty drink cans, and so on
- ☐ Lightweight stove with appropriate fuel
- ☐ Matches or lighter (even if your stove has an igniter)
- ☐ 1-liter and 1.5-liter pots with lids
- ☐ Lightweight mug
- ☐ Pocket knife
- ☐ Spork
- ☐ Granola bar, energy gel, or snack mix, in case something happens to your meal (like a bear decided your food canister is its favorite new toy)
- ☐ Small abrasive sponge
- ☐ Bandana

instance, our kids love to bring glow sticks and coloring supplies, so those live here too). Food gets packed in a separate bin so that we (hopefully) don't find a moldy orange at the bottom of the bin the next time we get ready to head out—although this is why using a clear bin can help. Bins with tight-fitting lids also offer a level of protection against small critters and the elements.

We also keep a stack of printed checklists in that bin. While on a trip, if we notice something has run out or gotten lost, we can make notes on the list and use it to help with the reset after the trip. Emily likes to use these list pages to add trip report notes as well. They have become a nice journal over time. Gently worn home goods are great for starting your base kit, especially for important but easy-to-forget items, like a can opener and corkscrew.

Campfire Base Kit

The items in this list are add-ons to the other base kits and should be included only when you're choosing to use an established campfire ring or raised firepit brought from home. These heavy, bulky items don't need to accompany you unless you're sure you'll be using them.

Backcountry Base Kit

Many trips that require nonperishable recipes also require lightweight, compact, and multi-use gear, useful in many situations. If you are planning a weight-restricted trip, you'll need to carefully curate these supplies in advance to ensure that the total weight stays within your preferred range. Everything you're schlepping should be essential. We keep all of these supplies in a separate bin in the garage and choose each individual item before leaving on a trip.

MEAL PLANNING

A key concept for camp cooking is to plan your whole menu—not just a collection of individual recipes—*before* your trip. This will streamline your cooking in many ways and allow you to effectively execute delicious and fulfilling meals rather than simply surviving on leftover fast food and snacks. Meal planning reduces food waste and saves you money and time by simplifying the number of ingredients and maximizing their use across multiple recipes. Preparation happens more quickly because you have shopped for—and need to chop—fewer types of ingredients overall, which gives you more time to focus on other aspects of your trip planning.

WHAT'S YOUR PREPPER PROFILE?

Preparation of some kind is essential to camp cooking. Everyone has a different approach to getting ready for a trip, and there's no wrong way to do it. There are, however, different things to keep in mind depending on how you prefer to prep. We offer some examples to help you determine what makes the most sense for your style.

The Way-Ahead Prepper (Emily's Style)

This type of person preps way before a trip is even planned and stores meals and ingredients for future use (maybe even a whole season at a time). This is a good choice for someone who goes on frequent trips, like Emily, who goes climbing and camping almost every weekend.

- Focuses on nonperishable recipes and long-term storage
- Dehydrates components that are multi-use, like a bunch of mushrooms that can be used throughout the season in different recipes
- Spends a week or two cooking ready-to-go meals and stores them in the freezer for use on multiple trips
- Builds premixed components like pancake mixes and spice mixes to have on hand at all times
- Preps other items like gear and fuel

- Has a ready-to-go base kit packed and stored in the garage for all types of trips
- Buys in bulk to allow for quick and easy resets

The Per-Trip Prepper (Aimee's Style)

This person likes to prep some components at home so that cooking is easier at camp. Chopping, mixing spices and sauces, and premeasuring are good to do a day or two ahead of your trip. Aimee loves to show up at camp ready to execute meals immediately with seasonal fresh produce.

- Makes use of fresh ingredients on hand at home for camp meals
- Prioritizes the relaxation aspect of the trip by getting a lot of the work done beforehand
- Makes a fresh meal plan for each trip, which allows for more creativity in the camp kitchen and customization of tools

The On-a-Whim Outdoorist (Mai-Yan's Style)

This person likes to seize any opportunity that arises, even at a moment's notice. They are fine figuring it out on the fly, and they aren't afraid to improvise. Mai-Yan lives the city life and always has something going on. She doesn't have kids and lives in a little space with limited storage options, so she prefers to plan on the go.

- Keeps our handy cookbook or printed recipes in the car or camp bin for easy access on the way out of town
- Chooses recipes that don't require a lot of specialty gear or ingredients

- Keeps an assortment of multipurpose spices in the base kit
- Looks for local ingredients to enhance meals

CREATING A MEAL PLAN

Whether you are going out for an afternoon or a week, you want food that makes you excited to eat at your destination. It's always a challenge to create an elegant solution for an outdoor meal that balances practicality and excitement. Enjoy the triumph of getting it right so you can focus on the outdoor experience, feeling nourished all the way through.

Meal Planning for Camp Cooking

1. Identify how many meals you need, and think through your trip considerations (see Camp Cooking Considerations). Will you be climbing until dusk one day? Make sure to have a recipe that's hearty and quick to prepare that evening. Will you be hanging around camp on another day? That's the perfect time for a slow campfire breakfast or an impressive dessert.
2. Choose a recipe you are excited about. Maybe it's a challenging recipe you've been wanting to try in your Dutch oven or something you think you'll really be craving after a long day out hiking. Start by writing up the list of ingredients for this anchor recipe.
3. Note the main ingredients, cooking techniques, and gear necessary for that recipe. What common threads can you identify to make meal prep easier? If you're planning on using your dehydrator, consider making more than one recipe that requires a

The basic premise of campification is to turn home-cooked meals into camp-friendly ones. We have shared this idea at our workshops for many years with a fun participatory exercise that asks the audience to share their favorite go-to home recipes. We then work together to identify the key components of the recipes and proceed to simplify them as needed to work for specific types of trips. You can do this for any type of meal and any type of adventure, and it is a good way to start menu planning rather than defaulting to what's usually classified as "camp food."

First, examine these three factors:

- Ingredients
- Recipe steps
- Gear required

One of our favorite examples to showcase the process is White Bean Chili Verde, so here's a quick guide for how we adjust the recipe for Car Camping and then more deeply for Backcountry Camping.

Home Recipe

White Bean Chili Verde

Oil
Onion, chopped
Green chiles, seeded and chopped
Garlic, chopped
Spices, such as oregano and cumin
Dried white beans, soaked overnight
Fresh tomatillos
Vegetable stock
Fresh toppings such as radishes, avocado, cilantro, plant-based sour cream, and lime
Homemade or packaged tortilla chips

Chop all of the vegetables, enjoying the convenience of your home trash and compost options for discarded trimmings and peels. In a large, heavy-bottomed pot, such as a stovetop-style Dutch oven, sauté the onions in some olive oil until soft, about 5 minutes.

Add the chiles and sauté until tender, about 5 minutes.

Add the garlic and sauté for about 1 minute.

Add the spices, and sauté until fragrant, about 30 seconds.

Add the beans, tomatillos, and stock, and simmer for $1^{1}/_{2}$ to 2 hours, until the beans are tender.

Serve topped with crunchy, cold, fresh toppings and tortilla chips.

Dutch Oven White Bean Chili Verde

Prechopped vegetables, leaving waste at home so you won't have to pack it out

Premeasured spice mix

Canned beans

Canned tomatillos

Bouillon Powder (page 287)

Limited toppings, 3 to 5 max

Homemade or packaged tortilla chips

Heat a Dutch oven on the grate of a campfire or the camp stove. Dump in the prechopped vegetables and sauté until tender.

Add the spices and sauté until fragrant.

Empty the beans and tomatillos into the pot, including their juices.

Add the Bouillon Powder and water to cover, and simmer until heated through, 20 to 30 minutes.

Serve with toppings and tortilla chips.

White Bean Chili Verde

Dehydrated aromatics and spices, premeasured and mixed

Dried bean flakes

Bouillon Powder (page 287)

Water

Limited toppings, 3 max

Put all the ingredients except the toppings together in a pot on a backpacking stove.

Bring to a boil, then turn down to a simmer.

Simmer until the vegetables are rehydrated and tender and the bean base is creamy, about 10 minutes.

Top with chips and/or squeezes of lime and chopped avocado.

Note: The toppings can include fresh limes and avocado for that fresh zing, but tortilla chips crushed with a bear canister "rolling pin" are great on their own.

6. Consider doing some batch processing or premeasuring and mixing ahead of your trip if that fits your prepper style.

Weekend Menu Plan Example

When going on a camping trip, it's important to plan not just a meal but a whole menu. The less you have to prep, the less likely you are to forget ingredients, misplace items, or be overwhelmed with food waste at camp. When meal planning, we like to make the most of home-prepped ingredients across multiple meals. This will help reduce cooler space and cooking time in camp. Here is a sample meal plan for a weekend car-camping trip that does just that.

DAY 1: ARRIVAL NIGHT DINNER

- Pot of beans, cooked at home
- Hot Cheesy Corn Dip (page 150)
- Grilled bread
- Maple Nut S'mores (page 216)
- Butter with a Side of Veggies (page 163)

The goal is to have a quick and easy dinner on the picnic table the first night, which is when many people arrive at camp. The beans can be reheated in a Dutch oven over a freshly made campfire, and the Hot Cheesy Corn Dip can be whipped up quickly as a great appetizer to keep everyone happy until dinner's on the table.

DAY 2: BREAKFAST

- White Bean Scramble—using leftover beans from the night before (page 114)
- Fresh fruit
- Cowboy coffee

dehydrator. Design your meal plan to maximize the use of all the things you're bringing. Don't pack your cast iron cookware for just one recipe or leave half a lemon unused. All these considerations should help steer you toward a second recipe idea.

4. Repeat this process using another ingredient from the first recipe or a versatile ingredient from the second. Keep going through this process until you have enough recipes for your trip.

5. Write down your final menu and a shopping list. Some ingredients may need to be sourced ahead of time. Make sure you record your meal plan on something you can take with you and access on your trip. Also consider which day is best for each recipe.

Cooking breakfast can be unmotivating while camping because it often precedes time-sensitive activities, such as long day hikes or packing to drive home. Using prepped ingredients, you can bring together a good breakfast with much less effort; it can even become the most memorable part of the trip.

Spicy Ranch Oyster Crackers

DAY 2: LUNCH

- Roasted Chile Peanut Butter Sandos— using prepared chiles from the Corn Dip and the bread from dinner (page 103)
- Chips

Lunch is essential to think about ahead of time, but it's often forgotten or thrown together in the morning before leaving camp. We usually have bread and peanut butter on hand, and that dull sandwich can be jazzed up if you prepare some extra roasted chiles when you make the Hot Cheesy Corn Dip.

DAY 2: DINNER

- Salisbury Seitan Smashed Potatoes (page 184)
- Summer Berry Custard (page 212)

DAY 3: BREAKFAST

- French Toast (page 118) with berries— using the remaining half carton of berries
- Cowboy coffee

Special Considerations for Backcountry Menu Planning

- Coordinate ingredients so you don't have to dehydrate or purchase too many specialty items.

- Write down your plan and take it along to eliminate excess decision fatigue by the end of a potentially long day.
- Match your meal type to the day's activity level; if you are doing high-energy output days or you'll be out late on the trail, this can be critical.
- Some meals from the On the Trail Recipes category can also work for backcountry scenarios.
- Plan your snacks as you would plan your meals. Have some emergency food as well—this can be repurposed snacks.

3-DAY BACKCOUNTRY SAMPLE MEAL PLAN

	DAY 0	DAY 1	DAY 2	DAY 3
Breakfast	Breakfast at home	Chai Oatmeal	Bacon Grits and Greens	Backcountry Tofu Scramble
		Golden raisins	Champurrado de Café	Instant coffee
		Instant coffee		
Snacks	Granola Bar Chews while on the road	Granola Bar Chews	Cracked Pepper Seitan Jerky	Indian spice snack mix
	Veggies and dip while on the road	Oyster crackers	Indian spice snack mix	Strawberry Balsamic Fruit Leather
		Cracked Pepper Seitan Jerky	Strawberry Balsamic Fruit Leather	
Lunch	Pick up on the road	Quiche Pie Bombs	Bagel with avocado	Bagel with shelf-stable hummus packet
		Hot sauce	Plant-based summer sausage	Plant-based summer sausage
			Olives	Olives
Dinner	Pioneer Stew with Grilled Lemon Bread at campsite*	French Dip Sandwiches	Matzo Ball Soup	Pick up dinner on the way home
		Peanut butter cup	Oyster crackers	
			Tahini Hot Chocolate	
		Emergency Meal: Patagonia Provisions Tsampa Soup + PROBAR Meal Bar		
Destination	Travel day to Tuolumne Meadows Lodge	Tuolumne Meadows Lodge to Glen Aulin	Glen Aulin to May Lake	May Lake to Sunrise and car
Distance	350 miles 6 hours' drive	8.0 miles Moderate	8.5 miles Strenuous	8.25 miles Strenuous
Camp Elevation	8700 feet	7800 feet	9270 feet	9400 feet

*Car Camping

OUTDOOR COOKING TECHNIQUES

Many camp cooking techniques are very similar to home cooking techniques; the following are more specific to outdoor cooking and dining.

ON THE TRAIL RECIPE TECHNIQUES

All recipes in the On the Trail category are meant to be cooked and prepared before you leave for the day. The most finicky part is packing them so that they aren't destroyed by the time you're ready to eat. Some must be wrapped up to hold the integrity of their shape; others need a leakproof container to keep them from making a mess en route.

Wrapping

Our favorite ways to wrap things like sandwiches or pie bombs involve both parchment paper and a bandana or oversize napkin. If you're planning on putting food in a backpack, wrap items rather than putting them in containers whenever possible since containers tend to be heavy and bulky. If you'll be bringing only one or two of an item (for example, one sandwich or two pie bombs), and the items are somewhat dry on the outside, wrapping is best.

We like to start by wrapping the food tightly in parchment paper, then wrapping a bandana or large cloth napkin around the parchment paper. The bandana accomplishes three things:

- It looks beautiful, which adds to the overall experience of eating well outdoors.
- It adds another layer of protection against any liquids oozing onto your gear.
- It keeps you from forgetting a bandana, which ends up being essential as a napkin, placemat, hair tie, or sun protector when the UV index is at its peak right after lunch.

Furoshiki, a Japanese wrapping technique that has become a popular way to wrap gifts, works perfectly here. See our step-by-step Furoshiki Wrapping Tutorial in the Appendix.

Leakproof Containers

Leakproof containers are a must when a food is wet or saucy, such as salads, pastas, and foods with dipping sauces. We use this term as a catchall in many recipes, rather than specifying a particular type—by all means, use what you already own if possible before going out and buying something new. Containers of any material (plastic, glass, metal, silicone) can work, though you'll want to consider weight and bulk if you're going to be carrying them any great distance. Untempered glass is the most breakable, but we rely pretty heavily on glass Mason jars because they are generally durable and inexpensive. The lids are reliably leakproof and interchangeable, whereas we've had many other types of container lids fail on us.

Other nice options are insulated metal food jars made by companies like Stanley. The screw-top lids are also reliable, and your food will stay hot or cold for much longer. These are heavier and higher-priced than other options, though.

There are quite a few reusable plastic or silicone bags on the market nowadays, which are shaping up to be a great option as well. The most popular brands tend to be higher priced, but they are worth it for their durability and shape options. Consider reusing takeout containers from your favorite restaurant if they're up to the task.

Whichever you choose, do a quick test before your trip by filling the container with water, then shaking and squeezing it upside down and all around. You want to be confident stuffing it into your pack and getting out the door. If the container shape is rigid, make sure it isn't poking you in the back or keeping you from being able to pack your other items neatly. We usually stow these containers last, so they're right in view and easy to access. This also protects the container and its contents from getting smashed if we carelessly drop the pack on a hard surface.

One more tip: You can often wrap a bandana or large napkin around a leakproof container, using the same Furoshiki wrapping technique. This provides another layer of protection, and once you unpack you'll have the cloth available for all its other uses.

How to Set Up a Picnic

Picnics are a time-honored type of day trip: a get-together with friends and family to relax in the outdoors, generally not far from your means of transport. It's just one meal, so you don't have to worry about making elaborate plans.

Here we share some of our tips to ensure you get to picnic with ease.

- Transportation is easiest using a wagon or cooler with wheels. Depending on the terrain, you could use a dedicated food backpack if necessary. Some backpacks are rigid-sided or even insulated for this very purpose. Remember, the less stuff you have to schlep, the happier you all will be.
- Your location should be chosen based on the flatness of the ground as well as the appropriate amount of sun and wind protection. Umbrellas or sun shades are a good option for exposed locations like the beach or the desert.

- A picnic blanket is essential no matter the terrain. It can add a festive element to the picnic and will encourage you to find a truly nice space to eat together. A blanket keeps everyone close enough for enjoyable conversation and can even make cleanup easier. Choose a tightly woven blanket, like a Mexican serape style, or one with a specific protective backing. For a larger group, bring two or three blankets and overlap the edges to expand your space.

- It's nice to make the effort to bring simple, pretty things that will enhance the look and feel of your picnic experience. Cloth napkins and reusable plates and utensils are good investments if you like to picnic regularly. Look for beautiful enamel and bamboo tableware to keep wasteful disposable paper and plastic options out of the forests and oceans.

- It's fun to have the kids pick up a few natural items to use as a centerpiece, as long as it's not against local regulations and these things aren't picked off of living plants. Heavier items like rocks, pinecones, or shells can also help hold down the blanket corners.

- Even if you're planning to picnic in your backyard, you should plan and prep ahead of time. You'll save yourself work during the picnic: searching the yard for tableware

or making too many trips back and forth to the kitchen.

• When planning your menu, choose a variety of sweet and savory recipes to keep things interesting. It's not cheating if you cook just one dish and pick up accompaniments from the grocery store.

• If you're doing a potluck, it's best to choose a theme so all the dishes work well together. We like to put ourselves in charge of the main dish to ensure that it doesn't get forgotten, and then let guests fill in the gaps with drinks and sides that don't matter as much if they are missing.

CAR CAMPING TECHNIQUES

Car camping is the closest style to cooking in your home kitchen, but the campfire and doing dishes are what really set it apart. Here are some techniques that will have you utilizing all the versatility of the campfire and make cleanup a breeze.

Cooking on a Campfire

We love campfire cooking, and there are quite a few recipes that can be made over a fire instead of on a stove. We still recommend having some sort of stove for tasks like boiling water and in case a campfire doesn't work out. We have found ourselves in situations where we planned to cook on the fire, only to find out they weren't allowed.

Cooking Fire Structure

Our favorite cooking fire setup is the log cabin structure, an efficient and stable setup that has yet to fail us.

See the step-by-step Log Cabin Campfire Tutorial in the Appendix.

Grate Cooking

You can use a grate over the campfire or even on a charcoal grill to mimic a stovetop for tasks like sautéing and heating stews. To adjust the heat, use your long tongs to move logs or coals under the grate closer to or farther from the pot. This is a "grate" option if you don't have a versatile stove and want to streamline what you need to pack. It also works well if all the burners on your stove are in use and you'd like your co-campers to help while they hang out around the campfire.

Almost any recipe that you can cook on the stovetop can also be cooked on the campfire or grill grate, but keep these things in mind:

- You may struggle with setting a campfire-style Dutch oven on stovetops that lack stability or have certain grate patterns that don't work well with the Dutch oven's feet. There are flat-bottomed Dutch ovens that are made for cooking on the grate or stovetop, however.
- If your recipe requires boiling water for pasta or rice, it will be difficult to achieve a high enough heat output for a long enough amount of time to do this on the campfire; our recipes will recommend the stovetop only in those cases.
- Some recipes have multiple steps that require continuous attention for stirring, flipping, or watching for doneness; we generally recommend that you make these over the stovetop instead of a grate, to avoid smoke-eye while you cook.

We generally like to have others attend to cooking appetizers over the grate while we focus on prepping the main meal in the camp kitchen. In this case, we often cook appetizers with a "low and slow" approach, using residual heat at the edge of the fire grate rather than directly over the heat. This lessens the chances of burning the food when you're entrusting it to less-focused guests and also protects your guests from getting smoked out.

Foil Pouch Cooking

Foil pouches are a great way to get to know campfire cooking, as you don't need to own any

ROASTING CHILES

This is a fun technique that harnesses the smokiness of the campfire. The simplest method is to place chiles right on the grate over high heat. Using long tongs, rotate the chiles every few minutes until the skins are bubbling and charred. If the chiles are small and might fall through the grate, use a cast iron skillet with no oil. Remove from the grate and set aside.

To use these chiles chopped in a recipe, you can steam them by placing the hot roasted chiles in a ziplock bag or a covered container for a few minutes, then peel the skin off by scraping it with a spoon. Another option is to serve them whole, skin-on, as a side, like in our Smoky SoCal Hash (page 124).

will have feet for standing above coals as well as a flanged lid for holding coals on top. This book is about *camp* cooking rather than Dutch oven mastery, so we are generally a little loose in our expectations of exact temperatures and even heating. The campfire is there for enjoyment and warmth as well as cooking, so we guesstimate how many coals pulled from the fire are equal to the amount of uniform charcoal briquettes determined by our Dutch Oven Baking Chart (see the Appendix). We prefer to feel our way through the process, and we stand behind our "rustic" burned edges. Camping is about letting go of the stresses of normal life, so campfire cooking should follow suit.

Car Camping Cleanup Without a Dishwasher (!)

Doing the dishes on your fun outdoor trip can feel like the worst part, but it's unavoidable. It's also one of the most important parts of camp cooking, because if we don't clean up properly, we aren't leaving the space better than we found it. This is a fundamental principle of Leave No Trace. As with everything in life, if you have the right tools and some tips and tricks at your disposal (get it?), it's a breeze to do it right and keep the wild, wild.

We've done dishes for hundreds of people at a time in remote locations after sixteen-hour workdays. For us, every detail matters in preventing dish-doing from becoming a sufferfest. You may not feel the need to go this far just for your family, but we wanted to let you know how serious you *could* get, and that it's worth it. For short trips, however, you can bring a dry

special equipment other than a roll of aluminum foil and some long tongs. Check out our tutorial in the Appendix to make our favorite version of a foil pouch, and start by experimenting with roasting vegetables in packets, since they are very forgiving and can withstand a little "rustic" char.

Campfire Baking

You can use a Dutch oven to create a reasonable facsimile of a baking oven over your fire, and we've made many a delicious baked dish on a campfire. You'll need to make sure you have a true baking Dutch oven, which bag or a bin to transport all your dirty dishes straight to your home dishwasher.

What you'll need:
- ☐ 1 folding table
- ☐ 4 dish bins
- ☐ 1 trash can or bag
- ☐ 1 scraper tool
- ☐ Biodegradable soap
- ☐ 1 sponge
- ☐ Plenty of water, warm and cold
- ☐ Lots of drying towels
- ☐ Strainer (we use a honey strainer, which is very fine mesh and fits nicely over a bucket)
- ☐ Bucket
- ☐ As many humans as possible

Setup

1. Set up your folding table and put all four dish bins on top in a line, with your trash can at one end of the table. A table is ideal so you don't have to bend over, which can be a pain in the back.
2. The first bin will stay waterless and act as a true bussing bin that people can put their dishes into after they scrape them.
3. Pour very warm water into the second dish bin, and add a squirt of biodegradable soap and a sponge. This is the bin you'll have your hands in for the majority of the time, so you'll want it to be a pleasant experience. Warm water will help release stuck-on food from the dishes. Tell yourself (or better yet, your recruits) that it's also like a spa treatment for your hands.
4. Pour cold water into the third dish bin. The dishes will need just a quick dip in this, so don't waste your fuel heating the water. The third bin is your rinse water and should generally stay pretty clean.
5. The fourth bin is for air drying clean dishes. We don't always use sanitizer (like bleach), but if you want to include a sanitize stage, you could use this bin for that purpose instead.

Dishwashing

1. Encourage your fellow campers to scrape their dishware as clean as possible into the trash can. (You can also encourage everyone to clean the dish with their bread or the "big gulp" method of pouring hot water into it and drinking that.) Any solid waste that goes into the water can be difficult to remove so it's best to keep it out in the first place.
2. Put a dish in the wash bin, give it a scrub, and dip it in the rinse bin.
3. Dry with dish towels; or leave it out to dry in the sun, as long as it's not windy enough to blow dust, leaves, and the like onto the clean dishes.
4. When you're done with the dishes, strain the soapy water to remove solid waste, walk it at least 100 yards away from camp and water sources, and scatter it rather than dumping it in one spot, to diffuse any strong smells.
5. Pack any trash out properly. Do not throw it into the fire pit or bury it underground, and definitely don't litter.

BACKCOUNTRY TECHNIQUES

Meals generally need to be prepared at home as much as possible for use in backcountry scenarios. Dehydrating and adjusting recipes to be as simple as "boil water" will make all the difference in many situations. But comfort matters too, so we also include considerations to make sure you're enjoying the whole back-country meal experience.

Backcountry Kitchen Comfort

When you're on a trip that has weight and/or space restrictions or lacks conveniences of any kind, it can feel daunting to cook. Squatting over a tiny, unstable stove in the cold and the dark after a long day can leave you wanting to just eat a granola bar and head to bed. There are a few ways to make the cooking experience feel like a comforting event in itself, and it may

even motivate you to go that extra quarter mile to reach a better view.

Make Yourself Comfortable

When you arrive at your campsite, set up the sleeping area and the kitchen area and make sure they are separated by plenty of distance (if that bear does come wandering through, you want it sniffing far away from your sleeping bag). Choose the most flat, wind-sheltered kitchen location you can find. Like the popular five-star rating system for pooping in the woods, you get extra stars for your camp kitchen if you can find a flat rock to use as a table.

If your trip is a chilly one, it's worth the weight to bring a little square of closed-cell foam to sit on so you're insulated from the cold ground while you cook. If you have even more room for luxury, there are plenty of ultralight chair options.

Be Fully Engaged

Set yourself up properly, and make yourself a drink first thing, like a warm mug of Golden Milk (page 268), or a party-starting Whiskey Sour (page 273). Once you're ready, commit to being actively engaged in the whole dining process, from cooking to cleanup. This is like visiting a fine-dining restaurant—it's not about hurrying through, it's about savoring.

Focusing completely on the cooking experience will allow you to put the love into the food that will elevate it from simple sustenance to the most memorable part of your trip. This is not the time to multitask with tent setup. If something starts to burn, you need to be avail-

able to quickly adjust the heat by lowering the flame or lifting the pot away from the stove. You want to be ready to add more water as soon as it's needed and put the finishing touches on at the end. Whoever is camping with you is a lucky eater!

Backcountry Cleanup

Remember, and remind others, to save a piece of bread or a scoop of rice to sop up that last little bit of food from the pot for a "camp clean" pot; this reduces how much trash you have to carry out.

If you need to, add some water to the pot and heat it up to make a nice little extra sip of "soup." Use your spork to release any stuck-on bits and stir it up. Whatever you ate originally will taste great as a warm soup sip.

Pack anything that may still have food residue or smell on it into a critter-proof container, keep it distanced from your tent, and enjoy the warm snuggly feeling of being nourished and comforted, no matter how far from home you are.

DEHYDRATING FOOD

Pulling water out of a recipe's ingredients is the simplest and most effective way to make food less perishable and lighter weight. This may feel overwhelming to someone new to the outdoors, but it can be achieved easily with some forethought, and it is essential for successful eating in primitive environments. There are some excellent dehydrated recipes in the Backcountry Recipes section, and you can dive straight into those without knowing much about dehydration. You don't need to own a dehydrator; you can purchase almost any individual ingredient already dehydrated and make our recipes or your favorites that way instead. But we wanted to also give you some general information and tips so you can experiment with dehydration on your own, as it will open up a world of flavor and fun.

Primitive Camping Situations

The most common situations we think about when considering dehydrated meals are multiday backpacking trips into the wilderness, but dehydrated recipes are also great for other types of adventures. Some of these scenarios include multiday kayaking or canoeing trips, bikepacking, and overlanding, which are often done on BLM land or other off-the-grid locations. It can even make sense to bring dehydrated recipes if you own a little two-door coupe and want to save baggage space for a weekend camping trip at an established campground.

We took the opportunity to prepare extra portions of most of the recipes we tested while developing this book and kept them on hand so we didn't have to figure out dinner after full days of work. We still have a good amount packed for our future trips, which is such a freeing feeling that we plan to continue prepping ahead in this way.

Equipment

When pertinent, our Backcountry Recipes will indicate if a dehydrator is required. Of course, having a dedicated dehydrator is the best option for high-quality execution, but you may already have other options in your kitchen. For example, a home oven, even without a dedicated "dehydrate" function, can be very effective at dehydrating simple recipes. Check to see how low the temperature goes and whether it will work for your recipe. To dehydrate using the oven, set the temperature to its lowest setting and keep the oven door propped open (a wooden spoon works great) to ensure airflow. Some air fryers have a dehydrate function. Right before the pandemic started, Emily's oven broke, but she was able to test all the Backcountry Recipes requiring dehydration with her air fryer, which worked perfectly.

The trays that come with a dehydrator are usually perforated so that air can adequately circulate around the food and evenly dry it. For some dehydrated foods, like fruit leather or sauces, you'll need to line the dehydrator trays with parchment paper or a silicone mat so that the more liquid foods don't drip through. Most dehydrator brands make a specialty fruit leather insert as well.

Time

It takes time to dehydrate foods completely. In our recipes, the dehydrating times listed are more of a guide than a hard-and-fast rule. Factors such as humidity, the size of the food you're dehydrating, and the equipment used can vary a great deal from one experience to the next.

When it comes to food items for successful dehydrating, smaller is better, and the more exposed the surface area, the faster it will dry. Another factor is how evenly the food is cut. If

Saag Tofu

you cut thick in some areas and thin in others, the pieces won't dehydrate evenly.

Temperature

The key to successfully dehydrating foods is to use a temperature high enough to remove moisture from the food quickly (to discourage growth of microorganisms), but not so high that the food's exterior is desiccated before the interior has a chance to fully dehydrate. In general, the following temperatures are used for dehydrating individual ingredients:

Herbs	95° F–105° F
Vegetables	115° F–130° F
Fruit	125° F–135° F

For dehydrating entire composed meals, the temperatures vary depending on the recipe. Figuring out the drying temperature takes a lot of trial and error, but that's the fun part. It's an aspect of cooking that we love: the inevitable process of experimentation.

Food Preparation

Before dehydrating vegetables, you'll generally want to blanch them. This means cooking them in boiling water for a brief time, usually just a few minutes for small cut veggies, and immediately plunging them into cold water to prevent them from cooking further once they're beautifully bright and perfectly tender. Blanching vegetables before dehydrating them slows or stops

naturally occurring enzyme activity, which could cause loss of flavor, color, and texture.

Quantity and Volume

You might be shocked at the reduced size of the yield when you dehydrate food. It's not unusual to lose more than half of the volume you started with. If you start with a full pot of curry, for instance, it might dry down to fit in a sandwich-size ziplock bag and probably weigh in at less than 10 ounces. This, after all, is the main advantage of dehydrating recipes, so don't worry if a whole week's worth of food fits in a tiny stuff sack.

Storage and Shelf Life

You want to make sure that foods are fully dehydrated. The worst thing would be that you get to camp, pull out your meal to cook it,

and find it's covered in mold. So the first step is to ensure that you've fully dried your meal. It should generally be crackly and dry to the touch all the way through. If you aren't sure, it's almost always better to overdry than to underdry.

After you're sure the meal is dry, you might consider sticking a desiccant packet in the bag with your food if you'll be storing it for a while. These help bring the humidity down in your bag by absorbing excess moisture. You can buy food-grade silica gel packets in bulk online or save them up from past packaged foods purchases.

Store dehydrated food in airtight containers, such as a well-sealed ziplock bag or a jar with a tight-fitting lid. If you're making your food far in advance, we suggest freezing it and pulling it out right before your trip. If you'll be eating it soon after dehydrating, it's fine to just store it in a cool, dry place. Properly stored, dehydrated foods will keep for months, if not longer.

Discard any food that shows signs of spoilage, such as off smells, unusual discoloration, or mold.

Tips for Dehydrating

- High-fat foods have the potential of going rancid.
- High-sugar foods can be difficult to get fully dry. This is fine for foods like fruit leathers, which are palatable *because* of the texture, but not great for long-preserving meals.
- Bananas get black and chewy.

Dehydrating Entire Meals Versus Ingredients

If you plan to dehydrate individual ingredients, choose small and similarly sized items so that they dehydrate evenly. This method is great for preserving large quantities of a single item. For instance, if you love to hoard kabocha squash (as Aimee does in the fall), you may want to make a bunch of dehydrated squash for future use.

Sometimes you are simply in love with a composed dish or sauce and don't want to have to figure out the dehydrated or powdered quantities of individual ingredients to get that flavor profile right for your next trip. This is a case for making the whole meal and then dehydrating it all at once. It's best to minimize the oil content of these types of recipes before dehydrating. Add that fat content back in at camp.

To Powder or Not to Powder

In some cases, the best way to ensure proper dehydration of a recipe is to grind it to a powder it at the end. This can make it extremely quick to rehydrate and also show that it is fully dry. Most powdered recipes will be fluffy and not clumpy if they are fully dry. However, you don't want to do this if you're looking for textural elements to stay intact. In some cases, you may want to powder only a portion of the whole recipe, like a sauce, then leave other parts unpowdered, like the vegetables.

THE RECIPES

The recipes are divided into four sections, with categories that reflect the type of camp amenities and gear you'll need to prepare them. Our recipes are designed for any type of outdoor experience, deep woods or in the heart of the city, and there are no rules for how to mix or match, other than your personal choice. The recipes include some outdoor-cooking-specific considerations not found in a typical home cookbook, such as cooking water, tools lists, and ingredient weights.

Each trip is unique—it won't always fit into a neat category—so browse through all types of recipes to find ones that will work best for you. For instance, you may be going on a climbing trip where you will have lunch on the hike to the base of your climb

Spicy Tomato Confit

during the day (see On the Trail Recipes), but that night you will be camping in a car campsite with a campfire (see Car Camping Recipes). Or you may also be car camping at a primitive site with no amenities, so something from the Backcountry Recipes may suit your needs.

We used the following criteria to define each recipe category:

ON THE TRAIL RECIPES

These recipes are designed to be packable and ready to eat. They assume that it would be inconvenient to pull out cooking gear to prepare your food, so the cooking and prep should be done ahead of time. You might enjoy On the Trail Recipes at a beach picnic, on a bike ride to your local park, while day hiking and climbing, or as snacks while on a multi-day backcountry trek.

Criteria

- Ability to withstand up to a half day in a backpack under temperate conditions
- Little to no preparation needed on the trail
- Sturdy ingredients better able to withstand the inevitable smooshing and jostling from being transported in a pack or pannier

CAR CAMPING RECIPES

These recipes are most similar to those you'd make in your home kitchen. They can typically be made entirely at camp, if you wish. You'll find recipes that use the campfire for cooking in this section. Examples of when you'd use Car Camping Recipes include car camping at a state park campground, horsepacking to a backcountry hut, or living the van life.

Criteria

- Access to amenities like a personal vehicle, potable water, and fire ring
- Generally few restrictions on weight, space, or perishability
- Designed for four servings unless otherwise noted

BACKCOUNTRY RECIPES

These recipes are traditionally intended for backcountry trips, but there are many other types of experiences that they may be well suited for. Backcountry Recipes tend to be simple to execute and lighter in weight; they are most amenable to long-term storage. Some

examples of times you'd use these are multi-day backpacking trips in the wilderness, off-the-grid overlanding (remote camping with an off-road vehicle) adventures, sea kayaking overnighters, or stocking your emergency survival bin for the next global pandemic lockdown.

Criteria

- Little to no reliance on ingredients that would perish quickly without refrigeration
- Use of lighter-weight ingredients, usually by prioritizing dehydrated or freeze-dried ingredients
- Simple, quick-cooking dishes that minimize effort, recipe steps, and fuel
- Minimization of food waste in recipe calculation, so that ingredient amounts produce portions that can be fully consumed in one sitting
- Generally designed for two servings, unless otherwise noted

STAPLE RECIPES

These recipes are meant to be made at home and are versatile enough to use in more than one way. Some are substitutes for popular perishable or animal-based products (like our favorite Nutty Parmesan, page 288), while others are things we find ourselves continually reaching for and needing to have available (like our Citrus Peel Powder, page 294). We recommend making these recipes at least once to see how useful you find them as you cook your way through home and camp life. Each Staple Recipe is referenced within other recipes throughout this book, highlighting our favorite ways to use them.

ICONS

You'll find icons with some recipes that indicate whether it requires dehydrating or significant prep time, or if it's designed to be cooked over a fire or coals.

 Appears on recipes that call for a **dehydration tool**. You can learn more about this in the Dehydrating Food section (page 53).

 Appears on recipes that require **extended prep time**, usually one hour or more. That prep may involve steps like soaking, freezing, marinating, or steeping. Note that we do not list prep time on all recipes in this book. We want each camp cook to be empowered to prep as much at home or at camp as they like, and this will add a great deal of variability from one person's experience to another for most recipes.

 Appears on recipes designed to be cooked with **the use of fire or coals**. This may be a campfire, grill, or similar.

HOW TO USE THE RECIPES

To make it easy to find the perfect recipe for your outing, we've added some key information. Some of this information is noted in only one or two recipes sections.

TOOLS: A quick list of the tools you should pack with your camping supplies to make the recipe. Note that we do not list tools that are only expected to be used in your home kitchen.

DEHYDRATION TIME: At-home dehydration time.

COOKING TIME: Any cooking time needed at camp for Backcountry and Car Camping Recipes only, based on sea-level elevation (see tips on altitude considerations on page 26). There is no at-camp cook time required for recipes in the On the Trail section.

COOKING WATER: Information provided for the Backcountry Recipes so you can properly plan when water access is limited.

NUTRITION INFO: Estimated calorie, fat, carbohydrate, and protein information *per serving* for Backcountry Recipes.

WEIGHT: Estimated weight of the *entire* packaged recipe, including standard ziplock bags. Listed for Backcountry Recipes only.

ON THE TRAIL RECIPES

SAVORY SNACKS

Spicy Ranch Oyster Crackers

lemon pepper, garlic, dill

Makes 8 servings
Cooking time: 10 minutes

1 teaspoon dried dill
1 teaspoon onion powder
1 teaspoon garlic powder
½ teaspoon lemon pepper
¼ teaspoon cayenne
¼ cup neutral oil
9-ounce package salted oyster crackers

My family has been making a ranch oyster cracker snack recipe for as long as I can remember. I've seen it on the counter at my mom's, grandmother's, and many uncles' homes through the years. It relies on an instant packet of ranch seasoning, which isn't plant-based or readily available in my pantry, so I wanted a recipe with the same flavor profile using ingredients I usually have on hand. Oyster crackers are very snackable and double as a nice topping option for a camp dinner after a day on the trail, and these will knock your socks off with zing. Thanks, family! —Emily

Preheat the oven to 250° F.

In a large bowl, combine the dill, onion powder, garlic powder, lemon pepper, and cayenne. Whisk in the oil.

Add the oyster crackers and stir to fully coat.

Spread out in a single layer on a baking sheet and bake for 10 minutes, stirring once about halfway through.

Let the crackers cool and pack them for your day trip, without eating too many at home first.

Tip: If you don't have lemon pepper, try adding ½ teaspoon of Citrus Peel Powder (page 294).

Spicy Ranch Oyster Crackers

Tea-Infused Tofu Bites (page 66)

Tea-Infused Tofu Bites

five-spice powder, black tea, soy sauce

Makes 4 servings

Cooking time: 10 minutes, plus overnight marinating

1 (16-ounce) block extra-firm or super-firm tofu, cut into bite-size cubes

2½ cups water

4 bags black tea

½ teaspoon ground ginger

½ teaspoon five-spice powder

2 bay leaves

1 tablespoon soy sauce

1 teaspoon dark soy sauce (optional)

1 teaspoon sugar

1 teaspoon salt

2 garlic cloves, thinly sliced

My dad was born and raised in Hong Kong, and it's been a long-time dream of his to show my brother and me his old stomping grounds. We eventually got it together and committed to making the journey there as a family in February 2020. It was going to be great—Chinese New Year celebrations, sightseeing, and all the culinary delights. As the trip date approached, political tensions with China led to increasingly violent protests, and a contagious virus was quickly becoming omnipresent. Needless to say, the trip was canceled. I was left with my foodie wish list and resolved to try to make some of the more attainable dishes myself, including the classic Chinese tea egg. This is a typical snack sold by street vendors—a hard-boiled egg infused with flavors of a rich, aromatic tea broth. This recipe takes all the delicious flavors of the tea broth and marries them with tofu instead for an elegant, portable, and healthy snack. —Mai-Yan

Arrange the tofu cubes in a single layer in an 8-inch-square or 2-quart baking dish. Set aside.

In a small saucepan, bring the water to a boil. Turn off the heat and steep the tea bags in the hot water for 5 minutes, then remove them.

Add the ginger, five-spice powder, bay leaves, soy sauce, dark soy sauce, sugar, salt, and garlic, and bring the mixture to a gentle boil over low heat for 5 minutes.

Pour the hot tea mixture over the tofu and cover. Marinate in the refrigerator overnight. The sauce should mostly cover the tofu cubes, but if it doesn't, consider flipping them halfway through the marinating process so they are evenly "browned."

When the cubes are done marinating, drain all the liquid and pack the cubes in a leakproof container. Make sure to pack a fork.

Nacho Kale Chips

bell peppers, nutritional yeast, smoked paprika

Makes 4 to 6 servings (6 ounces)
Dehydration time: 8 to 9 hours

1 cup unsalted cashews

1 cup chopped red, orange, or yellow bell pepper

2 tablespoons nutritional yeast

1¼ teaspoons salt

¼ teaspoon smoked paprika

1 tablespoon olive oil

2 tablespoons fresh lemon juice

Pepper

¼ cup water

2 large bunches kale, stemmed and torn into large bite-size pieces

These kale chips are a surefire way to get my kids to eat their greens. We can go through an entire batch in an afternoon between the four of us in my family. That's two bunches of kale, devoured like Cheetos! Eat them by the handful, or use them to top everything from soup to pasta. —Aimee

To make the sauce: Put the cashews, bell pepper, nutritional yeast, salt, smoked paprika, olive oil, lemon juice, a few sprinkles of pepper, and ¼ cup water in a blender. Blend until completely smooth, adding more water as needed to keep the blender moving, a tablespoon at a time.

To make the chips: Put the kale in a large bowl and pour the bell pepper cashew sauce over it. Use clean hands or tongs to toss and evenly coat the kale in the cashew sauce. It will be pretty wet.

Place the kale in a single layer on dehydrator trays.

Dehydrate at 135° F for 8 to 9 hours, or until completely dry.

Store in an airtight container.

Cheese Straws

Cashew Dream Sauce, puff pastry, everything bagel mix

Makes about 20 straws

Cooking time: 20 minutes

1 recipe Cashew Dream Sauce (page 288)

¼ teaspoon pepper

¼ teaspoon smoked paprika

¼ teaspoon cayenne

2 sheets (about a 1-pound package) vegan puff pastry, thawed in the refrigerator overnight

Flour, for rolling the pastry

About 4 tablespoons everything bagel mix

Cheese straws are a Southern staple and can be made plant-based with our favorite Cashew Dream Sauce. I like to experiment with different spice or seed mixes to add a little more pizzazz; I chose everything bagel spice mix here, but my Southern mama reminded me that cheese straws should *always* have cayenne pepper. —Emily

Make the Cashew Dream Sauce and add to it the pepper, smoked paprika, and cayenne.

Flour a board and roll out 1 sheet of puff pastry into a thin (about ⅛-inch-thick), even rectangle.

Spread half the rectangle lengthwise with a thin layer of cashew sauce. Sprinkle with about a tablespoon of everything bagel mix.

Fold the pastry in half to enclose the cashew sauce, and slice into strips ½ to 1 inch wide.

Repeat with second sheet of puff pastry.

Twist each strip 4 or 5 times and place on a baking sheet. Brush with additional cashew sauce, then sprinkle with the remaining everything bagel mix. Chill in the refrigerator for at least 10 minutes. Meanwhile, preheat the oven to 400° F.

Move the cheese straws directly from the refrigerator to the oven and bake until very golden brown, about 15 minutes.

Let cool completely and pack in an airtight container for your day trip.

Winter Vegetable Platter

beets, jicama, creamy tofu dip

Makes 4 to 6 servings

No cook recipe

1 beet (red or golden), peeled and thinly sliced

1 kohlrabi (softball-size or smaller), peeled and thinly sliced

1 small jicama, peeled and sliced

4 to 6 carrots (orange, purple, yellow), peeled and halved lengthwise

1 bunch radishes, stemmed and halved or sliced

TOFU DIP

8 ounces firm tofu

6 tablespoons neutral vegetable oil

6 tablespoons water

3 tablespoons nutritional yeast

2 tablespoons soy sauce

1 teaspoon fresh lemon juice

⅛ teaspoon garlic powder

Savory tofu dip has been a staple in my home ever since I tried it ten years ago at The Spot in Hermosa Beach, California. This restaurant has been around since the '70s, when being vegetarian was mostly for hippies. I've simplified the recipe over the years based on the items that I usually have on hand. This dip will totally work with the usual crudité suspects, but I encourage you to discover new textures and flavors to take advantage of the fresh seasonal vegetables available to you. Kohlrabi is crisp and crunchy and tastes like broccoli stem crossed with a hint of apple. Jicama is juicy and has the starchy sweetness and texture of an Asian pear. —Mai-Yan

Pack the vegetables in a leakproof container.

To make the dip: Crumble the tofu with your hands directly into a blender, and add the oil, water, nutritional yeast, soy sauce, lemon juice, and garlic powder. Blend until completely smooth. Adjust the seasoning with more soy sauce and/or nutritional yeast to taste.

Pack the dip in a leakproof container, ideally one with a wide mouth.

Keep everything refrigerated or in a cooler until ready to serve.

Tip: To get the best-looking vegetables for your day trip, choose types that won't discolor once they are chopped, and store them with a little bit of water to keep them hydrated.

Cracked Pepper Seitan Jerky

garlic, liquid smoke, freshly cracked black pepper

Makes 4 servings

Dehydration time: 1 hour to 1 hour 15 minutes

4 tablespoons soy sauce

2 tablespoons ketchup

2 teaspoons sugar

1 teaspoon liquid smoke

1 teaspoon garlic powder

½ teaspoon pepper

12 ounces sliced Seitan (page 292), ⅛ to ¼ inch thick

2 tablespoons freshly cracked pepper, for finishing

For those who are somewhat new to plant-based eating and concerned about protein intake, this is the snack for you! Seitan (pronounced SAY-tan) is made from vital wheat gluten and is high in protein with very little fat and carbohydrates. And it's delicious, because it can taste like whatever you want and has a satisfying "meaty" texture.

This jerky starts with marinated fresh seitan that is then lightly dehydrated. Once you've mastered this recipe, feel free to expand your arsenal and create your own jerky flavors. —Mai-Yan

In a medium bowl, mix the soy sauce, ketchup, sugar, liquid smoke, garlic powder, and pepper.

Add the seitan and stir to coat all sides.

Let it marinate for at least 1 hour and up to overnight, stirring occasionally to evenly coat the seitan.

Place the marinated seitan on trays in the dehydrator and season with freshly cracked pepper from a pepper mill.

Dehydrate the seitan for 1 hour at 160° F.

Check the seitan: It should be mostly dry with a bit of spring when pressed. Remove any pieces that feel ready. If the seitan still feels wet, dehydrate for another 10 to 15 minutes at the same setting.

Tip: The seitan tends to keep drying out on its own over time, so it's best to slightly underdry it to get the best texture.

Cracked Pepper Seitan Jerky

Herby Red Lentil Spread (page 74)

Herby Red Lentil Spread

cumin, parsley, Aleppo pepper

Makes 3 cups

Cooking time: 20 minutes

2½ cups water

½ cup red lentils, rinsed

½ cup bulgur

6 tablespoons olive oil, divided

1 onion, finely chopped

2 garlic cloves, minced

2 tablespoons tomato paste

1 teaspoon ground cumin

1 teaspoon salt

½ to 1 teaspoon Aleppo pepper (optional)

1 bunch fresh Italian parsley, finely chopped

½ cup chopped scallions

This recipe is adapted from a Turkish classic dish called *mercimek köftesi*, or lentil meatballs. To make this dish more portable, we've skipped the "meatball" assembly portion and decided to offer it as more of a spread. Although the ingredients are relatively straightforward, the combination of these flavors is unique and it's hard to resist eating more. If you have leftovers, the flavors will continue to develop and get better over time, so this is a great one to have in the fridge. —Mai-Yan

Bring 2½ cups of water to a boil in a 2-quart pot and add the lentils and bulgur. Turn down the heat to maintain a gentle simmer, partially cover with a lid, and cook for 10 minutes, or until all the water is absorbed.

Remove from the heat and let sit, covered, for 10 minutes to steam and finish the cooking process.

Meanwhile, in a skillet set over medium heat, heat 2 tablespoons of the olive oil. Add the onion and sauté until golden, 6 to 8 minutes. Add the garlic, tomato paste, cumin, salt, and Aleppo pepper, and cook for a minute more. Add 1 tablespoon of water to help scrape up any stuck-on tomato paste bits and mix those in. Turn off the heat.

In a large bowl, combine the cooked red lentils and bulgur, the spiced onion mixture, and the remaining 4 tablespoons of olive oil. Mix with a fork, mashing everything together until well combined.

Add the parsley and scallions and mix until evenly distributed.

Keep the spread refrigerated until you are ready to pack it for your outing.

Serve with crackers, hummus, and crudités.

Tip: If you're going on a picnic and are bringing a cooler, consider serving this with lettuce leaves for a refreshing, hand-held snack.

SWEET SNACKS

Almond Butter Granola Brittle

whole almonds, almond extract

Makes 4 cups

Cooking time: 30 to 35 minutes

3 cups rolled oats

1 cup raw almonds

⅓ cup shredded coconut

¾ teaspoon cinnamon

¼ teaspoon salt

⅓ cup creamy almond butter

½ cup packed brown sugar

¼ cup golden syrup, maple syrup, or agave syrup

6 tablespoons plant butter

1 teaspoon almond extract

We've been making various versions of granola brittle for years. Everyone loves it, it's super easy to make, and it travels well. Aimee set out to make a new flavor after trying Trader Joe's Almond Butter Granola. The toasted almonds, hint of coconut, and strong almond extract flavor all come together to make what is now my favorite version of granola brittle. I've made about seven batches of this since Aimee first asked me to test the recipe. The almond extract is the ingredient that makes it addictive. —Emily

Preheat the oven to 300° F. Line a baking sheet with parchment paper or a silicone baking mat.

In a large bowl, combine the oats, almonds, coconut, cinnamon, and salt.

In a small pot over medium-low heat, mix the almond butter, brown sugar, golden syrup, and butter. Whisk until the mixture is thoroughly combined and smooth. Remove from the heat and stir in the almond extract. Use a rubber spatula to scrape the mixture into the bowl with the oat mixture. Stir to mix well.

Pour the mixture onto the prepared baking sheet and bake for 30 to 35 minutes, stirring once or twice during the baking time to ensure that everything bakes evenly.

Cool the granola completely without stirring, then break it up into chunks. Store in an airtight container.

Tip: If you want this to stick together well and be more brittle-like, go for golden syrup. It will still be delicious with maple or agave syrup, but it may be a bit more crumbly.

Almond Butter Granola Brittle (page 75)

Pistachio Date Balls (page 78)

Crunchy Chocolate Chip Cookies (page 79)

Pistachio Date Balls

sweet and salty, cardamom

Makes about 30 1-inch balls

No-cook recipe

1½ cups shelled roasted salted pistachios, divided

2 cups soft Medjool dates, pitted

½ teaspoon ground cardamom

There are only three ingredients in these treats, but they're much more than the sum of their parts. The combination of salty pistachios, sweet dates, and herbal cardamom just works. The flavor reminds me of the dairy-heavy treats we used to buy at our favorite Indian sweet shop. We took these on a recent day trip to our local beach and had to fight the kids off to keep them from grabbing them straight out of the container. Sandy hands and communal food don't mix! —Aimee

In the bowl of a food processor, buzz ¼ cup of the pistachios until powdery. Don't process too long, or it will turn to nut butter. Transfer to a bowl and set aside; no need to wipe the food processor bowl clean.

In the bowl of the food processor, process the dates until they are broken down and form a paste. In processing, the dates will form a big ball around the blade of the food processor.

Add the remaining pistachios and the cardamom to the date paste and process until the mixture comes together. If you have a smaller food processor, it may help to do this in batches. In that case, try to break the date ball up into little chunks as you add smaller amounts of pistachios.

Turn the mixture out onto a clean work surface and pull off pieces to roll into 1-inch balls.

Roll each ball in the reserved finely ground pistachios and store in an airtight container.

Crunchy Chocolate Chip Cookies

walnuts, brown sugar, vanilla extract

Makes about 100 mini cookies

Cooking time: 15 minutes

2 cups all-purpose flour

1 teaspoon salt

¾ teaspoon baking powder

¼ cup plant butter

½ cup shortening

¾ cup sugar

¼ cup packed brown sugar

2 tablespoons plant milk

1 teaspoon vanilla extract

½ cup finely chopped walnuts

1 cup (6 ounces) chopped vegan chocolate (try for a mix of small shreds and slightly bigger chunks)

Turbinado sugar, for sprinkling *(optional)*

Aimee is our resident baker, and this recipe is her re-creation of the Famous Amos cookie. I doubted her. I doubted that I would want this many cookies. But of course I was wrong. There's something really fun about eating a one-bite cookie, plus they are very portable and shareable. Don't even think about halving this recipe—you will need all of them. —Mai-Yan

Preheat the oven to 350° F. Line two baking sheets with parchment paper.

In a medium bowl, stir together the flour, salt, and baking powder.

In the bowl of a stand mixer fitted with the paddle attachment (or with a hand mixer), cream together the butter, shortening, sugar, and brown sugar until very light and fluffy, about 5 minutes. Add the milk and vanilla extract and mix well.

Stir in the flour mixture, followed by the walnuts and chocolate.

Drop by scant teaspoons (each about ¼ to ⅓ ounce) onto the prepared baking sheets, leaving about 1 inch between the cookies. Sprinkle with turbinado sugar. Bake for 8 to 10 minutes, until the cookies are lightly browned and firm to the touch.

Let cool slightly before transferring to cooling racks to cool completely.

Date and Nut Quick Bread

orange zest, pecans, hazelnuts

Makes 1 loaf

Cooking time: 60 to 70 minutes

1½ cups chopped pitted dates

1 cup plus 3 tablespoons hot water, divided

¼ cup pecans, coarsely chopped

¼ cup hazelnuts, coarsely chopped

2 cups all-purpose flour

1½ teaspoons baking powder

1 teaspoon salt

1 tablespoon ground flaxseed

½ cup plant butter, softened

½ cup sugar

1 teaspoon orange zest

2 teaspoons vanilla extract

2 tablespoons hemp seeds

It might not sound that interesting, but this bread is really special. It's filled with nuts and seeds, but it doesn't taste too dense. The dates offer a mellow sweetness and pair nicely with the orange zest. Pack this bread for a long day hike or take it to a fancy picnic, and serve slices spread with orange marmalade alongside a thermos of tea. —Mai-Yan

Preheat the oven to 350° F. Grease a 9-by-5-inch loaf pan.

In a small bowl, cover the chopped dates with 1 cup of the hot water. Set aside.

Toast the pecans and hazelnuts on a baking sheet for 8 to 10 minutes or until lightly toasted and fragrant.

In a medium mixing bowl, whisk together the flour, baking powder, and salt.

In a small bowl, combine the ground flaxseed with the remaining 3 tablespoons of hot water and mix well.

Cream together the butter and sugar with a stand mixer fitted with the paddle attachment, or with a hand mixer. Beat on medium-high speed until light and fluffy. Add the flax mixture, orange zest, and vanilla and continue mixing until combined.

Add the flour mixture and mix until just combined. Stir in the dates with their soaking water, the toasted nuts, and the hemp seeds. Mix just until all the ingredients are incorporated. Scrape the batter into the prepared loaf pan.

Bake for 60 to 70 minutes, or until a toothpick inserted into the center of the loaf comes out clean. Cool on a rack for at least 15 minutes before removing the loaf from the pan.

Store in an airtight container at room temperature for up to 4 days or freeze for longer storage.

Tip: If you don't have a standard loaf pan, experiment using other shapes. Emily successfully made this using her toaster oven and a 10-inch cast iron skillet.

Granola Bar Chews

brown rice syrup, crisped rice cereal, nut butter

Makes about 36 squares

Cooking time: 25 to 30 minutes

2 cups crisped rice cereal

1½ cups rolled oats

1 cup roughly chopped toasted nuts, such as almonds or pistachios

1 cup dried fruit, such as blueberries, cranberries, or raisins

¾ cup well-stirred nut or seed butter, such as almond or sunflower

½ cup brown rice syrup

⅓ cup maple syrup

2 tablespoons coconut oil

1 teaspoon vanilla extract

¾ teaspoon salt

These Granola Bar Chews are a sort of choose-your-own-adventure treat. Many times I'll buy some nuts or dried fruit for a recipe and then the rest of the package sits around until it dries out or becomes rancid. This is a great way to use up all those last bits before that happens and turn them into something delicious. Mix and match whatever nut butter, nuts, and fruit you have on hand. The only must here is the brown rice syrup. It makes the texture perfectly chewy without being overly sweet. —Aimee

Preheat the oven to 350° F. Line a 9-by-9-inch (or similar size) baking pan with parchment paper long enough to extend above the sides of the pan (so that you can easily remove the bars after they're baked).

In a large bowl, combine the rice cereal, oats, nuts, and dried fruit.

In a saucepan, mix the nut butter, brown rice syrup, maple syrup, coconut oil, vanilla, and salt. Heat over medium heat until the mixture is well combined and bubbly. Remove from the heat.

Stir the hot nut-butter mixture into the cereal mixture and mix well. Spread evenly in the prepared baking pan and press down to ensure that it's even.

Bake for 25 to 30 minutes, or until golden brown. Let cool in the pan for 10 minutes before pulling up on the parchment to lift the bars onto a cutting board. Let cool completely before cutting into 1½-inch squares. Store in an airtight container.

Strawberry Balsamic Fruit Leather

*strawberries,
balsamic vinegar*

Makes 10 servings

Dehydration time: 4 to 6 hours

1½ **pounds strawberries, hulled**
3 to 4 **teaspoons balsamic vinegar**
Pinch of salt
Up to 3 tablespoons sugar

I think the addition of balsamic vinegar makes this special enough to warrant making your own fruit leather. If you didn't tell anyone what was in it, they probably wouldn't know it had the balsamic. They would just think it tastes like strawberries, but more delicious. This is a great way to use up strawberries that are almost past their prime, or ones that are just not that flavorful. The vinegar brings out the sweetness of the fruit without adding a bunch of extra sugar. —Aimee

Put the strawberries, 3 teaspoons of the balsamic vinegar, and a pinch of salt in a blender. Blend until smooth.

Taste and add sugar and additional vinegar as needed. The sweetness will intensify as the fruit dehydrates, so it doesn't need to be super sweet at this point.

Spread the fruit puree on dehydrator trays lined with silicone mats or parchment paper. Try to get it in a thin (about ⅛-inch-thick), even layer.

Dehydrate at 135° F for 4 to 6 hours, or until it's no longer sticky to the touch and easily peels off the parchment.

Allow to cool completely, then carefully peel the fruit leather off the parchment. Cut into pieces 1 to 1½ inches wide, roll in parchment paper, and store in an airtight container.

Tip: These instructions are for a dehydrator, but you can easily make fruit leather in the oven. Just preheat to the lowest temperature (usually around 170° F), make sure the fruit puree is not spread too thin, and keep a close eye on it so it doesn't get too dry.

Power Biscotti

energy-packed dried fruit, nuts, seeds

Makes about 18 biscotti
Baking time: 45 to 50 minutes

When I was growing up, my dad was very into racing. Triathlons, marathons, adventure races—he did them all. Energy bars weren't really a thing at that time. There were Power Bars, but not many other options. I made it my mission to come up with a homemade energy cookie that could fuel him when he was training, and biscotti seemed to be the perfect answer. I called them Power Biscotti, and he loved them.

Even now, with endless energy bar options, biscotti are one of my favorite trail foods. They can withstand being smashed in a

2 cups all-purpose flour

¼ cup arrowroot powder

1 teaspoon baking powder

½ teaspoon salt

1 cup sugar

⅓ cup plant milk

¼ cup neutral oil

1 teaspoon vanilla extract

½ cup dried cranberries, cherries, or blueberries (or a combination)

¼ cup chopped hazelnuts

2 tablespoons hemp hearts

2 tablespoons sesame seeds

2 tablespoons sunflower seeds

2 teaspoons poppy seeds

backpack, they stay fresh for weeks, and they are sweet, but not overly so. This version is loaded with seeds and fruit; feel free to mix it up and use whatever nuts, seeds, and dried fruit you have on hand. —Aimee

Preheat the oven to 350° F. Line a baking sheet with parchment paper or a silicone mat.

In a medium bowl, whisk together the flour, arrowroot, baking powder, and salt.

In a large bowl, whisk together the sugar, plant milk, oil, and vanilla extract. Add the flour mixture and stir just to combine. Stir in the dried fruit, hazelnuts, hemp hearts, sesame seeds, sunflower seeds, and poppy seeds. You may want to use your hands at this point.

Transfer the dough to the prepared baking sheet and shape it into a smooth, flat log 2 to 2½ inches wide. Use your hands or a bench knife to even out the edges so that the biscotti are neat. If the dough sticks to your hands, dampen them with a little water.

Bake the log for 30 minutes, until it's slightly puffed up and firm. Remove from the oven and set aside to cool for 10 to 15 minutes, leaving the oven on.

Use a sharp knife to cut the log into 1-inch slices.

Place the biscotti back on the baking sheet, cut side down, and return them to the oven. After 10 minutes, turn the biscotti over and continue baking for another 5 to 10 minutes.

Cool the biscotti slightly on the pan, then transfer to a wire rack to cool completely.

Store in an airtight container. Biscotti will keep for several weeks, but may soften in a humid climate. You can also freeze them for several months.

MEALS

Lemony Dill Chickpea Salad Sandwiches

mustard, dill pickles, hearty bread

Makes 4 sandwiches

No cook recipe

¼ cup plant-based mayonnaise

1 tablespoon fresh lemon juice

1 tablespoon dill pickle relish or chopped dill pickles

1 teaspoon whole-grain mustard

1 teaspoon dry dill or 1 tablespoon chopped fresh dill

½ teaspoon pepper

1 (14-ounce) can chickpeas, drained and rinsed

Salt

8 slices bread

Lettuce, pickle slices, and/or onion slices

Chickpea salad recipes are pretty common in vegan cookbooks and blogs, and they work as a great substitute for deli meats on sandwiches. Chickpeas are rich in protein and work well with many common sandwich flavors. I always want to have quick sandwich ingredients on hand for when I'm starving or squeezing in a last-minute hike, but some recipes are complicated enough to force me back to the old PBJ instead. I wanted this one to be very last-minute-outdoorist friendly, so I limited the list of chopped fresh ingredients. I also mashed the chickpeas more than usual, so the salad stays in the sandwich better, making it easier to follow Leave No Trace principles on the trail. —Mai-Yan

In a medium bowl, mix the mayo, lemon juice, pickle relish, mustard, dill, and pepper until well combined.

Add the chickpeas and mash well with a potato masher.

Season to taste with salt.

Spread ¼ of the mix onto a piece of bread. Top with crunchy lettuce, pickles, and/or fresh onion, followed by a second slice of bread. Repeat to make the remaining sandwiches and pack them for your trip.

Lemony Dill Chickpea Salad Sandwiches

Pretzel Sausage Rolls with Mustard Cheese Sauce (page 90)

Pretzel Sausage Rolls with Mustard Cheese Sauce

crescent roll dough, sausages, mustard cashew cheese sauce

Makes 16 rolls

Cooking time: 30 to 40 minutes

10 cups water

¼ cup baking soda

2 cans crescent roll dough

4 precooked plant-based Italian or kielbasa sausages, cut in half and again in half lengthwise to make 4 equal-size pieces

2 tablespoons plant milk

2 tablespoons pretzel salt or ½ teaspoon coarse salt

MUSTARD CHEESE SAUCE

1 cup raw cashews

¾ cup water

1 tablespoon fresh lemon juice

1 teaspoon nutritional yeast

½ teaspoon salt

1 garlic clove

2 tablespoons whole-grain mustard

As silly as crescent rolls in a can are, I'm a big fan. They are one of those "accidentally plant-based" items you can buy at practically any grocery store. They taste great to everyone and can be wrapped around everything. I have made pigs-in-a-blanket monsters of every kid I know (you're welcome, parents) and all of my climbing friends too, since they're my #1 most packed climbing trip food. I love to see what else can be done with them—especially for day trips!

This is pretty much my dream recipe, because I am also a big pretzel fan. It feels strange to be boiling your crescent rolls and turning them into a soggy mess, but then they magically transform into an amazing lunch! —Emily

Preheat the oven to 400° F. Line a baking sheet with parchment paper or a silicone mat.

In a large pot set over high heat, dissolve the baking soda in the water and bring to a rolling boil.

Place a sausage segment on a crescent roll, and roll it up as you would for pigs in blankets.

When the water is boiling, carefully lower 2 crescent dogs into the water using a slotted spoon and boil them for 30 seconds. Remove and put on the baking sheet.

Repeat with 2 rolls at a time until all the crescent rolls are boiled. They will look soggy and odd.

Brush the rolls with the plant milk and sprinkle with salt. Bake for 20 to 30 minutes, until golden brown. Remove and let cool completely before packing.

To make the sauce: Put the cashews, water, lemon juice, nutritional yeast, salt, garlic, and mustard in a blender and blend on high until very smooth. Taste and adjust seasonings as needed. Pack in a leakproof container.

Freezer Stash Tortellini

sweet potatoes, pine nuts, garlic

Makes 40 to 50 tortellini, or 8 to 10 servings

Cooking time: 3 minutes

1 package wonton wrappers (usually about 50 wrappers)

FILLING

2 large sweet potatoes

¼ cup pine nuts or cashews

1 tablespoon fresh lemon juice

Zest of 1 lemon

2 garlic cloves

2 tablespoons plant butter, at room temperature

1 tablespoon nutritional yeast

½ teaspoon salt

½ teaspoon crushed red pepper flakes

I used to rely heavily on fresh-packed cheese-filled tortellini when I needed food fast. Three minutes and I was set. I ate them at home after school and on my breaks at work, and eventually I realized I loved them cold as a light lunch or snack on climbing trips. But all packaged tortellini in the world seems to be filled with cheese, which is sad news for those avoiding dairy who also want a quick, easy meal.

When it comes to having great food, day trips can be challenging because they are often short and spontaneous. But if you do the prep work way ahead of time, you'll be ready. Make lots of these in advance and freeze them until you need them. They can also be added to a pot of soup at camp if you have any left over at the end of the day. —Emily

To make the filling: Preheat the oven to 400° F. Put the whole sweet potatoes on a baking sheet and bake until soft, 45 minutes to 1 hour. Let them cool for about 15 minutes, then scoop out the flesh into the bowl of a blender or food processor. You'll want about 2 cups total.

Add the nuts, lemon juice and zest, garlic, butter, nutritional yeast, salt, and red pepper flakes to the sweet potatoes and puree until the mixture is smooth.

To shape the tortellini: Set out one wonton wrapper on a cutting board with the points oriented into a diamond shape. Set a small bowl of water next to it.

Put 1 heaping teaspoon of the sweet potato filling in the center of the wonton wrapper. Dip your finger into the water and moisten the top edges of the wrapper; the water will act as glue.

Fold the bottom point of the wonton wrapper up to meet the top point, and press into a triangle, ensuring that the filling stays snuggled in the center. With a fork, crimp the edges of the triangle closed.

Dip your finger into the water again and touch it to the side points of the triangle. Bring these points together. This will form a ring shape, where the filling is like the jewel of that ring with the top point as a little flag pointing up.

As you work, set each piece on a baking sheet and repeat the process until all of the filling is used. Put the baking sheet in the freezer until the tortellini are fully frozen, about 1 hour. Transfer them to an airtight container and store in the freezer for up to a month.

To cook the tortellini: Bring a large pot of water to a boil over high heat. Add as many tortellini as you want (typically 5 per serving), and boil for 3 minutes, or until the tortellini float to the top.

Drain and drizzle with a little bit of olive oil to keep them from sticking. Top with Nutty Parmesan (page 288), fresh spinach, and/or marinara sauce and pack them up for the trail.

Tip: If you have extra filling or wrappers, you can freeze them for next time. Also, if you are adding the tortellini to your soup at camp, make sure they are preboiled or that your soup is boiling when you add them. This is important to ensure that the wonton wrappers take on the texture of pasta.

Chile Lime Rice Bowls

chipotle peppers, sesame-crusted tofu, roasted sweet potato rounds

Makes 4 servings

Cooking time: 30 minutes

¼ cup soy sauce

1 tablespoon minced chipotles canned in adobo

Juice of 1 lime

1 teaspoon toasted sesame oil

1 (16-ounce) block firm or extra-firm tofu, pressed and cubed

1½ cups brown rice

2 sweet potatoes, peeled if desired, and sliced into rounds about ¼ inch thick

⅓ cup olive oil, divided

Salt and pepper

1 large bunch asparagus, trimmed and cut into 2-inch pieces

1 tablespoon raw sesame seeds

CHILE LIME TAHINI SAUCE

Leftover tofu marinade (from above)

¼ cup tahini

Extra lime and chipotles

FOR SERVING

Extra lime slices

Cilantro, chopped *(optional)*

Wes and I adopted our three children in the summer of 2019. This was right at the end of our first cookbook tour, and our lives were absolute chaos. We were as shocked as anyone when just a few months later, in March 2020, we were told that all five of us would be staying home together for the foreseeable future. We chose to do an independent study program through school instead of the scheduled online meetings, which allowed us to spend one or two weekdays every week climbing and hiking as a family. This turned out to be a magical and very important experience for us.

Prepping for these frequent trips was the biggest challenge. We forgot the climbing gear more than once, dropped homework into crevasses before we thought to bring clipboards, and always had to figure out what everyone would eat. Rice bowls became a go-to because of their versatility and heartiness. We often used leftover vegetables from dinner to build them, and almost always used tahini as the base for a sauce. —Emily

In a large container or bowl, whisk together the soy sauce, minced chipotles, lime juice, and sesame oil to make the tofu marinade. Add the tofu cubes, ensuring that they are evenly coated with the marinade, and set aside.

Cook the rice according to the package instructions.

Meanwhile, preheat the oven to 400° F. Arrange the sweet potato rounds in a single layer on a baking sheet and brush with about 1 tablespoon of the olive oil. Sprinkle with salt and pepper, and begin roasting, setting a timer for 20 minutes.

Arrange the asparagus on a second baking sheet, drizzle with about 1 tablespoon of the olive oil, and sprinkle with salt and pepper. Set on another rack in the oven and roast all the vegetables until they are tender and beginning to char, 20 to 25 minutes for the sweet potatoes and 15 minutes for the asparagus. Flip the sweet potatoes over after they start to brown on one side, and stir the asparagus occasionally.

While the vegetables are roasting, remove the tofu from the marinade (reserve the marinade) and sauté in a skillet with the remaining olive oil over medium-high heat. Stir occasionally until

the tofu is browned on most sides. Remove from the heat and sprinkle with the sesame seeds. Stir to coat the tofu and let it sit in the hot pan to toast a bit as everything else finishes.

Add the tahini to the bowl of leftover tofu marinade and whisk to combine. Taste for flavor balance and add more lime juice and/or chipotle peppers as needed. If the sauce seems too thick, add 1 or 2 teaspoons of water to thin it out.

Once everything has cooled slightly, assemble the bowls. Portion the rice, veggies, and tofu among 4 containers and cover. Pack the tahini sauce in a separate leakproof container.

When you're ready to eat, add some sauce and a squeeze of lime to each container, sprinkle with cilantro, and enjoy.

Tip: If you can't find asparagus, choose any of your favorite vegetables that are in season. Some delicious options could be broccoli, Brussels sprouts, or red bell peppers.

Keep the sauce container in your fridge with the rice bowl container so that you don't forget it. If it fits inside the bowl, put it there.

Black Bean Torta Rolls

crescent roll dough, chile de árbol, cumin

Makes 16 rolls

Cooking time: 30 minutes

2 tablespoons olive oil

1 medium onion, diced

1 green bell pepper, diced

3 garlic cloves, minced

1 teaspoon oregano

½ to 1 teaspoon ground cumin

½ teaspoon salt

¼ teaspoon pepper

1 (8-ounce) can black beans, drained and rinsed

2 cans crescent roll dough

PICANTE SAUCE

8 to 10 dried chiles de árbol, or similar

6 tablespoons hot water

2 tablespoons tomato paste

1½ tablespoons white vinegar

1 garlic clove

½ teaspoon salt

½ teaspoon ground cumin

½ teaspoon oregano

Yes, another crescent roll recipe! This one is based on the Mexican torta ahogada—a sloppy sandwich made on a delicious bolillo roll topped with fresh vegetables like bell peppers and "drowned" in a picante red sauce. That's exactly what I want after a hot and sweaty active morning in the wilderness, but since that sandwich wouldn't survive in my pack, this is the next best thing. —Mai-Yan

To make the sauce: Put the dried chiles in a small bowl with hot water to soak for about 15 minutes. Put the chiles and their soaking water, tomato paste, vinegar, garlic, salt, cumin, and oregano in a blender and blend on high until smooth. Pour the sauce into a leakproof container.

To make the rolls: Heat the olive oil in a large skillet over medium-high heat. Add the onion and sauté until translucent, about 5 minutes. Add the bell pepper and sauté until tender, about 5 minutes.

Add the garlic, oregano, cumin, salt, and pepper and sauté until fragrant, about 2 minutes.

Add the beans and mix until well combined. Remove the pan from the heat and set it aside.

Preheat the oven to 400° F.

Unroll and cut the crescent rolls along the perforated lines. Spread about 2 tablespoons of filling across each one, then loosely roll them up starting at the widest part of the triangle. Carefully place the rolls on a baking sheet.

Bake for 10 to 15 minutes, until golden brown and puffed up. Let them cool completely before packing them for your trip. To serve, spoon some sauce over each roll or dip it in the sauce.

Mighty Meal Salad

massaged kale, seitan chicken, spice-roasted chickpeas

Makes 4 servings

Cooking time: 15 minutes

1 bunch kale, stems removed, washed and torn into small pieces

2 to 4 tablespoons olive oil, divided

8 ounces seitan or store-bought plant-based chicken, thinly sliced

1 (15-ounce) can chickpeas, rinsed and drained

½ teaspoon garlic powder

½ teaspoon chili powder

¼ teaspoon paprika

⅓ cup shelled pistachios

⅓ cup golden raisins

¼ cup sliced green olives *(optional)*

Extra squeeze of fresh lemon juice *(optional)*

TAHINI DRESSING

1 garlic clove

1 tablespoon chopped green olives

1 tablespoon olive brine

¼ cup tahini

2 tablespoons fresh lemon juice

1 to 3 tablespoons water

Salt and pepper

We've long experimented with how to bring fresh vegetables outdoors with us. We've had many failures, but have also learned some great lessons about what *can* work. Under temperate conditions, certain fruits and veggies do really well. We love to bring fresh citrus (whole in its peel) for a nice hit of acid to finish a dish, as we've done here. If you enjoy tucking into a nice big salad, kale is essential for your outdoor trips. It is the only green that can hold up for half a day as a predressed salad, and it will get more delicious as it marinates. —Mai-Yan

To make the tahini dressing: Put the garlic clove and chopped olives on a cutting board and mince very fine, adding a pinch of salt, and continue to mince and press into the cutting board with the flat side of your knife until it forms a paste. Transfer to a small bowl.

Add the olive brine, tahini, and lemon juice to the garlic-and-olive paste and whisk together to mix well. Add water, a tablespoon at a time, until the dressing is a bit thinner than the tahini was on its own. Season with salt and pepper.

To make the salad: Put the kale into a large bowl. Pour the dressing over the kale, and massage it well with your hands to fully coat all surfaces of the kale. Set aside.

Add 1 to 2 tablespoons of the olive oil to a pan. Cook the seitan for 5 to 10 minutes, until it's lightly browned. Remove the seitan from the pan, and set it aside to cool.

Add another tablespoon of olive oil to the same pan, then the chickpeas. Add the garlic powder, chili powder, and paprika, and stir to coat. Cook over medium heat until the chickpeas are starting to dry out and brown, 5 to 10 minutes. Set aside to cool.

Add the seitan, chickpeas, pistachios, raisins, and olives to the bowl of dressed kale. Mix well and pack in a to-go container with a wide enough opening to eat directly out of on your trip.

Tip: If you happen to have some of the Campfire Party Chickpeas (page 146) on hand, those would make a perfect substitution for the chickpeas here.

Italian Deli Sandwiches

lentil red pepper spread, oil and vinegar dressing, Italian vegetables

Makes 2 sandwiches

Cooking time: 25 minutes

2 (8-inch) sub rolls, or similar size

1 tablespoon red wine vinegar

1 tablespoon olive oil

½ teaspoon dried oregano

Salt and pepper

2 cups shredded romaine hearts

1 to 2 cups fresh baby spinach

6 slices plant-based provolone cheese (Violife brand recommended)

1 large tomato, sliced and seeded

4 tablespoons sliced pepperoncini

LENTIL RED PEPPER SPREAD

2 cups water

½ cup dried green, brown, or black lentils, rinsed

1 garlic clove

1 bay leaf

½ cup roasted red peppers, jarred or homemade

1 tablespoon olive oil

½ teaspoon salt

¼ teaspoon pepper

The first time I took my husband to meet my sister in Florida, I also took him to meet his true love—"Pub Subs" from Publix (the local market). If you have your own Publix, you understand. If you live in California, you need a sister-in-law like his. For Christmas that year, she shipped him disassembled Pub Subs. No one has beaten her at gifting since, and we have had to learn to make our own amazing sandwiches out here in the West. This version is the best we could do, and it's pretty darn good. —Emily

To make the lentil red pepper spread: In a small pot, add 2 cups of water to the lentils, garlic, and bay leaf and bring to a boil over high heat. Turn down the heat to a simmer and cook until the lentils are tender, about 25 minutes. Drain any leftover water completely and remove the bay leaf.

In a food processor, add the lentils (with the garlic), red peppers, olive oil, salt, and pepper and blend until smooth.

To assemble the sandwiches: Cut the bread in half lengthwise, without cutting all the way through, so the sandwich has a hinge that holds it together easily.

In a medium bowl, whisk together the vinegar, oil, oregano, salt, and pepper. Add the romaine and toss to fully coat. Set aside.

Start building your sandwich by spreading a thick layer of lentil red pepper spread on one cut surface of the roll. Layer a large handful of spinach on top.

Lay 2 or 3 slices of the provolone on top of the spinach. This will hold it down as you continue to build the sandwich. Layer half of the dressed lettuce on the cheese slices, then top with the tomato slices and pepperoncini.

Spread another layer of the Lentil Red Pepper Spread on the other cut surface, and top that with another thick layer of spinach. Press the whole sandwich together and wrap tightly in parchment or foil.

Tip: This sandwich is meant to be a bit juicy, so if it is going to hang out in your pack for more than a couple of hours, you may want to pack the dressing separately and douse the sandwich when you're ready to eat.

Roasted Chile Peanut Butter Sandos

peanut butter, maple syrup, Hatch chiles

Makes 2 sandwiches

Cooking time: 10 minutes

4 Hatch, Anaheim, or poblano chiles (or some combination), fire roasted (page 49)

1 or 2 jalapeños

4 slices of good-quality bread (pumpernickel, squaw, or whole wheat work well)

2 to 4 tablespoons natural peanut butter

1 or 2 tablespoons maple syrup

Salt

My friend Andrew and his family drive from California to New Mexico every year to buy as many freshly roasted Hatch chiles as they can fit into their freezers. Last year that amounted to forty pounds! They add them to pots of pinto beans, breakfast burritos, and even latkes.

On a beach camping trip, I was delighted when they introduced me to one of their favorite uses of the chiles: peanut butter and chile sandwiches. It sounds like a peculiar combination, but it works. Kismat and I are now hooked, and we keep a few roasted Hatch chiles in the freezer so we can make our version of Andrew's sandwiches all year. —Aimee

Cut the Hatch, Anaheim, and/or poblano chiles in half lengthwise and discard the seeds and stems.

Slice the jalapeños into smaller pieces.

Slather two slices of bread with peanut butter.

Layer the chiles on top of the peanut butter–slathered bread and carefully pour the maple syrup on top. Season to taste with salt.

Cover the sandwiches with the top slices of bread and pack for your trip.

Tip: Use a really good-quality bread—something that you'll be happy to eat untoasted.

Cornmeal Crust Pizzette

cornmeal tarts, bruschetta, grilled corn and red onion

Makes 8 pizzette
Cooking time: 15 to 20 minutes

1 teaspoon instant yeast
½ cup warm water
¾ cup all-purpose flour
¾ cup cornmeal
½ teaspoon salt
2 tablespoons olive oil

TOPPING OPTIONS:
BRUSCHETTA
1 cup cherry tomatoes, finely chopped
2 tablespoons olive oil
1 garlic clove, minced
½ teaspoon salt
Pinch of black pepper

CORN AND RED ONION TOPPING
2 tablespoons olive oil
1 teaspoon red wine vinegar
⅓ cup red onion, diced
½ cup sweet corn, fresh off the cob or frozen
1 teaspoon dried oregano
½ teaspoon salt
Pinch of black pepper
½ cup plant cheese or cashew cream

One of our favorite places to travel for Dirty Gourmet events is Portland, Oregon. We always make a point to eat at Dove Vivi, a cornmeal crust pizza restaurant. The pizza is like nothing else we've experienced, and they offered vegan cheese that was actually edible way before the world figured out how to make vegan cheese taste good. These little pizzette are a play on that pizza and are a fun lunch option for your day adventures. —Mai-Yan

In a large bowl, combine the yeast, warm water, flour, olive oil, salt, and cornmeal. Mix everything together to form a shaggy dough, then turn it out onto a clean work surface. Knead the dough for 8 to 10 minutes until it forms a smooth ball. Cover and let it rise at room temperature for 1 to 1½ hours or until approximately doubled in size.

To make the bruschetta topping: In a small bowl, combine the cherry tomatoes, olive oil, garlic, salt, and pepper. Set aside.

To make the corn and red onion topping: In a small bowl, combine the olive oil, vinegar, red onion, corn, oregano, salt, and pepper. Set aside.

Divide the dough into 8 balls. Cover and let rest for 15 minutes.

Preheat the oven to 475° F. Flatten each ball into a 4-inch diameter pizzetta. Form a small lip around the edge with your fingers. Arrange them on a baking sheet.

Top the pizzette with your topping of choice. For the bruschetta topping, top each pizzetta with about 2 tablespoons of bruschetta For the corn and red onion topping, first cover the crust with vegan cheese or cashew cream, then add the topping mixture. Bake for 15 minutes, or until the pizzette start to brown on top.

Kabocha Mushroom Pie Bombs

*kabocha squash, pie crust,
creamy mushrooms*

Makes 8 pie bombs
Cooking time: 70 to 95 minutes

CRUST

1½ cups all-purpose flour

¼ teaspoon salt

7 tablespoons plant butter, chilled
and cut into ½-inch pieces

¼ cup ice-cold water

FILLING

1 (3 to 4-pound) kabocha squash

2 tablespoons olive oil

1 large red onion, halved and sliced

8 ounces mushrooms, sliced

½ teaspoon salt

½ teaspoon smoked paprika

½ cup plant-based cream cheese,
at room temperature

Salt and pepper

I recently moved from the mountains to wine country. It's a big change, mainly in terms of weather, which in turn gives me better access to fresh produce. There's the cutest little farmstand right down the street from my house, and going there regularly makes me more aware of what fruits, veggies, and flowers are in season. One of my favorites is the kabocha squash. You can see it growing all along the highway around here, and I feel so lucky to get to cook with it throughout the winter. We made up the idea of pie bombs after Emily made one for a backpacking trip up Taboose Pass in the Sierra years ago. They are a great way to get something filling and creamy into your backpack but not *onto* your backpack, so we keep coming up with new versions. —Aimee

To make the crust: In a large bowl, mix the flour and salt. Add the butter pieces and, with your fingers, quickly mash them into the flour. Once every piece is mashed, add the ¼ cup of water and stir with a fork. Squeeze a handful of the dough to see if it holds together. If it doesn't, add additional water, 1 teaspoon at a time.

Alternatively, to make the dough in a food processor, mix the flour and salt in the food processor bowl and pulse to combine. Add the cold butter pieces and pulse until it forms coarse crumbs. With the motor running, add the water and process just until the dough holds together.

Shape the dough into a disk 5 to 6 inches in diameter. Wrap the disk in plastic wrap and refrigerate for at least an hour, or up to overnight.

To make the pie bombs: Preheat the oven to 400° F. Place the whole kabocha squash on a baking sheet and roast for 30 to 45 minutes, until it's very soft. Remove it from the oven and let it cool.

Lower the oven temperature to 350° F.

When the squash is cool enough to handle, cut it in half and remove the seeds. Scoop out the flesh and transfer it to a bowl. Mash it with a fork or potato masher and measure out 3 cups of squash. Set aside. Save any remaining squash for another use (you can freeze it for more pie bombs).

In a large skillet over medium heat, sauté the onion in olive oil until it is soft and caramelized, about 10 minutes. Add the mushrooms and sauté until they're softened, about 5 more minutes.

Stir in the mashed squash, smoked paprika, salt, and cream cheese, mixing until well combined. Season to taste with additional salt and pepper.

Generously coat 8 cups of a standard 12-cup muffin tin with cooking spray and set aside.

Lightly flour a clean surface and divide the pie crust into 8 even pieces. Using a lightly floured rolling pin, roll out each piece to form a $6\frac{1}{2}$- to 7-inch circle.

Place one dough circle in the muffin tin, making sure not to poke holes into the dough as you lightly press it down into the shape. Fill it with a heaping $\frac{1}{4}$ cup of the squash mixture.

Gently fold one side of the dough toward the center of the filling. Create a pleat by pinching the bottom edge of the folded dough. Take the pleat and gently press it down toward the center of the pie. Repeat this step going clockwise, until the filling is enclosed in the dough. Repeat this process for each pie.

Bake the pies for 40 to 50 minutes, until the tops are golden brown. Allow to cool before carefully removing them from the muffin tin.

Store refrigerated in an airtight container for up to 3 days.

Tip: You can definitely use store-bought pie crust if you are resistant to making your own. Check the ingredients list carefully, though, because most use lard or some sort of dairy. And don't be afraid of making pie crust—it really is easy!

Quiche Pie Bombs

pie crust, quiche filling

Makes 8 pie bombs
Cooking time: 45 minutes

CRUST

1½ cups all-purpose flour

¼ teaspoon salt

7 tablespoons plant butter, chilled and cut into ½-inch pieces

¼ cup ice water

FILLING

1 (16-ounce) package firm tofu

2 tablespoons chickpea flour

2 tablespoons nutritional yeast

¾ teaspoon salt

¼ teaspoon black salt (or regular salt)

¼ teaspoon ground turmeric

¼ teaspoon garlic powder

¼ teaspoon onion powder

1 cup broccoli, chopped

We live about 30 minutes from the beach now, which is a great quick escape for my family when we just need a break. It's not easy to eat on the beach, since sand gets into everything, so it's a perfect opportunity for foods that are self-contained and need no dishes. Pie bombs are great for that, and they are easy to customize to your liking. —Aimee

To make the crust: Mix the flour and salt in a large bowl until well combined. Add the butter cubes and, with your fingers, quickly mash the butter pieces into the flour. Once all are mashed, add the water and stir with a fork. Squeeze a handful of the dough to see if it holds together. If it doesn't, add additional water, 1 teaspoon at a time.

To make the dough in a food processor, put the flour and salt in the food processor bowl and pulse until well combined. Add the cold butter pieces and pulse until they form coarse crumbs. With the motor running, add the water and process just until the dough holds together.

Shape the dough into a disk 5 to 6 inches in diameter. Wrap the disk in plastic wrap and refrigerate for at least an hour or up to overnight.

To make the filling: In a large bowl, mash the tofu with a fork or potato masher until it's broken down, almost into a paste. Add the chickpea flour, nutritional yeast, salt, black salt, turmeric, garlic powder, and onion powder and mix well. Stir in the chopped broccoli.

Preheat the oven to 350° F.

Generously coat 8 cups of a standard 12-cup muffin tin with cooking spray and set aside.

Lightly flour a clean surface and divide the pie crust into 8 pieces. Using a lightly floured rolling pin, roll out each piece to form a 6- to 7-inch circle.

Put one dough circle into each muffin cup, making sure not to poke holes into the dough as you lightly press it down into the shape. Fill each with ¼ cup of the tofu mixture.

Gently fold one side of the dough toward the center of the filling. Create a pleat by pinching one side of the half circle that is already touching the dough. Fold the pleat toward the center of the pie. Repeat this step going clockwise, until the filling is enclosed in the dough. Repeat this step for each pie.

Bake the pies for 40 to 50 minutes, until the tops are golden brown. Allow to cool before carefully removing them from the muffin tin.

Store refrigerated in an airtight container for up to 3 days.

Tip: The black salt, also known as kala namak, *adds an eggy flavor, but you can just use regular salt if you can't find it.*

CAR CAMPING RECIPES

BREAKFASTS

Tropical Yogurt Bowls

coconut yogurt, tropical fruit, toasted nuts

Makes 4 servings
No cook recipe

TOOLS
4 (16-ounce) Mason jars
Spoon
Knife
Cutting board

2 tablespoons chia seeds
1 (24-ounce) container coconut yogurt (sweetened or unsweetened)
1 banana, sliced
2 mangos, cubed
2 cups blueberries
4 tablespoons shredded coconut, preferably toasted
4 tablespoons chopped toasted nuts
1 cup granola

Cooking breakfast on climbing days is tricky for me. We always leave home or our camp super early to get a good start, so I like a portable breakfast for the road or trail. I have my coffee before I eat breakfast, so it can be hard to come up with a recipe that will still taste good an hour or two after preparing it. No-cook breakfasts like these yogurt bowls are perfect for those days, as well as any day my kids want something special but I want to make something easy. The brightness of the fresh fruit and coconut yogurt really energizes you for your activity. —Emily

Stir the chia seeds into the yogurt and divide among Mason jars.

Portion the banana, mangos, and blueberries among the jars.

Just before serving, top the yogurt and fruit with coconut, nuts, and granola.

White Bean Scramble

canned white beans, spinach, turmeric

Makes 4 servings
Cooking time: 10 minutes

TOOLS

Camp stove
Can opener
Knife
Cutting board
Large skillet
Large wooden spoon

2 tablespoons olive oil
2 shallots, minced
4 garlic cloves, minced
2 (15-ounce) cans white beans with their canning liquid
½ teaspoon salt
¼ teaspoon ground turmeric
1 tablespoon nutritional yeast
Large handful of spinach, chopped
Salt and pepper
8 slices toast

Eating beans in the morning is a guaranteed way to make me feel great. They're savory and filling but don't make me feel sluggish after eating them because they are high in protein. I don't know why I don't eat them every day! This simple recipe comes together quickly and yields a really satisfying breakfast. I like to just barely mash the beans so that they stick to my toast but don't turn into hummus. —Aimee

Heat the oil over medium heat in a large skillet. Add the shallots and sauté until softened, about 5 minutes. Add the garlic and sauté for another minute.

Add the white beans with their liquid, and use a wooden spoon to lightly mash them as they warm up. You don't want them completely mashed, so leave them a bit chunky.

Add the salt, turmeric, and nutritional yeast, and stir to combine.

Stir in the spinach and continue cooking until the spinach is wilted.

Taste and adjust the seasoning with additional salt if needed, and lots of pepper. Spread the white bean mixture on the toast and serve.

Tip: You can buy a collapsible camp toaster that sits directly on top of your camp stove. Or toast your bread in a dry cast iron skillet or on the grate over a campfire.

Charred Tofu Breakfast Sandwiches

super-firm tofu, everything bagels, caramelized shallots

Makes 4 sandwiches

Cooking time: 15 minutes

TOOLS

Camp stove or grate

Shallow container for marinade

Knife

Cutting board

Skillet

Spatula

Spreader

---

1 (16-ounce) block super-firm tofu

6 tablespoons olive oil, divided

1 or 2 shallots, sliced

2 packed cups fresh spinach

Salt and pepper

4 bagels, preferably with "everything" topping

4 ounces vegan cream cheese

MARINADE

2 tablespoons cider vinegar

2 tablespoons soy sauce

1 teaspoon maple syrup

¼ teaspoon smoked paprika

¼ teaspoon cayenne pepper

I started eating vegetarian in 2011 when I was living with vegan friends. The rule was no meat in the house, and we loved cooking together, so I worked my way through Isa Chandra Moskowitz's *Veganomicon* cookbook and learned how to love tofu. I don't remember ever making an official decision to quit eating meat—it just happened gradually as more of my go-tos became plant-based. These days, a family-favorite standby is my childhood "egg-a-muffin" turned tofu breakfast sandwich. —Emily

Prepare the marinade by combining the vinegar, soy sauce, maple syrup, paprika, and cayenne in a shallow container.

Slice the tofu block from the short side into ½-inch slabs. Marinate the tofu for at least 10 minutes; if the marinade doesn't cover the tofu, gently flip the tofu pieces halfway through.

Add 1 tablespoon of the olive oil to the skillet over medium-low heat. Add the shallots and sauté, stirring occasionally, until they begin turning brown, about 10 minutes.

Add the spinach, salt, and pepper and cook until the spinach is wilted, about 3 minutes. Transfer to a bowl and set aside.

Increase the heat to medium-high and add about 1 tablespoon of olive oil to the skillet. Add the tofu slabs and grill on both sides until brown and crispy. You may have to do this in several rounds if your skillet is small. Set aside.

Add more olive oil to the skillet if needed, then grill the bagel slices, cut side down.

Spread cream cheese on one grilled side of each bagel. Top with 2 to 3 slabs of tofu per sandwich and a heap of greens. Top with the other bagel half.

Tip: I love tofu that's really charred, but I hate to breathe all that smoke in my kitchen, so I never go as far as I'd like to with it at home. Cooking at camp allows you to get a really good blackened crust on your tofu, which works well with the rest of the flavors in this sandwich.

French Toast

chickpea flour, maple syrup, cinnamon

Makes 4 servings

Cooking time: 15 minutes

TOOLS

Camp stove

Shallow bowl

Fork

Skillet or griddle

Spatula

---

1 cup chickpea flour

½ teaspoon salt, or black salt for extra eggy flavor

2 teaspoons cinnamon

1½ cups plant milk

2 tablespoons maple syrup

2 teaspoons vanilla extract

3 to 6 tablespoons plant butter or coconut oil

8 to 10 slices thick-sliced bread

FOR SERVING

Maple syrup

Plant butter

Fresh fruit, such as berries or banana slices *(optional)*

If you ever speak to someone about following a plant-based diet who's never considered it, you will likely hear a list of deal-breaker concerns that they couldn't imagine "living without." All vegans have gone through that same struggle and had to decide whether to hang on tight to animal products, live without our favorite foods, or figure out how to make a traditional recipe into a plant-based one that is satisfying enough to eat. This recipe satisfies #3 on that list. Chickpea flour takes the place of eggs and is close to a seamless mimic in this context. And substituting for eggs may be easier than figuring out how to take eggs on a camping trip without breaking them. Plant-based recipes truly are often the most camp-friendly foods, worth considering even if you aren't basing your whole diet on plants. —Aimee

---

AT HOME *(OPTIONAL)*

Combine the chickpea flour, salt, and cinnamon in a sealable container.

AT CAMP

Use a fork to stir together the chickpea flour mixture, milk, maple syrup, and vanilla in a shallow bowl.

Heat a skillet or griddle over medium-low heat. Melt about a tablespoon of butter in the skillet.

Dip both sides of a slice of bread in the batter, then place in the hot skillet.

Cook for 3 to 4 minutes, then flip the bread over. Cook for another 3 to 4 minutes, or until the batter is completely cooked and the toast is lightly browned.

Continue dipping and cooking the additional slices of bread, adding more butter to the skillet as needed.

Serve hot with butter, maple syrup, and fresh fruit.

Autumn-Spiced Fig Jam Toast

dried figs, molasses, fall spices

Makes about 1½ cups jam
Cooking time: 15 minutes

TOOLS
Camp stove
4-quart pot
Large spoon
Potato masher *(optional)*

1½ cups (8 ounces) dried figs, diced
¼ cup brown sugar
1 tablespoon molasses
½ teaspoon ground cinnamon
¼ teaspoon ground allspice
¼ teaspoon ground nutmeg
¼ teaspoon ground cloves
1 cup water
Zest and juice of one orange
Plant butter
Toast

Fig season is early September for the Mission fig tree we inherited when we bought our house a few years ago. The figs have to be harvested fast enough to beat the scrub jays and the squirrels, so for a few weeks we go out collecting every morning. I learned how to can for this tree. I stumbled upon a fig jam recipe somewhere and adapted it until it was the perfect flavor to start the fall season. This campified version uses dried figs and is so quick and simple that it can easily be made fresh at camp and enjoyed as a part of a fancy toast board. —Emily

AT HOME *(OPTIONAL)*

Put the figs, brown sugar, molasses, cinnamon, allspice, nutmeg, and cloves into a small container with a tight-fitting lid.

AT CAMP

Add the fig mixture, 1 cup of water, and the orange zest and juice to the pot, and bring to a boil over medium heat. Cover and cook for 5 to 10 minutes, stirring occasionally, using a potato masher or the back of the spoon if needed to further break down the figs. Continue cooking until the figs are softened and the mixture becomes jammy.

Let cool slightly and enjoy spread on buttered toast.

Tip: This recipe works well with fresh figs when they are in season.

Caramelized Banana Pancakes

ripe bananas, brown sugar, butter

Makes about 10 6-inch pancakes
Cooking time: 15 to 30 minutes,
depending on the size of the skillet
or griddle

TOOLS

Camp stove
Mixing bowl
Spoon or whisk
Ladle or other utensil to scoop up batter
Skillet or griddle
Spatula

3 cups Just Add Water Pancake Mix (page 297)
2 cups water
3 bananas, sliced
¼ cup brown sugar
¼ cup plant butter
Pinch of salt
Cooking spray or more butter

FOR SERVING

Maple syrup

Pancakes are so versatile and quick to make that they can be a great backdrop for special toppings to impress your crowd. We have made *literally* thousands of pancakes over the course of our career catering large camping events. We've made them in all kinds of ways and in all kinds of environments (even on a day so windy that fifty of them sat there on the griddles refusing to cook until our kitchen was encircled by Sprinter vans as a windblock). We've made them sweet, we've made them savory; we've topped them with fresh fruit in glamping situations and with entirely dried ingredients when backpacking. This combination is easy to execute, but feels oh so fancy. —Mai-Yan

Preheat the skillet or griddle over medium heat.

Put the pancake mix in the mixing bowl and add water. Mix or whisk well.

When the skillet is hot, spray it with cooking spray or melt a little butter.

Ladle on ¼ to ⅓ cup of pancake batter, enough to make an approximately 6-inch pancake. On a larger griddle or skillet you may be able to make more than one at a time. Cook until little bubbles form in the batter, about 2 minutes, then flip over. Continue cooking until the pancake is golden brown on the second side. Continue cooking the remaining pancakes in this way, stacking them on a plate as you go.

To make the banana topping: Melt the butter in a skillet, then sprinkle with the brown sugar and a pinch of salt. Arrange the banana slices on the sugar mixture, then gently stir to coat. Allow the bananas to heat through and caramelize a bit, 4 to 5 minutes.

Serve the pancakes with the caramelized bananas and, if desired, maple syrup.

Tip: You can make this using one skillet, but if you have two, fire up both burners of your stove and use them both. That way your pancakes are served hot and everything comes together more quickly.

Smoky SoCal Hash

fire-roasted chiles, hash browns, creamy cilantro sauce

Makes 4 to 6 servings

Cooking time: 30 minutes

TOOLS

Knife

Cutting board

Aluminum foil

12-inch skillet

Spatula

It takes a while to appreciate Los Angeles, but after over twenty years of living here, I have to admit I love this place. This Smoky SoCal Hash is an attempt to share a little taste of my personal LA experience: taco trucks on every corner and the roasted chiles that you can get as a side, Wahoo's creamy cilantro sauce, smoky smog and wildfires, 24-hour diners, and bountiful produce available year-round. It's fun to create an ode to your own favorite place using food. Try it for yours! —Mai-Yan

AT HOME

To make the sauce, put the tofu, oil, water, nutritional yeast, lime juice, garlic, cilantro, parsley, and salt in a blender. Blend on high until thick and creamy, about 30 seconds. Season to taste with additional salt.

Transfer the sauce to a leakproof container and keep refrigerated.

2 (4.2-ounce) boxes dehydrated hash browns

4 cups water

2 to 4 tablespoons neutral oil

1 (12-ounce) package Soyrizo

8 ounces fresh baby spinach

½ teaspoon ground pepper

CREAMY CILANTRO SAUCE

8 ounces firm tofu, crumbled

⅓ cup neutral oil

⅓ cup water

2 tablespoons nutritional yeast

3 tablespoons fresh lime juice

2 garlic cloves, minced

1 cup chopped cilantro

1 cup chopped parsley

½ teaspoon salt

FOR SERVING

4 whole jalapeño chiles or yellow peppers (güero chiles)

Avocado, cubed

Lime wedges

Hot sauce

AT CAMP

Place the chiles over the fire in a skillet, in a foil pouch, or directly over the grate. Roast them until the skin is charred on all sides. Set aside.

Meanwhile, rehydrate the hash browns according to the package instructions.

Once the hash browns are rehydrated, heat up 2 tablespoons of oil in your skillet over medium-high heat, and add the Soyrizo. Break it up with your spatula and add the rehydrated hash browns. Stir to combine.

Make an even layer of hash and press it down with the spatula. Let it brown for about 3 minutes without stirring.

When the bottom layer is crispy and golden brown, flip the hash in sections as needed, and rearrange it in an even layer, again pressing it down. Let the other side brown for 3 to 5 minutes or until crispy and golden brown.

Sprinkle the fresh spinach across the top of the hash, and flip sections of hash again to create a spinach bed underneath. Remove from the heat, drizzle with the sauce, and serve immediately with all of the garnishes.

Tip: We prefer to use the dehydrated hash browns because they don't take up room in the cooler and won't go to waste if our breakfast plans suddenly change. That said, this recipe will also work with fresh hash browns, often found in a cold case at the grocery store.

Tofu Florentine

spinach, tomato, plant-based hollandaise sauce

Makes 4 servings

Cooking time: 10 minutes

TOOLS

Camp stove

Knife

Cutting board

1-quart pot

12-inch skillet

Tongs or spatula

Spoon

2 tablespoons oil, divided

1 (16-ounce) block extra-firm tofu, cut into 8 half-inch-thick slabs

Salt and pepper

6 ounces (about 6 cups) fresh baby spinach

4 English muffins

8 tomato slices

HOLLANDAISE SAUCE

¼ cup plant butter

½ cup plant-based mayo

2 tablespoons nutritional yeast

1 teaspoon Dijon mustard

¼ teaspoon salt

Freshly ground pepper

Pinch of cayenne

Juice of half a lemon

Most recipes we develop start with practicality as the first ingredient, but here's one where fanciness takes priority. Don't worry—practicality is still the second ingredient, because we're camping. This is a different take on replacing eggs and cheese for breakfast, and it's a fun one that you can pull off even if you've got a full day of activity planned and need to get out quick. —Emily

AT HOME *(OPTIONAL)*

Pack the butter for the sauce by itself in a leakproof container.

In another leakproof container, mix the mayo, nutritional yeast, Dijon, salt, pepper, and cayenne.

AT CAMP

In the pot set over medium-low heat, melt the butter. Stir in the mayo mixture and heat just until warmed through. Remove from the heat, cover, and set aside.

Heat a tablespoon of the oil in the skillet over medium-high heat. Working in batches, fry the tofu until golden brown, about 3 minutes per side. Season with salt and pepper, place on a plate or work surface, and set aside.

To the same skillet, add a drizzle of oil and then the spinach. Season with salt and pepper, and cook just until wilted, turning with tongs to ensure it all cooks down. If your skillet isn't big enough to add all the spinach at once, work in batches. Transfer the spinach to a plate.

Add the remaining oil to the skillet and then the English muffin halves, cut side down, and grill until toasted. Set aside.

Assemble the open-faced sandwiches by placing the English muffins cut side up on serving plates. Top each with a slice of tomato and then a slice of tofu. Divide the spinach among the muffins and drizzle with the hollandaise sauce. Serve immediately.

Camp-Fried Donut Hole Party

canned biscuit dough, maple syrup, freeze-dried strawberries, instant coffee

Makes 8 servings
Cooking time: 10 to 15 minutes

TOOLS
Camp stove
Cutting board
Knife
Skillet
Tongs
Paper towels
Plate

If you've been to one of our workshops in the past couple of years, you likely sampled one of these beauties. A great camp breakfast can sometimes feel tricky to pull off since we're often itching to get out on a hike or on the road before traffic catches up. We love to demonstrate how lazy you can be and still impress with a special breakfast. These donut holes also make the perfect blank slate for experimentation with local or seasonal flavors (topping recipes follow the main recipe). The secret to frying them outdoors is to use only small amounts of oil. Cleanup is easy with a quick skillet wipe using paper towels, with no used frying oil to transport. —Emily

AT HOME

Pack the unopened can of biscuit dough in a waterproof container, such as a ziplock bag, for storing safely in your cooler.

Measure the oil into a Mason jar. You may have leftover oil to pour back in afterward, so don't bring too much extra.

AT CAMP

Pour about a quarter of the oil into a skillet and heat it over medium-low heat. You aren't deep-frying here; you need just

1 (1-pound) can biscuit dough

½ to ¾ cup vegetable oil

MAPLE-DRIZZLED DONUTS

TOOLS

Skillet

Spoon

¼ cup apple butter or jam

¼ cup maple syrup

DUSTED DONUTS

TOOLS

2 paper bags

Serving plate

COFFEE POWDER

½ cup powdered sugar

1 teaspoon micro-ground instant coffee

STRAWBERRY DUST

¼ cup freeze-dried strawberries, crushed to a powder

¼ cup granulated sugar

enough to coat the bottom of the skillet. The heat will be lower than other frying experiences.

Open the can of biscuit dough and cut each biscuit into quarters. Line the plate with paper towels.

Use 1 piece of dough to test the oil for readiness. It is ready when you see tiny bubbles forming around the edges of the biscuit dough. When this happens, add about 7 more pieces.

Actively turn each donut hole in the oil with the tongs as each edge browns. These can burn easily, so don't walk away. You may need to turn down the heat to low.

When the donut holes are golden brown on all sides (30 seconds to 2 minutes depending on your heat level), transfer them from the oil to the paper towels.

Continue frying until you use all the biscuit dough.

While the donut holes are still hot, add your topping(s) of choice.

To make maple-drizzled donuts: In the skillet over low heat, stir together the apple butter and maple syrup.

As soon as the mixture starts to bubble, remove from the heat and drizzle it over the plate of donut holes.

To make dusted donuts: Nest one paper bag inside the other. Fill the internal bag with either the powdered sugar and coffee or strawberry powder and sugar.

After the donut holes have drained and cooled a bit, add them to the bag. Fold the top of the bags closed tightly, and shake the donuts around to fully coat them in the powdered mix.

Pour the donuts out onto a plate and serve.

Tip: When buying canned biscuit dough, read the ingredients carefully, as some of them contain dairy, but most of the popular brands fit into the "accidentally vegan" category, even if the flavor is listed as buttermilk.

Sticky Bun Turnovers

puff pastry, brown sugar, cinnamon

Makes 4 to 8 turnovers, depending on the size of your pie iron

Cooking time: 4 to 7 minutes per turnover

TOOLS

Food storage container or bowl

Fork

Cutting board or other clean surface

Pie iron(s)

Knife

Spoon

———

½ cup packed brown sugar

½ cup chopped toasted pecans or walnuts

1 tablespoon flour

2 teaspoons cinnamon

Pinch of salt

2 tablespoons plant butter, soft-ened

1 (1-pound) package vegan puff pastry

Cooking spray

I used to be really into brown sugar and cinnamon Pop-Tarts. I would toast them until they were just shy of burnt, then method-ically eat the edges before savoring the sugary center. It's been years since I've eaten one, but I can still clearly conjure up the taste. These remind me of those Pop-Tarts, but they're more grown up, and obviously more delicious. It's always fun to cook with a pie iron because it produces a little packet that you can't otherwise create in the outdoors. These can be saved as portable leftovers—if you ever manage to have any left over. —Aimee

AT HOME *(OPTIONAL)*

Combine the brown sugar, nuts, flour, cinnamon, and salt and pack in a food storage container.

AT CAMP

Get a campfire going until it forms hot coals.

Add the butter to the container of the brown sugar mixture. Use a fork to incorporate the butter into the sugar mixture.

Place a sheet of puff pastry on a clean work surface. Cut it into an even number of pieces to fit your pie iron. Set aside.

Set the pastry pieces and brown sugar mixture near where you'll assemble the turnovers.

Meanwhile, preheat the pie iron(s) over the campfire. Once the pie iron is hot, carefully open it and spray it with oil.

Set the pie iron on a flat, heat-proof surface and lay 1 piece of pas-try in the bottom. Scoop 1 to 2 tablespoons of the sugar mixture onto the pastry. Cover the filling with an additional piece of pastry and use a fork to tuck in any loose edges. Close the pie iron and lock it in place. You can also build the pies on a clean work surface, then transfer them to the pie iron.

Cook the pastry over hot coals for 4 to 7 minutes, turning often. Don't peek for the first 4 minutes; if you open it too soon, the pas-try might not puff up as intended. The cooking time depends on how hot the fire is and where you place the pie iron, so check it often—especially the first one you cook. If you wait too long, you

may not realize it's burning. When the pastry is puffed up and golden brown, it's done. Transfer the pastry to a plate and let cool slightly before serving.

Tip: The sugar gets very hot, so be extra careful when you pull one out of the pie iron!

One-Pan Breakfast Tacos

Soyrizo, black beans, green chiles

Makes 10 to 12 tacos
Cooking time: 20 minutes

TOOLS
Camp stove or grate
12-inch skillet
Spatula
Tongs

2 tablespoons neutral oil
1 large russet potato, peeled if desired, cut into ½-inch cubes (about 2 cups)
1 (12-ounce) package Soyrizo
1 (15-ounce) can black beans, drained
1 (4-ounce) can diced green chiles
Salt and pepper
10 to 12 6-inch corn or flour tortillas

FOR SERVING
Plant-based feta cheese
Avocado
Shredded cabbage
Pico de gallo
Lime wedges
Hot sauce

Breakfast burritos just feel like camping food to me, but they're a little complicated to pull off. There are so many different components, and then you have to figure out how to roll them into tidy burritos without all the counter space you have at home. Tacos are the answer! The filling is made all in one skillet, and you don't have to worry about rolling burritos. They're delicious with just one or two toppings, or you can go all out with the full toppings spread. —Aimee

Heat the oil in the skillet over medium-high heat. Add the potato cubes and sauté, stirring often, until softened and lightly browned, about 10 minutes.

Stir in the Soyrizo, black beans, and chiles, and cook for a few more minutes to heat everything through. Season with salt and pepper.

Heat the tortillas directly over the flame of a camp stove or in a skillet.

Place a scoop of filling on top of each tortilla and top with any or all of the suggested toppings. Fold up and enjoy!

APPETIZERS

Chili Crisp Roasted Nuts

Sichuan Chili Oil, mixed nuts, aromatics

Makes 2 cups

Cooking time: About 25 minutes

TOOLS

Campfire grate or camp stove

Knife

Cutting board

Cast iron skillet

Metal spatula or spoon

Heatproof gloves

---

1 cup roasted cashews

1 cup roasted peanuts

1 shallot, sliced

4 garlic cloves, sliced

2 tablespoons Sichuan Chili Oil (page 291) or other chili oil

1 tablespoon white sesame seeds

Salt

I was lucky enough to test this recipe in Joshua Tree National Park during a rare stint of snow in the desert. The white-blanketed yuccas were beautiful, but it was also quite cold, so I was glad to be cooking at the campfire. This recipe is a different take on our original recipe for Spiced Nuts with Shallots in *Dirty Gourmet: Food for Your Outdoor Adventures,* and it may be even more delicious. We are currently as obsessed as everyone else with chili crisp, and this is basically a deconstructed version. We suggest specific nuts, but it really doesn't matter whether you use salted or unsalted, raw or roasted nuts. The nuts will get roasted and smoky, and you can adjust the level of salt at the very end. The recipe keeps well and makes for an addictive snack for the drive home. —Mai-Yan

Scoot some embers from the main campfire to create a pile of coals under the campfire grate.

Place the skillet on the grate over the embers. Add the nuts, shallot, garlic, chili oil, and sesame seeds to the skillet and mix well.

Roast the nuts, stirring often, and rotate the skillet occasionally to ensure even heating.

Continue roasting the nuts until they are fragrant and the garlic and shallots are softened and slightly caramelized, about 25 minutes. Season to taste with salt. You can continue roasting and caramelizing for much longer if the heat is very indirect and people are enjoying grazing around the fire.

Tip: There are always plenty of people happy to help with the job of stirring at the campfire, so this is a great one to delegate once you get your fire set up. If you are camping with fire restrictions, you can also make this on your camp stove over a low flame.

Pie Iron Asparagus Turnovers

Nutty Parmesan–rubbed asparagus, puff pastry pockets

Makes 4 to 8 turnovers, depending on the size of your pie iron

Cooking time: 6 to 8 minutes per turnover

TOOLS

Pie iron(s)

Cutting board or other clean surface

Bowl

Knife

Fork

---

1 bunch (about 1 pound) asparagus, trimmed and cut into 1-inch pieces

2 teaspoons olive oil

2 tablespoons Nutty Parmesan (page 288)

Pepper

Salt

1 (1-pound) package vegan puff pastry

¾ cup chopped or shredded plant-based cheddar

Cooking spray

Emily once visited me for a few days and on the last day of her stay, while I was away at work, she assembled an asparagus tart and left it in my fridge with a sweet note. It was such a nice surprise; now I always think of that tart when I come across asparagus. I've transformed that idea here into turnovers that you can make in a pie iron. I especially like to use asparagus, since it cooks so quickly. A longer-cooking vegetable wouldn't cook through before the puff pastry burns. —Aimee

In a bowl, toss the asparagus pieces with the olive oil, Nutty Parmesan, and a sprinkle of pepper. Taste and season with salt and more pepper if needed.

Place a sheet of puff pastry on a clean work surface. Cut it into an even number of pieces to fit the pie iron. Set aside.

Set the pastry pieces, asparagus, and cheddar near where you'll assemble the turnovers.

Meanwhile, preheat the pie iron(s) over a campfire. Once the pie iron is hot, carefully open it and spray it with oil.

Set the pie iron on a flat, heat-proof surface and lay one piece of pastry in the bottom. Top with about a heaping tablespoon of asparagus and a tablespoon of cheese. Cover the filling with another piece of pastry and use a fork to tuck in any loose edges. Close the pie iron and lock it in place.

Cook the pastry over hot coals for 6 to 8 minutes, turning the pie iron often. The cooking time will depend on how hot the fire is and where you place the pie iron, so check it often. When the pastry is puffed up and golden brown, it's done.

Continue cooking the rest of the turnovers until you run out of ingredients, spraying the pie iron again as needed.

Cut in halves or quarters to serve as hors d'oeuvres.

Tip: Cook time will get shorter with each round as the pie iron gets hotter. Open up the pie iron to check on the color of the puff pastry after a couple of minutes and adjust the cook time accordingly.

Pie Iron Asparagus Turnovers

Ginger Chile Corn Fritters (page 138)

Ginger Chile Corn Fritters

fresh corn, cornmeal batter, ginger

Makes 10 fritters

Cooking time: 15 to 20 minutes, depending on the size of your skillet

TOOLS

Camp stove

Knife

Cutting board

Cast iron skillet

Mixing bowl

Plate

Paper towels

Spoon

Metal spatula

¾ cup chickpea flour

¼ cup cornmeal

¾ teaspoon salt, plus more to taste

¼ teaspoon pepper

1 cup corn (from frozen or fresh)

½ medium bell pepper, minced

1 medium shallot, minced

2 scallions, thinly sliced

¼ cup chopped cilantro

2 teaspoons minced fresh ginger

1 jalapeño or serrano chile, minced (leave the seeds in if you like it spicy)

½ cup water

¼ to ½ cup neutral oil

We live for peach season, fig season, and citrus season. But no fresh produce is more strictly seasonal than corn. Even the least inspiring markets in the least corny parts of the country fill their produce sections with mountains of unhusked fresh corn for a few weeks in the summer. When you can't stop yourself from buying most of that corn mountain, you need some corn recipes! Corn fritters are delicious but can feel a bit heavy, so here I've added fresh ginger, cilantro, and scallions to brighten them up. —Aimee

AT HOME *(OPTIONAL)*

Put the chickpea flour, cornmeal, salt, and pepper into a container with a tight-fitting lid.

AT CAMP

In the mixing bowl, combine the corn, bell pepper, shallot, scallions, cilantro, ginger, and jalapeño. Add the chickpea flour mixture and stir to combine. Add the water and stir until the vegetables are coated in the batter. If the mixture seems dry, add more water, a little at a time, until you end up with a liquidy batter coating all the vegetables.

Heat about ¼ cup oil in the skillet over medium-high heat and line a plate with paper towels. Drop approximately ¼-cup scoops of the corn mixture in the skillet. Cook for 3 to 4 minutes, then flip. Cook for an additional 3 to 4 minutes, until the fritters are browned and crispy on both sides.

Put the fritters on the paper towels and sprinkle with additional salt if desired. Continue cooking all the fritters, adding additional oil as needed.

Bean Curd Ribbon Salad

dried tofu, sugar snap peas, fresh ginger

Makes 6 servings

Cooking time: 15 minutes, plus 1 hour chilling

TOOLS

Grater or microplane

Lidded jar

4-quart pot with lid

Tongs

Knife

Cutting board

Mixing bowl

---

1 (6- or 7-ounce) package bean curd sticks

1 cup diagonally sliced sugar snap peas

3 scallions, sliced

1 tablespoon chopped cilantro

Salt

DRESSING

1-inch piece of fresh ginger, grated

4 tablespoons soy sauce

2 tablespoons rice vinegar

2 tablespoons Sichuan Chili Oil (page 291) or similar

1 teaspoon toasted sesame oil

¾ teaspoon sugar

1 garlic clove, minced

This chilled salad is made from dried bean curd sticks, a staple in Cantonese cuisine and something that I grew up eating as part of my dad's home cooking. Like most soybean products, it doesn't have a lot of flavor, but it makes up for it in texture. Once rehydrated, it's not at all like soft blocks of tofu, but rather chewy and slippery, like a noodle that won't get mushy on you. It gets an umami bomb dressing with a delicate balance of zingy fresh ginger paired with just a hint of sesame and chili oil. If you're a textural eater like me, you will love this one. —Mai-Yan

---

AT HOME *(OPTIONAL)*

Mix together all of the dressing ingredients in a jar with a tight-fitting lid. Keep refrigerated or in your cooler until you are ready to toss the salad.

AT CAMP

Bring a large pot of water to a boil.

Break the bean curd sticks in half by hand and add them to the pot of boiling water. Use the tongs to push the floating pieces down into the water.

Once the water returns to a rolling boil, turn off the heat and cover. Let the bean curd soak for 10 minutes, stirring often to give all the bean curd pieces a chance to be submerged in the hot water. Once the bean curd is fully rehydrated, it will be light yellow and will have lost all rigidity.

Drain the water from the bean curd sticks, then slice them crosswise into thin ribbons. Put them in a bowl.

Add the snap peas, scallions, cilantro, and dressing to the ribbons and mix it well. The ribbons will not have a strong flavor at this point, but resist the urge to salt the salad right away.

Chill the salad for at least 1 hour to let the flavor develop and infuse into the ribbons. Taste before serving and add salt to taste.

Bean Curd Ribbon Salad (page 139)

Ember-Roasted Shallot Dip

Ember-Roasted Shallot Dip

lots of shallots, sour cream, chopped chives

Makes about 2 cups
Cooking time: 15 to 25 minutes

TOOLS
Heavy-duty aluminum foil
Cutting board
Knife
Bowl
Spoon

———

5 large shallots
1 head garlic
1 teaspoon olive oil
1 cup plant-based sour cream
2 tablespoons chopped chives
½ teaspoon salt
¼ teaspoon pepper

FOR SERVING
Potato chips
Raw vegetables, such as carrots and celery

If you're nervous about ember-roasting vegetables, this is a great way to dip your toe. The shallots and garlic are small, so they roast quickly, and it's easy to give them your full attention and avoid burning them. Plus, the protective skins of these aromatics will likely protect the flesh even if the skins do burn. If you don't have a campfire, you can sauté the shallots and garlic over low heat until they're caramelized. The result will be slightly different, but equally delicious. I like to sauté them at home to bring on picnics.
—Aimee

Place the whole shallots and head of garlic (without removing the skins) on 2 or 3 pieces of heavy-duty aluminum foil. Drizzle with the oil, wrap tightly, and place the foil pouches directly in the embers of a campfire. (See our Foil Pouch Tutorial in the Appendix for more information.)

Roast the shallots and garlic, turning them frequently, until they're softened, with charred skins. The skins will likely burn, and that's fine, but make sure you pull them out before the fleshy insides burn. Remove from the fire and set aside to cool.

Cut the ends off the shallots and garlic and squeeze out all the softened flesh onto a cutting board. Use a knife to roughly chop and mash the flesh. Transfer to a bowl.

Add the sour cream, chives, salt, and pepper to the bowl and stir until well combined.

Taste and adjust the seasoning.

Serve with potato chips and/or fresh vegetables.

Oyster Mushroom Canapés

torn king oyster mushrooms, miso butter, fresh parsley

Makes 4 servings

Cooking time: 10 minutes

TOOLS

Camp stove

Mixing bowl

10-inch skillet

Cutting board

Knife

---

2 tablespoons white miso

1 tablespoon soy sauce

1 tablespoon olive oil

¼ cup water

18 ounces king oyster mushrooms

2 or 3 slices sourdough bread

¼ cup plant butter

4 garlic cloves, minced

¼ cup chopped fresh Italian parsley

Salt and pepper

Writing a cookbook requires lots of recipe testing, and for us, that means lots of camping trips. We tested this one on a trip to the Mojave Desert that will forever be remembered primarily for the wind. We started the trip with perfect weather but were quickly warned of what was coming by an eerie and strong gust of wind. That first gust was followed a few hours later by incessant 30+ mph winds. Everything from our tabletops to our tents blew over and we soon decided to pack it up early. The word "canapé" is derived from the French word meaning "couch," because the toast looks like a couch for the topping, and we love to remember ourselves daintily nibbling these fancy little canapés while the chaos went on around us. —Aimee

AT HOME (OPTIONAL)

Make a marinade by mixing the miso, soy sauce, olive oil, and water in a jar with a tight-fitting lid. Seal and keep refrigerated until ready to use.

AT CAMP

Use your fingers to tear and shred the mushrooms into small pieces. Place the mushrooms in a bowl with the marinade, toss to coat, and allow to sit for about 30 minutes.

While the mushrooms are marinating, toast the bread in a dry skillet. Cut each slice of bread into 4 triangular toasts.

Melt the butter in a skillet set over medium-high heat. Add the mushrooms in their marinade and sauté until the liquid from the mushrooms evaporates and the mushrooms brown slightly, 7 to 10 minutes.

Stir in the garlic and parsley, and season to taste with salt and pepper.

Top each toast with a pile of mushrooms and serve.

Tip: King oyster mushrooms can be a little hard to find, but it's worth seeking them out for this recipe. Their flavor and texture really take this simple recipe to the next level. Try your local Asian market, and while you're there, grab some other varieties to experiment with.

Tofu Satay with Peanut Sauce

extra-firm tofu, peanut butter, chili-garlic marinade

Makes 4 servings

Cooking time: 15 minutes

TOOLS

Leakproof container

Mason jar

Knife

Cutting board

Fork

8 skewers

Camp stove or grate

Skillet or grill pan

Spatula

---

1 tablespoon neutral oil, plus more for grilling

3 tablespoons soy sauce

2 tablespoons brown sugar

1 tablespoon rice vinegar

1 tablespoon chili-garlic sauce or 1 garlic clove, minced

Juice and zest of 1 lime

1 (16-ounce) block extra-firm or super-firm tofu

½ cup natural creamy peanut butter

¼ to ½ cup hot water

1 cucumber, sliced, for serving

We've got a lot of experience with skewers. The idea of food on a stick is an icon of outdoor cooking in many people's minds, so it has crept into our large-scale catering menus over the years. We really should hire some interns for the job, but we naively sit for eight-hour skewering sessions each time, somehow forgetting the pain and suffering that occurred each time before. The praise we get once the eating starts is always worth it, however, and we still love them for any event of fewer than two hundred people. —Emily

AT HOME (OPTIONAL)

In a leakproof container, make a marinade by whisking together with a fork 1 tablespoon of the oil and the soy sauce, brown sugar, rice vinegar, chili-garlic sauce, and lime juice and zest.

Cut the tofu into 8 strips by first halving it crosswise, then cutting each block into 4 long strips. Put the tofu strips in the marinade and cover to marinate for at least 15 minutes. Keeping the tofu in the container, carefully pour off the marinade into a Mason jar.

Add the peanut butter to the marinade and mix with a fork until well combined. Add hot water, 1 tablespoon at a time, until you reach the desired consistency for the sauce—thin enough to dip and thick enough to coat the bite.

AT CAMP

Carefully insert a skewer through the center of each strip of tofu, lengthwise.

Heat a grill pan or large skillet over medium-high heat and add about 1 tablespoon of vegetable oil.

Grill the tofu on at least 2 sides until brown and crispy, 4 to 5 minutes per side. Add more oil if necessary to prevent sticking.

Serve hot or cold with the dipping sauce and sliced cucumbers.

Tip: The marinade adds tons of flavor to the tofu and doubles as the base for the dipping sauce, so there's no waste!

Campfire Party Chickpeas

Chex Party Mix seasoning, chickpeas

Makes 3 cups

Cooking time: 15 to 20 minutes

TOOLS

Camp stove or grate

Can opener

Skillet

Spatula or spoon

---

2 tablespoons plant-based Worcestershire sauce

2 teaspoons paprika

1 teaspoon dried oregano

½ teaspoon pepper

¼ teaspoon salt

2 tablespoons plant butter

2 garlic cloves, minced, or ½ teaspoon garlic powder

2 (14-ounce) cans chickpeas, rinsed and patted dry

I am a major Chex Mix fan. My mom still makes it for me every time I visit, and now I've got Aimee roped into that role too! The last time I went to visit Aimee, she made some with store-bought dehydrated chickpeas as an ingredient, which I thought was genius. I ended up eating most of the chickpeas out of the mix and realized they would be delicious to share simply on their own with the same spice mix. We love having quick-cooking appetizers to stall whining while dinner is being prepared, and these fit that profile nicely. They also work great as a topping for salad or pasta that needs a little last-minute jazzing. —Emily

---

AT HOME *(OPTIONAL)*

Mix together the Worcestershire sauce, paprika, oregano, pepper, and salt in a leakproof container.

AT CAMP

Melt the butter in the skillet over low heat, either on the camp stove or on a grate set over a campfire.

Add the spice mixture and minced garlic and stir until fragrant, about 1 minute.

Add the chickpeas and stir to coat them in the sauce. Cook over medium-low heat for about 10 minutes, until the chickpeas have absorbed the sauce and are lightly browned.

Season to taste with additional salt and pepper and serve as an appetizer or snack.

Tip: If you want that smoky flavor but are not making these over the fire, use smoked paprika.

Fried Pickles

dill pickles, cornmeal, Cajun spices

Makes 4 to 6 servings
Cooking time: 15 to 20 minutes

TOOLS
Lidded container
Fork
Cast iron skillet
Camp stove
Plate
Paper towels
Tongs

⅔ cup all-purpose flour
⅓ cup cornmeal
¼ cup cornstarch
1½ teaspoons pepper
1 teaspoon smoked paprika
1 teaspoon garlic powder
1 teaspoon onion powder
1 teaspoon salt
¼ teaspoon cayenne pepper
1 cup water or sparkling water
Neutral oil for frying
20 to 30 dill pickle chips

FOR SERVING
Plant-based ranch dressing

I hate frying in my house because it makes the whole house smell like a fast-food restaurant, but it can be such a fun addition to a meal once in a while. Any time I have a hankering, I try to do my frying outside; for me, this is the only way to do it. Pickles are a really fun thing to fry, since you don't have to make too many of them to satisfy a group. Pair them with Dirty Rice and Beans (page 173) and some sautéed greens for a great dinner, whether camping or just in your backyard. —Aimee

AT HOME *(OPTIONAL)*

Stir together the flour, cornmeal, cornstarch, pepper, smoked paprika, garlic powder, onion powder, salt, and cayenne in a container with a lid (a 4- to 6-cup-capacity food storage container is ideal so that you can add the water and batter the pickles in it, keeping the cleanup mess contained until you're somewhere you can deal with it best).

AT CAMP

Add the water to the flour mixture and stir with a fork to create a smooth batter.

In a cast iron skillet set over medium-high heat, heat ½ to 1 inch of oil. Line a plate with paper towels.

Dip a few pickle chips at a time in the batter and use a fork to lift them out and shake off the excess batter before adding to the hot oil.

Fry the battered pickle chips until golden brown, 2 to 3 minutes, flipping halfway through the cooking time to ensure that both sides are cooked through.

Use tongs to remove the pickles from the hot oil and place them on the paper towels. If desired, sprinkle with salt while they're still hot. Continue this process until you use up all your pickle chips and/or batter.

Serve hot with ranch dressing.

Hot Cheesy Corn Dip

charred corn, red onion, green chiles

Makes 6 to 8 servings
Cooking time: 15 minutes

TOOLS
Knife
Cutting board
Skillet
Camp stove
Spoon

---

1 recipe Cashew Dream Sauce (page 288)

1 tablespoon olive oil

1 medium red onion, diced

1 cup corn kernels

⅓ cup diced fire-roasted Hatch, Anaheim, or poblano chiles (page 49)

1 teaspoon chili powder, plus more for garnishing

½ teaspoon salt

½ teaspoon pepper

½ cup water

2 scallions, sliced, for garnishing

Tortilla chips, for serving

One holiday season, my mother was invited to attend a party while I was visiting. She needed to bring an appetizer and wanted my help, but she wanted it to be traditional. We made a hot cheesy corn dip that she transported in her miniature Crockpot. I was happy to see her text that she'd arrived safely, but then I opened the attached photo—of the corn dip all over the floorboard of her car. At least it was still a memorable dish! This dish is as satisfying as any traditional cheesy corn dip you've spilled all over your car, yet also plant-based and campfire scented. —Emily

---

AT HOME

Make the Cashew Dream Sauce and pack it in a jar or leakproof container in a cooler.

AT CAMP

Heat the oil in a skillet set over medium-high heat. Add the red onion, corn, chiles, 1 teaspoon of the chili powder, and the salt and pepper. Sauté until the vegetables are tender and charred, about 10 minutes, stirring occasionally.

Once the corn and red onion are cooked, stir in the Cashew Dream Sauce and ½ cup water. Turn the heat down to low. Cook for about 5 more minutes, until the sauce has thickened to a cheesy consistency.

Remove the skillet from direct heat and sprinkle with a dusting of chili powder and sliced scallions. Serve immediately with chips.

Tip: Eat immediately, straight from the grate of the campfire—don't try to transport it! If it thickens too much as it sits, you can stir in a few tablespoons of water and reheat.

SIDE DISHES

Spicy Tomato Confit

cherry tomatoes, whole garlic cloves, fresh herbs

Makes 6 to 8 servings
Cooking time: 1 hour

TOOLS
Cast iron skillet
Campfire grate
Metal spoon or spatula

½ cup olive oil
2 cups whole cherry tomatoes
1 cup whole, peeled garlic cloves
1 sprig fresh rosemary
1 sprig fresh thyme
3 dried whole chiles, árbol or Japones, or similar
½ teaspoon salt
½ teaspoon pepper
1 loaf grillable bread or crackers, for serving

When you're recipe planning, it's hard enough to come up with a meal idea to feed your hungry crew in the wild. Adding a side dish can feel both overwhelming and unnecessary, but we think it can also be the secret to your success—if you pick the right dish. This one works perfectly alongside a Dutch oven meal like a big pot of beans. It is very hands-off, letting you focus on the main meal while someone else occasionally stirs. Start it right when you start the fire, and let it cook down to a beautiful, deeply colored spread. The intensity of the flavor means just a bit goes a long way—in case your neighbors smell what's happening on your fire and you want to share. —Emily

Get a campfire going until it forms hot coals.

In a skillet, stir together the olive oil, cherry tomatoes, garlic, rosemary, thyme, chiles, salt, and pepper.

Scoot some embers from the main campfire to create a pile of coals under the campfire grate. Place the skillet on the grate over the embers.

Stir occasionally, mashing as you stir, until all of the ingredients have broken down into a thick spread, about 1 hour.

Spread on campfire-grilled bread or crackers.

Tip: Leftovers are lovely as a sandwich spread for tomorrow's day trip or added to a morning hash or scramble.

Garlic Pull-Apart Bread

store-bought pizza dough, fresh garlic and herbs

Makes 6 to 8 servings

Cooking time: 40 to 45 minutes

TOOLS

Parchment paper and scissors or Dutch oven liners

10-inch Dutch oven

Small pot

Cutting board

Knife

Spoon

½ cup plant butter

¼ cup minced Italian parsley

6 garlic cloves, minced

3 tablespoons nutritional yeast

½ teaspoon salt

2 (1-pound) balls store-bought pizza dough

Even though you *could* make dough for this pull-apart bread at camp (and it would be delicious), using store-bought pizza dough is just so much more practical. You can still get your hands a little dirty, and you'll get a big reward of fresh bread baked on your campfire. —Aimee

Get a campfire going until it forms hot coals.

Cut the parchment paper to fit your Dutch oven or use a precut liner. Use enough parchment paper so that it goes up the sides of the Dutch oven a few inches and can act as a sling; this will help you to remove the bread when it's time to eat.

In a small pot, melt the butter. Remove from the heat and stir in the parsley, garlic, nutritional yeast, and salt.

Break off 1½-inch balls of pizza dough (about the size of a ping-pong ball) and dip each ball, one by one, in the butter mixture, arranging them in the prepared Dutch oven as you go.

Cover and allow to rest for 30 minutes to 1 hour.

Adjust the campfire to make room to set the entire Dutch oven next to the fire on a level surface. Set it over a bed of about 7 small coals and put 14 coals on the lid.

Bake for 40 to 45 minutes, checking it every 10 to 15 minutes and adjusting the heat as necessary. To ensure that the bread bakes evenly, rotate the entire Dutch oven a half turn about 20 minutes into the baking time, and turn the lid a quarter turn once or twice in the other direction.

The bread is done when it's golden brown and a knife inserted in the center comes out clean.

Use the parchment paper to carefully lift the bread out of the Dutch oven, and serve immediately.

Fun-dipped Fruit Salad

jicama, watermelon, chili powder

Makes 16 servings
No-cook recipe

TOOLS
Knife

Cutting board

Mixing bowl

Toothpicks

1 whole pineapple (about 4 pounds), skin removed, cubed

1 small watermelon (about 4 pounds), rind removed, cubed

1 jicama, peeled and cubed

2 cucumbers, peeled if desired and cubed

½ cup fresh lime juice

MEXICAN SPICE DIP
1 tablespoon chili powder, such as ancho chile powder

2 tablespoons sugar

1 teaspoon salt

¼ teaspoon cayenne *(optional; use if you would like a little more spice)*

Fresh lime wedges, for serving

This salad was inspired by the fresh fruit cups drizzled with chile lime seasoning and chamoy sauce sold by street vendors all over Los Angeles. We originally made this salad for an REI campout on Angel Island in San Francisco Bay, which required schlepping a whole weekend's worth of food for about three hundred people on a ferry. This salad's original quantities were twelve pineapples, six large watermelons, twelve jicamas, and twenty-five cucumbers—that was just *one* of the dishes we had to prepare for that event! We had a lot of fun during our catering days, but honestly, I don't miss the hard labor. What I *do* miss is this fruit salad, so here it is, scaled *way* down for your next summer weekend getaway. —Mai-Yan

AT HOME *(OPTIONAL)*

Stir together the chili powder, sugar, salt, and cayenne in a leak-proof container.

AT CAMP

In a mixing bowl, toss together the pineapple, watermelon, jicama, cucumbers, and lime juice.

Serve with Mexican spice dip and fresh lime wedges.

Tip: Although this may seem like too much fruit salad, it will keep for the whole weekend in your cooler, and you'll be happy to have a refreshing snack to reach for at any time.

Spicy Pickled Vegetables

serrano chiles, pickling spices, crunchy root vegetables

Makes 2 cups
No-cook recipe

TOOLS
Mason jar
Knife
Cutting board

6 radishes, quartered
1 jalapeño or serrano chile, sliced
4 garlic cloves, peeled
1 carrot, sliced into coins diagonally
¼ large red onion, sliced
½ teaspoon peppercorns
1 bay leaf
½ teaspoon salt
⅔ cup white vinegar

We have always loved going to local taquerias and loading up on the fresh pickled jalapeños and carrot slices alongside our burritos. Aimee took this one step further for a Dirty Gourmet event a few years ago and pickled a bunch of different kinds of vegetables to use as taco toppings. Her recipe includes a lot of beautiful pickling spices, but we've found that the vegetables bring out a lot of complex flavor on their own and the recipe works simply as a campified side. These are delicious on their own, as a topping to any Mexican dish, or on a bright soup. No cooking needed. —Emily

Fill a Mason jar with the radishes, jalapeño, garlic, carrot, red onion, peppercorns, bay leaf, and salt. Pour in the white vinegar and top off the jar with water, ensuring that the liquid covers all the vegetables. Store for up to a week in the cooler.

Mushroom Pilaf

mushrooms, spinach, dried woody herbs

Makes 6 to 8 servings
Cooking time: 25 minutes

TOOLS
3-quart pot
Camp stove
Knife
Cutting board
Large spoon

2 cups white rice
1 teaspoon dried thyme and/or rosemary
1 bay leaf
1¼ teaspoons Bouillon Powder (page 286) or bouillon cube equivalent
½ teaspoon pepper
2 tablespoons olive oil
1 shallot, chopped
8 ounces mushrooms, sliced
4 cups water
2 cups fresh baby spinach
½ teaspoon salt

Side dishes aren't often considered for camping meals, but there are many trips where I'm stumped for what to make other than something quick-grilled on the campfire. It's nice to have a hearty side dish to round that stuff out. This recipe is great alongside some grilled bread and plant-based sausage. It is always sort of an epiphany how fantastic such a simple dish can be, and it makes preparing for a camping trip much less of a chore. —Emily

AT HOME *(OPTIONAL)*

Put the rice, thyme, bay leaf, bouillon, and pepper in a lidded jar.

AT CAMP

Heat the oil in a pot over medium heat. When the oil is shimmering, add the shallot and mushrooms and sauté until softened and beginning to brown, about 7 minutes.

Add the rice mixture and salt, stirring, for about 2 minutes, until toasted and fragrant.

Add 4 cups of water, bring to a boil, and simmer, covered, until all of the water is absorbed and the rice is tender, about 15 minutes.

Add the spinach and stir until it's wilted. Serve immediately.

Mushroom Pilaf

Smashed Cucumber Salad (page 162)

Smashed Cucumber Salad

Korean banchan, sesame, garlic, gochugaru

Makes 4 servings
No cook recipe

TOOLS
Knife
Cutting board
Mixing bowl
Spoon

———

2 English cucumbers
6 garlic cloves, minced

DRESSING
4 tablespoons soy sauce
4 tablespoons rice vinegar
2 tablespoons sugar
2 tablespoons sesame oil
1 tablespoon coarse gochugaru flakes or Aleppo pepper
2 teaspoons toasted sesame seeds
½ teaspoon salt, plus more to taste

A typical Korean meal is served with *banchan*, a collection of small side dishes that accompany the meal. Kimchi is standard, but the other offerings change all the time and can include creamy potato salad and crispy sprouts. The one Daniel and I fight over all the time is the cucumber salad. This recipe is a shareable version that balances salty, sweet, and acid with the earthiness of the cucumbers and *gochugaru*. You might wonder why you should bother with smashing them. This helps remove the cucumber seeds and, more important, breaks up the skin and flesh, creating lots of nooks and crannies for the dressing to seep into. And a bonus is that smashing is fun! —Mai-Yan

---

AT HOME *(OPTIONAL)*

Stir together the dressing ingredients in a leakproof container.

AT CAMP

Cut the cucumbers lengthwise and then into 1-inch sections.

Place the flat part of the knife on a cucumber piece and smash it lightly using your other hand. Repeat for all the cucumber pieces.

Add the cucumbers to the bowl along with the garlic and add the dressing ingredients. Stir to combine. Serve immediately or store chilled for up to 2 hours for the best crunch.

Tip: Gochugaru is made from dried Korean red chile peppers; it's sweet and slightly smoky but typically not spicy. Aleppo pepper has a similar texture but does come with some heat; if using the substitution, begin with less and add more to taste.

Butter with a Side of Vegetables

We strive to eat seasonally whenever possible, since produce tastes *so much* better when it's fresh, so we want to share a loose concept for how to cook great vegetables all year round. Because everything tastes better with butter, we've whipped up five compound butter flavors to enhance your veggie feast.

What follows is a guide for which vegetables to look for during each season. If you see something you don't recognize on the shelves or at the farmers' market, ask about it! Different regions tend to have local specialties that will make your feast uniquely yours. —Dirty Gourmet

CHOOSING THE VEGGIES

SPRING VEGGIES: These vegetables are tender and delicate. They don't need much preparation or extensive cooking. Many can be sautéed in a skillet or grilled. Pair these with lemon herb butter.

SUMMER VEGGIES: Summer's bounty is begging to be grilled. Imagine a big pile of veggies stamped with grill marks and crispy charred edges. (You can also easily prepare them in a foil pouch. See the tutorial in the Appendix.) You'll be impressed by how many veggies you can eat. Pair these with balsamic or aleppo butters.

FALL VEGGIES: Fall's harvest brings hearty squash and dark, leafy greens. Bring out your cast iron skillet or play with some interesting foil pouch combinations. These veggies will taste great with masala butter.

WINTER VEGGIES: In winter you'll want to stay as close to the fire as possible, so we like to embrace foil pouch cooking. Fortunately, winter veggies are some of our favorites to cook in a foil pouch. Top these with miso butter. While you're at it, put that miso butter on everything!

COMPOUND BUTTER
FIVE WAYS

LEMON HERB BUTTER

½ cup plant butter, softened

1 teaspoon lemon zest

1 tablespoon fresh lemon juice

¼ cup finely chopped fresh dill

¼ teaspoon salt

BALSAMIC BUTTER

½ cup plant butter, softened

2 garlic cloves, minced

2 tablespoons balsamic vinegar

¼ teaspoon salt

ALEPPO BUTTER

½ cup plant butter, softened

2 garlic cloves, minced

2 teaspoons ground Aleppo pepper

4 sun-dried tomato halves, minced

¼ teaspoon salt

MASALA BUTTER

½ cup plant butter

1 teaspoon tomato paste

½ teaspoon sweet paprika

½ teaspoon ground cumin

½ teaspoon coriander

1 whole dried chile, like Kashmiri or chile de árbol

1 garlic clove, minced

¼ teaspoon salt

¼ teaspoon pepper

MISO BUTTER

½ cup plant butter

4 teaspoons miso paste

4 scallions, thinly sliced

TO MAKE THE COMPOUND BUTTERS

LEMON HERB BUTTER: In a small bowl, use a fork to mix together the softened butter, lemon zest and juice, dill, and salt until well combined.

BALSAMIC BUTTER: In a small bowl, use a fork to mix together the softened butter, garlic, balsamic vinegar, and salt until well combined.

ALEPPO BUTTER: In a small bowl, use a fork to mix together the softened butter, garlic, Aleppo pepper, sun-dried tomatoes, and salt until well combined.

MASALA BUTTER: Melt the butter in a small skillet over medium heat. Stir in the tomato paste, paprika, cumin, coriander, dried chile, garlic, salt, and pepper. Cook for about 1 minute, stirring constantly, until the spices are fragrant and everything is well combined. Remove from the heat and allow to cool until the butter mixture solidifies.

MISO BUTTER: In a small pot set over medium heat, cook the butter and miso, stirring constantly, until the butter melts and the miso is dissolved. Remove from the heat, stir in the scallions, and allow to cool until the butter mixture solidifies.

TO PACK COMPOUND BUTTERS

All these compound butters can be simply packed in a jar. But if you'd like to have sliceable logs like those pictured, lay a piece of parchment paper about 12 by 12 inches on a work surface. Scrape the butter mixture onto the paper and roughly shape it into a log. Wrap the paper around the log, twisting the ends to close. Store in the cooler until ready to use.

MAINS

One-Pot Sausage and Broccolini Pasta

plant-based Italian sausage, broccolini, shallots

Makes 4 servings
Cooking time: 30 minutes

TOOLS
Camp stove
Large pot
Spoon
Plate or bowl

---

2 to 4 tablespoons olive oil

4 plant-based Italian sausages, crumbled or chopped

3 large shallots, diced

4 garlic cloves, minced

1 teaspoon salt

¼ teaspoon crushed red pepper flakes, or to taste, plus more for serving

3 cups water

8 ounces pasta, such as penne or orecchiette

2 small bunches broccolini, chopped (about 3 cups)

2 tablespoons Nutty Parmesan (page 288), plus more for serving

Here's a quick dinner that cooks all in one pot. No pasta draining required! The first time I made pasta like this, I was sure it wouldn't work, but it magically comes together every time, and every time I am still in awe. The starchy pasta water helps to create a sauce that's light but nicely sticks to the pasta. When I make this recipe and think back on my typical childhood camp meal of pasta with jarred marinara sauce and Parmesan from the green can, I can see how far my camp cooking has come. This recipe is also one that Emily and I both make all the time at home. Even at home, it's so nice to have fewer dishes to wash. —Aimee

---

In a large pot over medium-high heat, heat 2 tablespoons of the olive oil. Add the sausages and cook until lightly browned, 4 to 6 minutes, adding more oil if needed. Transfer to a plate, leaving any extra oil in the pot, and set aside.

Add the shallots to the pot and cook over medium heat until softened and slightly browned, about 5 minutes. Stir in the garlic and cook for another minute.

Add the salt, crushed red pepper flakes, and water and bring to a boil over high heat.

Add the pasta and stir until well combined. Turn down the heat to medium-low, cover, and simmer for 12 minutes.

Stir in the broccolini, cover, and continue cooking for a few more minutes, until the pasta is cooked through and the broccolini is bright green.

Remove from the heat and stir in the crisped sausage and 2 tablespoons of Nutty Parmesan.

Serve with additional Nutty Parmesan and crushed red pepper flakes if desired.

One-Pot Sausage and Broccolini Pasta

Turkish Flatbread (page 168)

Turkish Flatbread

sumac, plant-based meat crumbles, tahini

Makes 4 to 5 servings

Cooking time: 15 minutes

TOOLS

Cutting board

Knife

Campfire grill or camp stove

Medium skillet

Spatula

Aluminum foil *(optional)*

Tongs *(optional)*

2 tablespoons olive oil, divided

1 small yellow onion, finely chopped

2 cups (10 ounces) plant-based meat crumbles

2 garlic cloves, minced

3 large tomatoes, finely chopped

½ cup roasted red pepper, chopped

3 tablespoons chopped flat-leaf parsley

1 tablespoon tomato paste

1½ teaspoons sumac

1 teaspoon paprika

½ teaspoon ground cumin

½ teaspoon crushed red pepper flakes

Salt

4 to 5 flatbreads or naan

FOR SERVING

Tahini

1 shallot, thinly sliced

Toasted pine nuts

Lemon, sliced in wedges

This recipe is inspired by Daniel's time living in Berlin, where he would pick up Turkish flatbread (*lahmacun*) most days for the equivalent of a couple bucks. As part of my research for this recipe, I reached out to my Turkish friend Rengin to get insider information. She shared that this dish is usually made in a large wood-fired oven with a thin layer of spiced meat baked right into the dough. The whole thing is typically topped with lots of fresh leafy greens, tomatoes, and raw red onions. For our campified plant-based version, we kept the rich spiced tomato base and went with shallots for a slightly milder allium. Our addition of tahini and pine nuts is totally nonregulation, but it has Rengin's approval. —Mai-Yan

Heat the skillet over medium heat and add 1 tablespoon of oil. Add the onions and cook, stirring occasionally, until they are translucent, about 7 minutes.

Add the meat crumbles, garlic, tomatoes, roasted red peppers, parsley, tomato paste, sumac, paprika, cumin, red pepper flakes, and another tablespoon of oil and mix well. Cook the mixture for 5 minutes, stirring occasionally. Season to taste with salt.

If you want to warm up the flatbread, wrap each separately in foil. Set each individually on the campfire grill out of direct heat or over a low flame on the camp stove for a few minutes.

Place the flatbread on a cutting board and spread about ½ cup of spiced crumble mixture all the way to the edges. Cut into quarters and top with tahini, shallot slices, pine nuts, and a squeeze of lemon.

Tip: Frozen crumbles work well for this recipe and will act as an additional ice pack in your cooler.

Mexican Lime Soup

poblano chile, onion, tortilla strips

Makes 4 servings
Cooking time: 20 minutes

TOOLS
Knife
Cutting board
Large pot
Camp stove
Large spoon
Ladle

———

2 tablespoons vegetable oil

1 red onion, quartered and sliced

1 large poblano chile, seeded and diced

1 teaspoon dried oregano

1 teaspoon salt

½ teaspoon dried thyme

½ teaspoon pepper

5 garlic cloves, minced

5 scallions, chopped

3 tablespoons Bouillon Powder (page 286) or bouillon cube equivalent

8 cups water

1 cup soy curls, or similar, broken into bite-size pieces

3 to 4 limes

½ cup fresh cilantro, chopped

1 cup tortilla strips or chips, for topping

During the height of the pandemic in 2020, Daniel and I did all fifty-two walks in the book *Secret Stairs: A Walking Guide to the Historic Staircases of Los Angeles* by Charles Fleming. This was our escape, exploring local neighborhoods and discovering places we had never seen or even heard of before. We did most of the walks at night, relishing the quiet hush of the city and the breeze on our rarely unmasked faces. I savored glimpses of how others were coping with the pandemic in their homes with rainbow drawings taped up in windows and work desks awkwardly placed in living rooms.

I sought some escapism in the kitchen too, as standard recipes became too familiar or difficult to source. This recipe is one that made me feel both comforted and nostalgic. First made for us by Daniel's mom, Paula, *Sopa de Lima* is a recipe she discovered while traveling in Mexico. Over a hot bowl of soup, I was reminded that adventure is a mindset and possible without hopping on a plane or driving for hours. —Mai-Yan

In a large pot over medium heat, heat 2 tablespoons of the oil. Add the red onion, poblano chile, oregano, salt, thyme, and pepper and sauté until the onions are translucent but not browned, 5 to 7 minutes.

Stir in the garlic and scallions and cook for a few more minutes, until fragrant.

Add the bouillon, water, and soy curls, increase the heat to high, and bring to a boil.

Turn down the heat to low, add the juice of 2 of the limes, and taste. Add more lime juice if needed, and salt to taste.

Simmer the soup for another 10 minutes for the flavors to meld.

Stir in the cilantro and serve topped with tortilla strips.

Tip: You know that package of tortillas that's been hanging out in the back of the fridge—the one that doesn't quite have enough tortillas to make a full meal but is still probably good for "something"? Well, it's time to break it out and make homemade tortilla strips! Just cut the tortillas into thin 2-inch strips, and toss them in a pan with hot oil. Season with a bit of salt and chili powder and cook on medium-high heat until they are nice and crispy.

Mexican Lime Soup (page 169)

Cajun Grits Bowl (page 172)

Dirty Rice and Beans (page 173)

Cajun Grits Bowls

spinach, smoky sausage, Old Bay

Makes 4 servings

Cooking time: 30 minutes

TOOLS

Knife

Cutting board

Aluminum foil

4 campfire skewers

Camp stove

Large pot with lid

---

4 plant-based sausages

1 cup grits

4 cups cool water

3 teaspoons Bouillon Powder (page 286) or bouillon cube equivalent

1 teaspoon Old Bay Seasoning

½ teaspoon salt

½ teaspoon pepper

⅓ cup tahini

Juice of 1 lemon

12 ounces spinach, frozen or fresh, chopped

FOIL POUCH VEGETABLES

1 large onion, sliced

1 bell pepper, sliced

1 tablespoon olive oil

Salt and pepper

Writing a cookbook has many perks. All the new recipes and ideas are at my fingertips, begging to be tested, which makes it so easy to meal plan. It also encourages me to think about my favorite dishes from locales where I've eaten, and how to re-create satisfying camp versions of them. I often think of Shrimp and Grits, and this recipe is my vegan camping answer. We actually make it at home a lot too, but it's more fun to make at camp because the campfire adds an extra smoky flavor. —Emily

---

To make the foil pouch vegetables: Lay out a 2-foot-long sheet of aluminum foil and put the pepper and onion slices, olive oil, salt, and pepper in the center. Fold up into a foil packet (see the tutorial in the Appendix).

Place the packet on the campfire grate over medium-high heat and let cook, flipping once, until the vegetables are charred and tender, about 10 minutes. Set aside.

Meanwhile, skewer the sausages and roast over the campfire until crispy on the outside and cooked through, about 10 minutes. When cool to the touch, chop into rounds and set aside. If you forgot your skewers, these can be cooked in a foil packet.

In the pot on the camp stove, stir together the grits, water, bouillon, Old Bay Seasoning, salt, and pepper. Bring to a boil over medium-high heat. Turn down the heat to low and simmer, stirring occasionally. Cook until the grits are creamy and thick, about 20 minutes.

When the grits are cooked, add the tahini and lemon juice and stir until well combined.

Stir in the spinach. If you're using fresh spinach, you'll need to add it in batches, adding more as it cooks down.

To serve, put about 1 cup of grits in each bowl and top with vegetables and sausage.

Tip: If you've got some helpers, enlist one person to grill the veggies and sausage while someone else cooks the grits, so dinner comes together more quickly.

Dirty Rice and Beans

red beans, brown rice, trinity mix

Makes 8 servings
Cooking time: 1 hour

TOOLS

Camp stove or grate
Knife
Cutting board
Large pot or Dutch oven
Spoon

---

1 pound dried red beans, soaked overnight
3 tablespoons olive oil
1 medium onion, chopped
1 green bell pepper, chopped
4 stalks celery, chopped
2 cups brown rice
2 bay leaves
2 teaspoons salt
1 teaspoon black pepper
½ teaspoon smoked paprika
½ teaspoon garlic powder
½ teaspoon ground white pepper
¼ teaspoon oregano
¼ teaspoon cayenne
1 tablespoon vegan Worcestershire sauce

FOR SERVING

Sliced scallions
Sliced radishes
Lemon wedges
Vinegar-based hot sauce

Obviously, we are drawn to any dish with the term "dirty" in it. We also love meals that can be made all in one pot. In this recipe we use traditional Cajun-style red beans. They need to be presoaked, but they can be cooked at the same time and in the same pot as the rice, reducing dishwashing duty to simply wiping the pot out with that last piece of bread. —Emily

AT HOME *(OPTIONAL)*

Rinse the beans and soak overnight in water. Drain and store in a leakproof container for transporting in your cooler to camp.

AT CAMP

Heat the olive oil in a large pot or Dutch oven over medium-high heat. Add the onion, bell pepper, and celery and sauté until softened, about 5 minutes.

Add the rice, bay leaves, salt, black pepper, paprika, garlic powder, white pepper, oregano, and cayenne and continue cooking for about 1 minute.

Add the beans and enough water to cover the mixture by 1 inch.

Bring to a boil over high heat. Turn down the heat to a simmer, cover, and cook until the beans and rice are tender, about 1 hour. Add the Worcestershire sauce. Add toppings such as scallions, radishes, lemon juice, hot sauce, and more Worcestershire, if desired.

Tip: If you have a favorite Cajun seasoning, use 2 teaspoons of that in place of our spice mix.

(Almost) Instant Saucy Noodles

kecap manis, bok choy, wheat noodles

Makes 4 servings

Cooking time: 10 to 15 minutes

TOOLS
Camp stove

Medium pot

Tongs

Knife

Cutting board

---

8 ounces Chinese wheat noodles

1 cup dried sliced shiitake mushrooms

2 heads of baby bok choy, washed and quartered lengthwise

1 head of broccoli, chopped into bite-size pieces

SAUCE
2 tablespoons neutral oil

3 teaspoons Bouillon Powder (page 286) or bouillon cube equivalent

2 teaspoons kecap manis

2 teaspoons chili-garlic sauce

¼ teaspoon ground ginger

¼ teaspoon ground nutmeg

¼ teaspoon garlic powder

¼ teaspoon ground cumin

FOR SERVING
3 scallions, chopped

4 tablespoons fried onions or shallots

This recipe is inspired by Indomie brand *mi goreng*, instant noodles coated with a super flavorful sticky sauce. These are more like a stir-fried noodle dish than a soupy bowl of ramen. The dish is designed to be a one-pot meal made with almost any quick-cooking vegetables that can be blanched directly in the noodle water. While many different types of noodles would work, our favorite is medium-thin *mein* or wheat noodles. We highly recommend serving this with our Sichuan Chili Oil (page 291). —Mai-Yan

---

AT HOME *(OPTIONAL)*

Stir together the oil, bouillon, kecap manis, chili-garlic sauce, ginger, nutmeg, garlic, and cumin and put into a leakproof container.

AT CAMP

Bring a pot of water to a boil.

Add the noodles and dried mushrooms and cook according to the package instructions.

When 2 minutes of cooking time remains on the noodles, add the fresh vegetables to the boiling water and blanch until bright green and tender.

Drain the noodles and vegetables and return them to the pot.

Pour the sauce into the pot and mix well so all of the ingredients are coated.

Serve garnished with scallions and fried onions or shallots.

Tip: Kecap manis is a delicious, sweet soy sauce used in Indonesian cooking. You can find it at Indonesian markets or online.

Pioneer Stew with Grilled Lemon Bread

mushrooms, apples, root vegetables

Makes 4 to 6 servings

Cooking time: 1 hour

TOOLS

Camp stove or grate

Large pot or Dutch oven

Cutting board

Knife

Spoon

Foil or cast iron skillet

---

6 tablespoons plant butter

1 onion, quartered

4 garlic cloves, whole

2 portobello mushrooms, quartered

4 cups water

½ cup red wine

1 pound potatoes, cut into large chunks or whole if small

1 sweet potato, cut into large chunks

3 carrots, cut into large chunks

1 apple, quartered

2 teaspoons Bouillon Powder (page 286) or bouillon cube equivalent

2 or 3 sprigs of fresh woody herbs, such as rosemary or thyme *(optional)*

1 teaspoon salt

Grilled loaf of bread, such as French bread, for serving

1 or 2 lemons

Some of our favorite pioneers are those who find practical and elegant solutions that seem too simple to be innovative. Indigenous American culture has relied on the "three sisters" (corn, beans, and squash) to maximize space for essential crops; Australian Aboriginal people used silviculture practices to protect all parts of their forests. Regenerative farming is being relearned and used on a much larger scale as we recognize the importance of sustainable practices. These ideas don't require major technological advances—just a different mindset.

This recipe celebrates the importance of simplicity and fully utilizing resources. There isn't much preparation required—at home or at camp—and we recommend cooking it over the campfire, which will serve double duty as a heat source for you and your food. It is comfort in its simplest form, allowing you to appreciate the elegance of simply existing within the natural world. —Emily

---

In a pot set over medium heat on the stove or over the campfire grate, melt the butter. Add the onion, garlic, and mushrooms. Sauté until the onions are softened, about 10 minutes.

Increase the heat to high and add the water, wine, potatoes, carrots, sweet potato, apple, bouillon, herbs, and salt. Bring the mixture to a boil, then turn down the heat to medium-low. Cover and simmer until all the vegetables are tender, about 45 minutes.

Meanwhile, slice the lemons into halves or quarters. Grill them alongside big pieces of bread on a grate set over the fire or in a cast iron skillet. Once everything is charred and heated through, rub the lemon over the cut sides of the bread.

Serve the stew in bowls with lemon bread.

Pioneer Stew with Grilled Lemon Bread

Sunflower Ramen (page 178)

Sunflower Ramen

sunflower butter, shiitakes, edamame

Makes 4 servings
Cooking time: 15 minutes

TOOLS
Camp stove
Large pot
Knife
Cutting board
Ladle or spoon

---

4 tablespoons miso
2 tablespoons soy sauce
2 tablespoons unsweetened sun-flower butter
1 tablespoon toasted sesame oil
4 teaspoons Bouillon Powder (page 286) or bouillon cube equivalent
½ teaspoon ground ginger
1 tablespoon neutral oil or plant butter
1 shallot, minced
4 garlic cloves, minced
10 cups water
8 ounces shiitake mushrooms, sliced
1¼ cups shelled edamame (from frozen)
8 ounces dried ramen noodles

FOR SERVING
Sliced scallions
Sichuan Chili Oil (page 291)

I never would have thought of using sunflower butter as an ingredient in my cooking until I had a bowl of ramen from Ramen Hood in downtown LA. Their ramen broth is made with sunflower seeds, which adds a subtle creaminess that I love. In this camp-friendly version, I use sunflower butter instead of seeds, so it doesn't require a blender, but you still get a rich and creamy broth made right at camp. I love this loaded with shiitake mushrooms, but switch it up with whatever veggies you prefer. —Aimee

AT HOME *(OPTIONAL)*

In a leakproof container, mix the miso, soy sauce, sunflower butter, sesame oil, bouillon, and ginger until well combined.

AT CAMP

Heat the oil or butter in a large pot over medium heat. Add the minced shallot and sauté until softened but not browned, about 5 minutes. Add the garlic and cook for about 1 minute.

Add the miso mixture to the pot and stir until well combined. Add the water. Increase the heat to high, cover the pot, and bring to a boil.

Add the mushrooms, edamame, and ramen and return the mixture to a boil. Turn down the heat and simmer until the noodles are cooked through.

Top with scallions and Sichuan Chili Oil.

Tip: Swap out the sunflower butter for tahini or cashew butter if that's what you've got on hand. The results will be different, but equally delicious!

Smothered Seitan Sandwiches

sliced and spiced seitan,
grilled peppers and onions,
secret sauce

Makes 4 servings

Cooking time: 20 minutes

TOOLS
Knife
Cutting board
Camp stove or grate
Skillet
Tongs or spatula
Plate

---

1 loaf Seitan (page 292), sliced thin
1 teaspoon smoked paprika
1 teaspoon minced garlic
½ teaspoon salt
½ teaspoon pepper
3 tablespoons olive oil, divided
1 onion, sliced
1 bell pepper, sliced
8 slices sourdough bread

SECRET SAUCE
¼ cup vegan mayonnaise
2 tablespoons chopped dill pickle
1 tablespoon ketchup
½ teaspoon mustard
½ teaspoon salt
½ teaspoon pepper

I tried making my first seitan loaf years ago. I didn't knead it long enough and did not enjoy the texture, so I never made it again. When Mai-Yan asked me to test this seitan recipe, I wasn't thrilled, but I took on the challenge. Slicing it thin and drenching it in sauce makes it irresistible, and we now make a couple loaves a week. This sandwich has the saucy, drippy qualities you want in a good grilled burger, and it also works great as a hot breakfast or even cold as a day-trip lunch. —Emily

---

AT HOME *(OPTIONAL)*

Make the secret sauce by combining the mayo, pickles, ketchup, mustard, salt, and pepper in a leakproof container.

Put the seitan slices, smoked paprika, garlic, salt, pepper, and 1 tablespoon of the olive oil in another leakproof container and massage to coat each slice in spice.

AT CAMP

Heat the remaining 2 tablespoons of oil in a skillet over medium-high heat. Sauté the onion and bell pepper together until softened and starting to brown, about 5 minutes. Remove from the skillet and set aside.

In the same skillet, cook the spice-rubbed seitan slices until they are starting to brown and the edges are getting crispy, about 5 to 10 minutes. Remove from the skillet and set aside.

In the same skillet, grill the bread slices until lightly toasted, 2 to 3 minutes on each side.

To assemble the sandwiches, spread 1 tablespoon of sauce on one side of each piece of bread. Divide the seitan, peppers, and onions between 4 bread slices and top with remaining slices.

Tip: Grill up all of the seitan even if you aren't planning to use it up in sandwiches right away. It's great to snack on by itself or to eat as cold cuts later.

Smothered Seitan Sandwiches (page 179)

Spicy and Sweet Tempeh Stir-Fry

Spicy and Sweet Tempeh Stir-Fry

tempeh, sweet soy sauce, peppers, shallots

Makes 4 servings
Cooking time: 20 minutes

TOOLS
Knife
Cutting board
12-inch cast iron skillet
Spatula

1½ to 2 cups uncooked white rice

6 tablespoons neutral oil

16 ounces tempeh, cut into matchsticks

2 red bell peppers, cut into matchsticks

1 to 2 chiles, such as Thai bird, serrano, or jalapeño, thinly sliced diagonally

1 large cucumber, sliced, for serving

SAUCE

1 shallot, minced

6 tablespoons kecap manis (sweet soy sauce)

1 teaspoon salt

1 teaspoon sugar

3 garlic cloves, minced

1-inch piece of fresh ginger, peeled and minced (about 1 tablespoon)

2 bay leaves

Tempeh, a high-protein fermented soybean product, is a staple of Indonesian cuisine. If you're not familiar with tempeh, consider this your gateway dish. Even if you have tried it and said "not my favorite" (like Aimee and Emily), this dish could win you over. It's for spice lovers, but the recipe is balanced with sweetness for those still building up their spice tolerance. —Mai-Yan

AT HOME *(OPTIONAL)*

Measure all the sauce ingredients into a leakproof container such as a Mason jar.

AT CAMP

Cook the rice according to the package instructions. Set aside until ready to serve.

Pour the oil into the skillet and heat it over medium-high heat. When the oil is shimmering, carefully add the tempeh to the oil, starting with a few matchsticks to test the temperature. The temperature is right if small bubbles form around the tempeh when it hits the oil. Fry the tempeh, occasionally flipping the matchsticks around, until all the pieces are golden brown, around 10 minutes.

Add the bell peppers and chiles and sauté until slightly tender, about 2 minutes.

Finally, add the sauce and mix well so all of the ingredients are fully coated. Lower the heat to medium and stir-fry for another 5 minutes to meld the flavors and cook the sauce ingredients.

Serve with the rice and sliced cucumber.

Roasted Fennel and Sausage Bake

fresh fennel and apple,
nutty breadcrumb topping,
Italian sausage

Makes 4 servings
Cooking time: 40 minutes

Despite my being very particular, Aimee manages to find me the perfect gift every year. It's always a cookbook, and Joshua McFadden's *Six Seasons: A New Way with Vegetables* is still one of my go-tos. One day I'd ended up with a lot of fennel in my fridge and I reached for this book and campified his fennel recipe to work with a Dutch oven. If, like me, you instinctively run from recipes that pair fruit with vegetables, hold your horses! This is a solidly savory recipe, and a great beginner Dutch oven campfire-cooking recipe. It can be made mostly on the stovetop or grate, and it bakes just enough to develop a nice, crispy browned topping. —Mai-Yan

TOOLS

Dutch oven
Camp stove or campfire grate
Large spoon
Knife
Cutting board
Lid lifter
Long tongs
Heatproof gloves

---

1 to 2 tablespoons olive oil

14 ounces uncooked sweet or mild Italian vegan sausages, sliced into coins

2 garlic cloves, smashed

½ teaspoon chile flakes

1½ to 2 pounds medium fennel bulbs, thinly sliced

1 pound red potatoes, sliced thinly into half moons

1 apple, Fuji or similar, cored and thinly sliced into half moons

1 teaspoon salt

¼ teaspoon pepper

¼ teaspoon dried thyme

⅔ cup water

TOPPING

½ cup panko bread crumbs

½ cup hazelnuts or almonds, roughly chopped

1 teaspoon nutritional yeast

AT HOME (OPTIONAL)

Stir together the panko, nuts, and nutritional yeast in a leakproof container.

AT CAMP

Get a campfire going until it forms hot coals.

Set the Dutch oven carefully on the camp stove so it is stable. Heat it over medium-high heat and add 1 tablespoon of olive oil.

Add the sausages and brown them for about 5 minutes, stirring occasionally.

Turn down the heat to medium and move the sausages away from the center of the Dutch oven. Add another tablespoon of olive oil in the cleared area, if needed, and add the smashed garlic and chile flakes. Stir until fragrant, about 1 minute.

Add the sliced fennel, potatoes, apples, salt, pepper, thyme, and water. Mix everything well, scraping up any little bits stuck to the bottom of the pot. Adjust the heat so that the liquid gently simmers. Cover and cook for 10 minutes, stirring occasionally.

Add the topping mix to cover the ingredients and place the Dutch oven on the campfire grate, away from any direct flames.

Cover the Dutch oven and place about 15 coals on the lid. Check on the topping after 10 minutes; if the topping already looks browned, remove some or all of the coals from the lid. Bake for another 10 minutes, or until the topping mix is browned and the vegetables are cooked.

Salisbury Seitan Smashed Potatoes

mushroom gravy, seitan steaks, ember-roasted potatoes

Makes 4 servings

Cooking time: 1 hour

TOOLS

Campfire grate or camp stove

Knife

Cutting board

Aluminum foil

12-inch skillet

Large spoon

Long tongs

Heatproof gloves

Plate or bowl

Spatula

———

4 baking potatoes, such as russet

2 to 4 tablespoons plant butter or olive oil, divided

1 loaf Seitan (page 292), cut into 8 slices

24 ounces mushrooms, like baby bella or white button, sliced

1 medium onion, sliced

2 tablespoons chopped fresh parsley

Many people new to the idea of plant-based eating worry that the food won't be hearty or filling enough. This becomes even more nerve-wracking when thinking about what to eat on high-energy days outdoors. We created this recipe as the "meat and potatoes" of camp cooking. We like to stack this whole meal so it can be eaten out of one dish, leaving you feeling warm and comforted. Thanks to the gravy, you don't need all the standard baked-potato toppings, so there are fewer ingredients floating around in your cooler. —Emily

AT HOME *(OPTIONAL)*

Stir together the flour, bouillon, thyme, mustard, garlic, pepper, and smoked paprika in a leakproof container.

AT CAMP

To bake the potatoes, let the campfire start to build up a bed of embers. Wrap the potatoes in foil and put them directly over the embers along the edge of the fire. Roast, turning them every 15 minutes or so, until they are tender throughout, about 1 hour.

Meanwhile, make the Salisbury Seitan. In a skillet set over medium-high heat, melt 1 tablespoon of butter or oil. Add the seitan slices and brown for about 5 minutes on each side. Remove the seitan from the skillet and set aside.

Add another tablespoon of butter or oil and the sliced mushrooms. Cook until the mushrooms release their water and start to brown, 5 to 7 minutes.

Add the sliced onion. Cook the mixture until the onion has softened, 5 to 7 more minutes.

Add the dry spice and flour mixture and stir to coat the vegetables evenly.

Add the water and Worcestershire sauce, stir until well combined, and turn the heat down to a simmer.

Once the sauce begins to thicken a bit, add the seitan slices to the gravy. Cook, rotating occasionally, until cooked through, about 10 minutes.

MUSHROOM GRAVY

3 tablespoons all-purpose flour

3 teaspoons Bouillon Powder (page 286) or bouillon cube equivalent

1 teaspoon dried thyme

1 teaspoon ground mustard

½ teaspoon garlic powder

½ teaspoon pepper

¼ teaspoon smoked paprika

2 cups water

1 tablespoon vegan Worcestershire sauce or soy sauce

When the potatoes are finished cooking, unwrap and put them on a plate or in a bowl. Smash the potatoes to flatten them, using a spatula, the back of the skillet, or a bowl.

To serve, spoon about ¼ of the gravy mixture and 2 slices of seitan over each potato and sprinkle with fresh parsley.

Tip: If you're short on time, you can substitute plant-based ground beef for the seitan.

Sukiyaki

saucy vegetables, soba noodles, rice wine

Makes 4 servings

Cooking time: 15 minutes

TOOLS

Mason jar

Camp stove

Knife

Cutting board

4-quart high-sided skillet or Dutch oven with lid

Tongs and/or long cooking chopsticks

———

6 ounces soba noodles

8 ounces sliced mushrooms

8 ounces firm or baked tofu, sliced

1 small yellow onion, thinly sliced

3 or 4 bunches (12 ounces total) baby bok choy, individual stalks pulled off

4 cups sliced napa cabbage

8 scallions, sliced

SAUCE

1½ cups water

½ cup mirin

½ cup sake

½ cup soy sauce

1 tablespoon sugar

We first made this for an inspiring Portland, Oregon, event called Snow Peak Way. The outdoor brand Snow Peak designed it to showcase their philosophy and products for their most loyal fans. We had the pleasure of featuring their camp-kitchen setups in several cooking classes while also catering all the employee meals. Our goal was to provide the crew with nourishing and hearty meals that would also be beautiful enough to measure up to Snow Peak serving ware. This sukiyaki delivered on all fronts, with an on-brand nod to Japanese tradition. This is meant to be a family-style meal that is best enjoyed with all of your favorite people (like all meals). —Mai-Yan

AT HOME *(OPTIONAL)*

Stir together the water, mirin, sake, soy sauce, and sugar in a Mason jar.

AT CAMP

Have the mushrooms, tofu, onion, bok choy, cabbage, and scallions prepped and ready.

Put the sauce ingredients in the pot and bring to a boil.

Add the noodles to the boiling sauce and let them simmer for 3 minutes, stirring so the noodles don't stick to the bottom.

Place the mushrooms, tofu, onion, bok choy, and cabbage in neat side-by-side piles in the pot and garnish with the scallions.

Adjust the heat to maintain a simmer and cover for 5 to 10 minutes, until the veggies are softened.

Serve family-style in bowls with serving tongs, ensuring that everyone gets a little of everything (don't be a noodle hog!). This is meant to be more saucy than soupy, so don't worry if there's not a lot of liquid left.

Seitan Adobo

soy sauce, vinegar, garlic

Makes 4 servings
Cooking time: 25 minutes

TOOLS
Camp stove
Knife
Cutting board
Vegetable peeler *(optional)*
4-quart pot
2-quart pot with lid
Spoon

———

1½ to 2 cups uncooked white rice
¼ cup neutral oil
1 large onion, diced
1 (12-ounce) loaf Seitan (page 292), halved and thinly sliced
8 garlic cloves, minced
1 large potato, peeled *(optional)* and cut into 1-inch cubes
1 teaspoon peppercorns
3 bay leaves
2 cups water
4 to 5 tablespoons white vinegar
3 to 5 tablespoons soy sauce
2 teaspoons sugar

TOMATO CUCUMBER SALAD
1 cup halved cherry tomatoes
1 English cucumber, chopped
Juice of 1 lime
Salt and pepper

Mai-Yan and I made this the night before my kids' first backpacking trip in Sequoia National Park. They were little, so it was going to be a chill three-mile hike, and they were beyond excited about it. Unfortunately, I threw my back out that night and almost canceled the trip. I couldn't let my kids down, though, so I ended up leaving my pack in the car, hiking out with everyone, and then Mai-Yan and Kismat went back to the car to grab my pack. They did an unexpected nine-mile hike just for me. The trip went well, but one of the most memorable parts of it was this adobo. I'd first had it at Ichiza Kitchen, a tiny vegan restaurant in Portland, Oregon, and my mind was blown. I'm so happy I figured out this campified version to share. —Aimee

———

Cook the rice according to the package instructions. Set aside until ready to serve.

Heat the oil in a large pot over medium-high heat. Add the onion and seitan and cook until the onion is softened and the seitan is browned in spots, about 10 minutes.

Add the garlic and stir for another minute.

Add the potato, peppercorns, bay leaves, water, 4 tablespoons of the vinegar, 3 tablespoons of the soy sauce, and the sugar. Bring to a boil, then turn the heat down to low and cover.

Cook until the potatoes are softened, 15 to 20 minutes.

Meanwhile, make the salad. Combine the tomatoes, cucumber, and lime juice. Season to taste with salt and pepper and add more soy sauce and vinegar if desired.

Serve with the rice and the tomato cucumber salad.

Tip: Any rice will work for this recipe, but we love to eat this with short-grain white rice.

Dutch Oven Zucchini Casserole

zucchini boats, Italian-seasoned plant-based ricotta, cashew cream

Makes 4+ servings

Cooking time: 45 minutes

TOOLS

10-inch Dutch oven

Mixing bowl

Spoon

Knife

Cutting board

Metal spatula

2 pounds zucchini

1 recipe Cashew Dream Sauce (page 288)

1 cup cherry tomatoes

½ cup Italian-style bread crumbs

TOFU RICOTTA STUFFING

1 block (14 ounces) firm tofu, pressed

¼ cup Nutty Parmesan (page 288)

2 or 3 garlic cloves, minced

1 teaspoon Italian seasoning

½ teaspoon salt

½ teaspoon pepper

When I told Aimee and Mai-Yan that I was thinking about changing my idea for ricotta-stuffed pasta into ricotta-stuffed zucchini boats, they strongly protested. I told Wes I was going to try making it for dinner that night, and he turned into a whiny kid being told to eat his vegetables. But I held strong and served it up—and no one could get enough. When we think of zucchini boats, we think of a low-fat, bland, unsatisfying dinner, but these are not those zucchini boats! The recipe works great for camping because it's much more forgiving than pasta and still gets crispy on top and creamy on the inside. The tofu ricotta is simple to make and also satisfies protein needs. —Emily

AT HOME *(OPTIONAL)*

In a mixing bowl, combine the tofu, Nutty Parmesan, minced garlic, Italian seasoning, salt, and pepper. Squish it until the ingredients are well combined. Keep refrigerated until ready to use. This can be done in a ziplock bag as well.

AT CAMP

Get a campfire going until it forms hot coals.

Slice each zucchini in half lengthwise. Scoop out the flesh, leaving no more than ¼-inch thickness, so there's enough of a trough to stuff with the filling. Set the scooped-out flesh aside.

Divide the ricotta stuffing among the zucchini boats evenly, pressing it down to pack the troughs.

Arrange as many as you can in a single layer on the bottom of the Dutch oven. You may want to cut each boat into halves or thirds to fit them better.

Pour half of the cashew sauce over the stuffed zucchini boats. Sprinkle with half of the tomatoes and all the scooped zucchini flesh.

Create a second layer by arranging the rest of the stuffed zucchini on top of the first, then top with the rest of the cashew sauce and tomatoes.

Top the Dutch oven with its lid and set it over a bed of about 8 small coals. Place the equivalent of about 17 coals on the lid.

Bake for about 40 minutes, turning the whole Dutch oven about a half turn in one direction and the lid a quarter turn in the other direction every 15 to 20 minutes, until the zucchini is tender. Remove the lid and dump the coals into the fire.

Sprinkle the bread crumbs over the top of the casserole. Replace the lid and top with about 10 fresh coals. Bake for about 5 more minutes, until the bread crumbs are browned.

White Bean Chili Verde

white beans, Anaheim and poblano chiles, tomatillos

Makes 6 servings
Cooking time: 30 to 40 minutes

TOOLS
Knife
Cutting board
4-quart pot or 10-inch Dutch oven
Camp stove or grate
Tongs
Spoon

¼ cup olive oil
1 large yellow onion, diced
2 Anaheim chiles, fire roasted (page 49) and diced
2 poblano chiles, fire roasted (page 49) and diced
6 garlic cloves, minced
2 teaspoons ground cumin
1 teaspoon dried oregano
1 pound tomatillos, husks removed and quartered
3 (15-ounce) cans white beans, drained
5 teaspoons Bouillon Powder (page 286) or bouillon cube equivalent
Salt and pepper

SUGGESTED TOPPINGS
Tortilla chips
Roasted pepitas
Hot sauce
Sliced radishes
Sliced avocado
Plant-based sour cream

Chili is always a welcome and hearty meal to enjoy in the outdoors. It is thicker than other stews and loves lots of toppings, which we think are the secret to making soups and stews more interesting. This is a lighter-than-average version that feels very fresh and bright thanks to the tangy tomatillos. I make it at home all the time, but the chiles beg to be roasted over the coals of a campfire whenever possible. —Emily

Heat the olive oil in a pot or Dutch oven over medium-high heat. Add the onion and sauté until it begins to soften, about 5 minutes. Add the chiles, garlic, cumin, and oregano, and sauté until they are fragrant, about 1 minute.

Add the tomatillos and continue cooking until they start to soften and break down, 10 to 15 minutes.

Add the beans and bouillon. Bring the chili to a boil, then turn down the heat to low and simmer, covered, stirring occasionally, for another 10 to 15 minutes. Season to taste with salt and pepper.

Serve with as many toppings as you'd like.

Tip: You can prepare this at home for a backcountry meal by spreading the chili as thin as possible on as many dehydrator trays as needed and lightly smashing some of the beans. Dehydrate at 145° F for 8 to 12 hours, until fully dry and crumbly. You may want to reduce the oil content and add it back in later.

Jackfruit Goulash

paprika, crushed tomatoes, green peas

Makes 4 servings
Cooking time: 30 minutes

TOOLS

Camp stove
Knife
Cutting board
Can opener
12-inch skillet
2-quart pot

¼ cup plant butter

2 (20-ounce) cans of young jack-fruit in brine, drained and quartered

1 medium onion, sliced

3 garlic cloves, minced

2 tablespoons paprika

1½ teaspoons salt

Pinch of cayenne

1 (28-ounce) can crushed tomatoes

½ cup ketchup

2 teaspoons vegan Worcestershire sauce

1 cup peas, frozen or defrosted

8 ounces farfalle pasta or other short pasta

This dish is one step up from your default "pasta red sauce" weeknight dinner. Goulash is originally from Hungary, but we aren't going to pretend like this one has much to do with that, aside from the copious amounts of paprika. The paprika and tomato flavors in this particular version are bold, complemented well by the texture and familiarity of the pasta. The original recipe—a "Mom recipe" I pulled from Daniel's family cookbook—calls for beef cubes, but in this version we use jackfruit, which is naturally cube-like and ready to eat right out of the can. Jackfruit is generally underrated; although it requires some manipulation to remove the briny flavor that it's typically canned in, it's a great ingredient to play with. —Mai-Yan

---

In the skillet over medium-high heat, melt the butter. Add the jackfruit and onion and cook, stirring occasionally, for 10 minutes, until the onion slices are translucent and soft.

Add the garlic, paprika, salt, and cayenne. Stir to coat all the ingredients and let simmer for 2 minutes.

Stir in the crushed tomatoes, ketchup, Worcestershire sauce, and peas. Bring the contents to a boil, then turn the heat down to low and let simmer, stirring occasionally, for 15 minutes.

Meanwhile, fill a pot with water and bring to a boil. Add the pasta and cook according to the package instructions.

Drain the pasta and serve topped with the goulash.

White Bean Chili Verde (page 192)

Jackfruit Goulash (page 193)

Emergency Bean Soup (page 196)

Emergency Bean Soup

quick-cooking beans, grains, spice-infused oil

Makes about 4 servings

Cooking time: 30 to 45 minutes, depending on your bean choices

TOOLS

Camp stove

16-ounce Mason jar

2-quart pot

Spoon

Knife

Cutting board

Small skillet

---

1 cup any combination of quick-cooking beans, such as lentils, mung beans, or split peas

½ cup any quick-cooking grain, such as quinoa, millet, bulgur, or farro

2 tablespoons Bouillon Powder (page 286) or bouillon cube equivalent

½ teaspoon salt

8 to 10 cups of water

SPICED OIL MIX

2 tablespoons olive oil (individual packets preferred)

1 small shallot

1 teaspoon garlic powder

1 teaspoon cumin seeds

1 teaspoon mustard seeds

½ teaspoon red chile flakes

We strongly advise always having some sort of backup food in case something goes terribly wrong on your trip. Some examples: Your fresh corn spoiled in the backcountry before you got to use it, your van got stuck forty miles deep into Death Valley's backcountry, or you just want to extend your trip an extra night (all of which have happened to us). You could, of course, bring granola bars or instant ramen, but wouldn't it be great if it were something special that you'd be proud to share instead? This one could be your hero. —Emily

---

AT HOME *(OPTIONAL)*

Combine the beans, grains, bouillon, and salt in a Mason jar.

Put the garlic powder, cumin seeds, mustard seeds, and red chile flakes into a ziplock bag. Place the whole shallot and oil packet in the bag as well.

Store in your camp bin, vehicle, or shed for future use.

AT CAMP

Pour the contents of the soup mix jar into a pot with 8 to 10 cups of water.

Bring the water to a boil, then lower the heat, cover, and simmer, stirring occasionally, for 30 to 45 minutes, until the beans and grains are tender.

Peel the shallot and slice cross-wise. Heat the oil in a skillet over medium heat. Add the sliced shallot and cook, stirring frequently, until softened, about 4 minutes. Add the spice mix and cook for another minute, until fragrant. Stir into the soup and serve immediately.

Tip: If you're packing this soup and don't have any trips planned in the near future, consider replacing the fresh shallot with shelf-stable fried shallots.

DRINKS

Sparkling Botanical Sun Tea Cocktail

ginger ale, green tea, gin

Makes 8 drinks

TOOLS

1-liter pitcher

Cheesecloth and kitchen string, or sachet, if using loose leaf tea

Jigger or shot glass

Spoon

———

1 liter water

¼ cup dried hibiscus flowers

5 teaspoons loose leaf jasmine green tea or 3 tea bags

4 cups ice cubes

4 cups ginger ale

8 ounces botanical gin

Fresh thyme sprigs, for garnish

Ever since our dirtygourmet.com blog launch party in Leo Carrillo State Park back in 2009, we have been evolving our camp party hosting skills—always striving for maximum impact with minimal effort. The best expression of all these ideas is probably our workshop titled "Entertaining Outdoors: Elevating the Outdoor Meal," which we taught in collaboration with the Stanley brand, featuring their camp cookware. It was a weekend-long outdoor event and we had prepared a giant vat of hibiscus tea, served with fresh limes and Martinelli's sparkling cider to cool everyone off during the hot afternoon. Next thing we knew, the tea was being spiked and the drinks were no longer mocktails. That's when the real party started! We loved that drink and have refined it to better show off its botanical qualities. —Mai-Yan

AT HOME *(OPTIONAL)*

If using loose leaf tea, you'll need to create a sachet for the sun tea ingredients. Enclose the hibiscus flowers and tea in an 8-by-8-inch piece of cheesecloth and twist it shut, leaving a bit of room for the contents to move around. Close the sachet tightly with a kitchen string.

AT CAMP

To make the sun tea: Add the hibiscus flowers, tea, and water to a pitcher and cover. Leave in the direct sunlight where it won't get knocked over. On a hot, sunny day, the sun tea will be ready in about an hour.

When the tea reaches your desired intensity of flavor, remove the sachet or tea bags from the pitcher.

To make each cocktail, put ½ cup of ice in a cup, followed by ½ cup sun tea, ½ cup ginger ale, and 1 ounce gin. Stir and garnish with a sprig of fresh thyme.

Sparkling Botanical Sun Tea Cocktail (page 197)

Iced Oat Chai Latte

Iced Oat Chai Latte

cinnamon, cardamom, oat milk

Makes 4 cups of concentrate, enough for about 8 drinks

Cooking time: 20 minutes

TOOLS

2-quart pot

Spoon

Camp stove

Fine mesh sieve

1-quart Mason jar with lid

4 1-pint Mason jars with lids, for serving

CHAI CONCENTRATE

⅔ cup Chai Sugar (page 295)

2 tablespoons sugar

6 cups water

4 tablespoons loose leaf black tea

CHAI LATTES

4 to 5 cups oat milk, preferably full-fat

Ice

Several years ago we decided to take a last-minute trip to Death Valley in late spring. We knew it would be hot, but we were determined to go. All the good tent campsites were booked and we weren't prepared to backcountry camp, so we were stuck in a parking lot full of RVs. We took short hikes with the kids, but mostly we drove around all weekend. It sounds like a miserable trip, but witnessing the beauty of Death Valley is always worth it. Luckily, I came prepared with iced chai concentrate, homemade almond milk, and lots of ice. In the afternoons, we would pull over to the side of the road, shake up some chai lattes, and then keep on driving. Now that I have discovered oat milk, I don't usually bother with homemade almond milk. —Aimee

AT HOME (OPTIONAL)

In a pot over high heat, add the Chai Sugar, sugar, and water and bring to a boil. Turn down the heat to low and simmer, uncovered, for about 15 minutes.

Add the tea and simmer for an additional 5 minutes.

Remove from the heat and strain the mixture through a fine mesh sieve into a quart Mason jar. Store in your cooler.

AT CAMP

Add about ½ cup of chai concentrate and ½ cup of oat milk to a pint Mason jar. Top off the jar with ice. Seal the lid tightly and shake until well combined. Serve immediately.

Bitters Sangria Fizz

fresh berries, bitters, grapefruit

Makes 4 to 6 servings

TOOLS

Paring knife or small knife

Cutting board

1-quart jar with lid

---

1 grapefruit

2 cups mixed berries, such as strawberries, blueberries, blackberries, or raspberries

1 tablespoon bitters

1 tablespoon sugar

Ice

36 to 48 ounces sparkling water

We followed the pandemic trend of cutting back on our drinking—after we had followed the pandemic trend of drinking more than usual. All of us got into experimenting with nonalcoholic versions of our favorite drinks, which were fun but never quite satisfying enough. Then Emily shared a *New York Times* article about mindful drinking, and how adding a bitter component to your mocktail makes it more of a slow sipper, which is a lot of what people are looking for in a "drink." Bitters is an easy-to-find ingredient that will do the trick, while also bringing out the flavor of the fresh fruit. —Aimee

---

Section the grapefruit by thinly slicing off the top and bottom to form a flat base. Set one base on a flat surface and pare all the skin off from top to bottom, attempting to remove as much pith as possible without cutting into the fruit. Then, holding the grapefruit in one hand, slice into each segment along its edges toward the core, and remove the flesh without the membrane around it. Repeat the process around the whole fruit.

Put the grapefruit slices into the jar.

Squeeze any remaining juice from the fruit into the jar with the grapefruit.

Cut any large berries so that they're all about the same size. Add the berries, bitters, and sugar; seal the jar; and gently rotate it to coat all the fruit.

Let sit for 30 minutes or up to overnight, allowing the flavors to meld.

When ready to drink, scoop about ½ cup of fruit into a small jar or glass. Add a scoop of ice and top with 6 to 12 ounces of sparkling water.

Campfire Bloody Mary

canned tomato or vegetable juice, fresh prepared horseradish, roasted chile garnish

Makes 4 servings

TOOLS
Knife
Cutting board
32-ounce jar with lid

2¾ cups tomato or vegetable juice
¾ cup vodka
2 tablespoons prepared horseradish
2 tablespoons fresh lemon or lime juice
1 tablespoon vegan Worcestershire sauce
2 teaspoons hot sauce, such as Tabasco
½ teaspoon celery salt
½ teaspoon pepper

FOR SERVING
Ice
Celery sticks
Olives
Lemon or lime wedges
Campfire-roasted jalapeño or serrano (page 49)

I think the best time to drink a Bloody Mary is while camping. It is a common choice for a morning after late-night fun, and what's more conducive to staying up late having fun than a campfire gathering? I'm generally not a fan of all the twists that different Bloody Mary recipes add to the traditional one, but here's my own twist: a roasted chile garnish. It's an appropriate addition to the setting and accentuates the smokiness and spiciness already present in the base recipe. You mix the vodka right into the drink mix before storing it in the cooler, so it's ready to go exactly when you want it, without having to fuss with extra bottles or measuring. —Emily

AT HOME *(OPTIONAL)*

Mix together all the ingredients except for the garnishes in a jar.

Chop the garnishes and store them in a sealed container in the refrigerator or cooler.

AT CAMP

Divide the mixture into 4 to 6 small jars or mugs.

Add a small scoop of ice to each drink.

Garnish and enjoy.

Orange Mojito

fresh-squeezed orange juice, sparkling water, mint

Makes 4 servings

TOOLS
16-ounce Mason jar

---

1 cup fresh orange juice

¼ cup fresh lime juice

12 mint leaves

2 cups lime-flavored sparkling water

6 ounces light rum *(optional)*

Ice *(optional)*

I've lived most of my life in citrus country. I grew up in Orange County, Florida, and now live in Southern California. I am lucky to have navel orange, tangerine, and lime trees in my backyard, as well as lemons, grapefruits, and tangelos hanging over walls throughout my neighborhood. We usually pick our first oranges on Christmas Day and then use them to help us transition out of holiday mode. The kids (and Kismat) basically just sit in the yard eating them straight from the tree, but I take the opportunity to come up with new citrusy recipes. This one was created on a whim as part of a camping picnic, and the kids loved it so much (the "faux"-jito version, of course!), they've been making them for themselves throughout citrus season ever since. —Emily

AT HOME *(OPTIONAL)*

Squeeze the orange and lime juices into a Mason jar and add the mint leaves. Pack the jar in the cooler for your adventure.

AT CAMP

Shake up the juice and mint in the jar to distribute the steeped mint flavor (similar to muddling without the need for an extra tool).

Distribute the juice mixture among 4 small jars or glasses. Add to each about 1½ ounces of rum and a handful of ice, then fill the jar to the top with sparkling water.

Tip: We've been talking up Mason jars and their myriad uses for years. Here's another good use. We had these for a picnic, and it was nice to be able to put a lid on our drinks when not in active use.

Orange Mojito

Spiced Apple Whiskey Smash (page 206)

Spiced Apple Whiskey Smash

apple cider, rye whiskey, spiced simple syrup

Makes 1 serving

Cooking time: 10 minutes

TOOLS

Cocktail shaker or Mason jar with lid

Muddler

Jigger or shot glass

½ cup ice cubes

1 lemon wedge

1½ ounces rye whiskey

3 ounces apple cider or unfiltered fresh apple juice

¼ to ½ ounce spiced simple syrup

1 apple slice, for garnishing *(optional)*

1 cinnamon stick, for garnishing *(optional)*

SPICED SIMPLE SYRUP (MAKES ENOUGH FOR 4 TO 8 DRINKS)

½ cup water

½ cup sugar

3 whole cloves

1 cinnamon stick

1-inch piece of orange peel

4 peppercorns

Cocktail making is a whole *thing*. It's all about getting the perfect ratios of ingredients and often requires some specialized ingredients and tools. Luckily for me, Daniel has dipped his toes into this world. Without diving into the deep end, we've found a lane that works for us: three- to four-ingredient cocktails with mostly off-the-shelf, good-quality ingredients. This is one of our go-to summer drinks that works well into fall when fresh apple cider becomes readily available. —Mai-Yan

AT HOME

In a small saucepan, bring all the simple syrup ingredients to a boil.

Lower the heat and simmer for 5 minutes. Remove from the heat and let cool completely.

Strain the solids out of the syrup and transfer to a lidded jar. Close snugly and keep refrigerated until ready to use.

AT CAMP

Add the ice cubes to the serving cup.

Put 1 lemon wedge into the cocktail shaker and muddle.

Add the whiskey, apple cider/juice, and simple syrup to the shaker. Close and shake to mix.

Pour over the ice and garnish with an apple slice and a cinnamon stick.

DESSERTS

Berry Cream Cheese Cooler Cake

fresh berries, plant-based whipped frosting, cookie cake

Makes 8 servings

No cook recipe

TOOLS

Mixing bowl

Wooden spoon or whisk

Rubber spatula

9-by-9-by-3-inch (or similar size and volume) waterproof container with a lid

---

1 (8-ounce) container plant-based cream cheese, softened

⅔ cup powdered sugar

¼ cup plant butter, softened

1 (9-ounce) container of plant-based whipped cream, such as Truwhip Vegan or Cocowhip

1 (9-ounce) package vegan vanilla wafers or 2 sleeves graham crackers

2 cups raspberries, blueberries, and/or sliced strawberries

We liked the idea of a cooler cake so much, we decided to make *two*! The S'mores Cooler Cake (page 209) is perhaps a more typical camping dessert, but this one is fresh and light and still sets in your cooler as an icebox cake would in your fridge, with no need for cooking. I tested this out on an icy cold winter day in Death Valley, and we happily gobbled it up, but it's best served at a shady summer picnic. If you can't get your hands on fresh berries, it would also be great with bananas or stone fruit. —Aimee

---

In a mixing bowl, use a whisk or wooden spoon to beat together the cream cheese, powdered sugar, and butter until the mixture is light and fluffy. You'll have to put some muscle into it without a mixer!

Gently fold in the whipped cream.

Arrange a single layer of the cookies (or graham crackers) across the bottom of the container.

Spread about ¼ of the cream cheese mixture in a thin layer on the cookies, then sprinkle with about ½ cup of the berries.

Add another layer of cookies, another ¼ of the cream cheese mixture, and another ½ cup of berries.

Repeat these layers until all the ingredients are used up. Save out a few cookies as well as berries for a fancy top.

Cover with the lid and store in the cooler.

Allow the cake to set for at least an hour before serving.

Berry Cream Cheese Cooler Cake (page 207)

S'mores Cooler Cake

S'mores Cooler Cake

*graham cracker crust,
cream cheese filling,
marshmallows, chocolate*

Makes 8 to 12 servings

No cook recipe

TOOLS

Mixing bowl

Wooden spoon or whisk

Rubber spatula

Knife

Cutting board

9-by-9-by-3-inch (or similar size
and volume) waterproof container
with a lid

---

2 to 3 sleeves graham crackers

**1 (8-ounce) container plant-based
cream cheese, softened**

¼ cup plant butter, softened

**1 (9-ounce) container of plant-
based whipped cream, such as
Truwhip Vegan or Cocowhip**

½ cup powdered sugar

Pinch of salt

1 cup mini vegan marshmallows

**1 (3-ounce) bar vegan chocolate,
finely chopped**

Sprinkles *(optional)*

We celebrate most of our family's big events camping. It's a great way to get a lot of people together without anyone having to clean house. Many of these events *require* cake, but I don't bake. Aimee came up with the genius idea of trying an icebox cake but doing it in the cooler. I tried it out for my daughter Anastasia's eighth birthday, and I couldn't believe how successful it was. The graham crackers that started off crunchy turned soft and cakey, and the whole thing can easily be assembled at camp. I will be making cooler cakes for all camping events requiring cake from now on. —Emily

Set the cream cheese, butter, and whipped cream out to soften while you're hanging out at camp.

Once these are softened but before they start melting, add the cream cheese, butter, powdered sugar, and pinch of salt to a mixing bowl and mix well.

Gently fold the whipped cream into the cream cheese mixture. Set aside.

Arrange a single layer of the graham crackers across the bottom of the container.

Spread about ¼ of the cream cheese mixture in a thin layer on the graham crackers. Sprinkle on about half of the marshmallows.

Add another layer of graham crackers, another ¼ of the cream cheese mixture, and half of the chopped chocolate.

Add another layer of graham crackers, another ¼ of the cream cheese mixture, and the remaining marshmallows.

Finish with a layer of graham crackers and the remaining cream cheese mixture and chopped chocolate. Generously decorate with sprinkles for a festive final touch.

Cover with the lid and chill the cake in the cooler for an hour so the crackers can soften and turn into cake.

Bourbon Apple Bread Pudding

apples, bourbon whiskey sauce, pecans

Makes about 8 servings

Cooking time: About 1 hour

We love the opportunity to show how forgiving our recipes are. This recipe was tested on a trip to Indian Cove Campground in Joshua Tree National Park. It was the third and final recipe being made on the campfire, and we were rushing to get it started before our coals got used up. Mai-Yan opened the can of coconut milk and immediately spilled all of it over the ground, the photo equipment, and the dog. We improvised, using the smidgen of coconut milk powder we had diluted with too much hot water. This "bread pie" (as the kids called it) turned out incredibly delicious and was served to ten happy people under the stars. —Aimee

AT HOME *(OPTIONAL)*

In a small container, stir together the sugar, cornstarch, cinnamon, and salt.

In another small container, stir together the coconut milk, plant milk, bourbon, and vanilla.

2 small containers

Can opener

Mixing bowl

Fork or whisk

Dutch oven with lid

Parchment paper, cut into an 11-inch round

Cooking spray

Lid lifter

Heatproof gloves

Long tongs

Small pot

Spoon

⅔ cup sugar

¼ cup cornstarch

½ teaspoon cinnamon

¼ teaspoon salt

1 (15-ounce) can coconut milk

1½ cups plant milk

2 tablespoons bourbon

2 teaspoons vanilla extract

1 (1-pound) loaf of French bread (or similar), cut into 1-inch cubes

1½ cups peeled, chopped apples

BOURBON SAUCE

¼ cup plant butter

½ cup brown sugar

Pinch of salt

2 tablespoons bourbon

½ cup toasted pecans, chopped, for serving

AT CAMP

Get a campfire going until it forms hot coals.

In a mixing bowl, stir together the sugar mixture with the coconut milk mixture. Use a fork or whisk to eliminate any lumps of cornstarch.

Spray the Dutch oven with cooking spray and line it with parchment paper.

Layer half of the bread and apples in the Dutch oven, making sure the apples are evenly distributed, then add the remaining bread and apples. The Dutch oven will be very full at this point, but once you pour in the milk mixture, it will all fit.

Pour the milk mixture over the top, pressing the bread down so that it's fully coated. Cover the Dutch oven with its lid.

Adjust the campfire so there's room to place the entire Dutch oven next to it on a level surface. Set it over a bed of about 7 small coals and set 14 coals on the lid. You may need to replace the coals about halfway through if they break down and turn to ash.

Bake for about an hour, checking after about 20 minutes to make sure it's not burning. To ensure that the bread pudding bakes evenly, rotate the entire Dutch oven a half turn and turn the lid a quarter turn several times during the baking time.

The bread pudding is done when the top is golden brown and the center is cooked through.

While the bread pudding bakes, make the sauce. Melt the butter in a small pot and stir in the brown sugar and pinch of salt. Simmer for a few minutes, stirring to dissolve the sugar. Remove from the heat and stir in the bourbon.

To serve, sprinkle the warm bread pudding with pecans and drizzle with the bourbon sauce.

Tip: Hold the can of coconut milk with two hands.

Summer Berry Custard

fresh berries, vanilla custard

Makes 4 servings
Cooking time: 10 minutes

TOOLS
Leakproof container
Small bowl
1-quart pot
Whisk
Knife
Cutting board
Mixing bowl

1⅓ cups oat milk, divided
2 tablespoons cornstarch
½ teaspoon vanilla extract
¼ cup granulated sugar
4 cups ripe berries, like strawberries, blueberries, or blackberries
1 to 2 teaspoons sugar, depending on berry type and ripeness
4 speculoos cookies *(optional)*

One way to make outdoor cooking special is to use really fresh local ingredients, because they don't need much to show off their flavor. Many people ask us about foraging, and we suggest avoiding it unless you are 100-percent positive you can properly identify the plant. If you were to try it, though, freshly foraged berries would be really exciting here—either on their own or mixed in with purchased berries. A simple creamy custard is the perfect accompaniment for any fresh berries you can find, and it can easily be made at camp. This can be served warm right away or chilled if you want to prepare it ahead of time. It will keep nicely for up to a day ahead. —Mai-Yan

To make the custard: In a small bowl, whisk together ⅓ cup of the oat milk, the cornstarch, and the vanilla until it forms a slurry. Set aside.

Put the remaining 1 cup of oat milk in a pot and bring to a gentle simmer on medium-low heat.

Whisk in the sugar and the slurry and continue stirring vigorously until mixture is thickened. Turn the heat off and set aside.

If you're serving the custard chilled, transfer it to a leakproof container and put it in the cooler for an hour or more. The custard will need a quick whisk before serving.

If using strawberries as part of your berry mix, remove the stems and dice the berries.

Reserve a handful of whole berries as garnishes, and add the remaining berries and sugar to a large bowl. Mash them with a fork to release their juices.

Divide the custard into 4 bowls, about ¼ cup each, top with the macerated berries and a cookie, and serve.

Celebration Cookie Cake

chocolate chips, sprinkles, cookie dough

Makes 8 to 10 servings

Cooking time: 20 to 25 minutes

TOOLS

10-inch Dutch oven with lid
Parchment paper
Mixing spoon
Bowl
Medium pot
Lid lifter
Long tongs
Leak-proof container *(optional)*

2¼ cups all-purpose flour
1 teaspoon baking soda
½ teaspoon salt
¾ cup packed brown sugar
¼ cup granulated sugar
1 tablespoon ground flaxseed
3 tablespoons hot water
¾ cup plant butter
2 teaspoons vanilla extract
1 cup vegan chocolate chips
Sprinkles

Baking cookies on a campfire was something I'd never even considered, but baking a giant cookie actually makes a lot of sense! Emily came up with this idea, based on those giant chocolate chip cookies you see at mall cookie shops. They're always loaded with frosting, which makes them cloyingly sweet, but there's no need for fussing with frosting in a camping context—it'll already be pretty exciting to pull your sooty Dutch oven off the campfire and reveal a giant cookie to the kids. —Aimee

AT HOME *(OPTIONAL)*

Mix together the flour, baking soda, and salt in a leakproof container.

Pack the sugars in another leakproof container.

AT CAMP

Get a campfire going until it forms hot coals.

Line the Dutch oven with parchment paper.

Mix together the flaxseed and the 3 tablespoons of hot water in a bowl. Set aside.

In a medium pot over low heat, melt the butter.

Remove from the heat and mix in the flax mixture, the combined sugars, and the vanilla.

Stir in the flour mixture and the chocolate chips.

Transfer to the prepared Dutch oven and top with sprinkles.

Adjust the campfire to make room to place the entire Dutch oven next to the fire on a level surface. Set it over a bed of about 7 small coals and set 14 coals on the lid of the Dutch oven.

Bake for 20 to 25 minutes, checking to make sure it's not burning after about 10 minutes. To ensure that the cookie bakes evenly, rotate the entire Dutch oven a half turn about 10 minutes into the baking time. Give the lid a quarter turn once or twice during the baking time.

The cookie is done when it's golden brown and a knife inserted in the center of the cookie comes out clean.

S'moresgasbord

Makes 1 serving each

We're back at it with another round of gourmet s'mores that will surely be a hit around the camp-fire. We still love the classic s'more, but we're excited to give you a mix of new flavors including plant-based versions of our favorite spreads.

You know how it's done! Sandwich your roasted marshmallow and toppings between two graham cracker squares. Eat immediately!

TOOLS FOR ALL
Camp stove
1-quart pot
Spoon

CLASSIC S'MORES
1 roasted vegan marshmallow
1 square of vegan chocolate
2 graham cracker squares

MAPLE NUT S'MORES
3 tablespoons chopped toasted salted nuts
1 tablespoon maple syrup
1 roasted vegan marshmallow
1 square of vegan chocolate
2 graham cracker squares

STRAWBERRIES AND CREAM S'MORES
1 tablespoon condensed coconut milk
1 tablespoon crushed freeze-dried strawberries
1 roasted vegan marshmallow
1 square of vegan chocolate
2 graham cracker squares

VIETNAMESE COFFEE S'MORES
1 tablespoon condensed coconut milk
⅛ teaspoon microground instant coffee
1 roasted vegan marshmallow
1 square of vegan chocolate
2 graham cracker squares

DARK CHOCOLATE ORANGE S'MORES

1 tablespoon orange marmalade

1 roasted vegan marshmallow

1 square of vegan dark chocolate

2 graham cracker squares

MILK CHOCOLATE GANACHE S'MORES

1 roasted vegan marshmallow

1 tablespoon milk chocolate Ganache (recipe follows)

2 graham cracker squares

GANACHE

1 cup coconut cream

1 cup vegan semi-sweet chocolate chips

Pinch of salt

AT HOME (OPTIONAL)

To make the ganache: Warm the coconut cream in a small pot set over medium heat or in a bowl in the microwave. Stir in the chocolate chips and a pinch of salt. Store in a jar in the refrigerator or cooler until ready to serve. This will keep, refrigerated, for about a week.

Maple Nut S'more

Strawberries and Cream S'more

Salted Caramel Coconut S'more

Cinnamon Apple S'more

SALTED CARAMEL COCONUT S'MORES

1 tablespoon toasted coconut shreds

1 tablespoon Salted Caramel (recipe follows)

1 roasted vegan marshmallow

1 square of vegan chocolate

2 graham cracker squares

SALTED CARAMEL

1 cup sugar

5 tablespoons water

¼ cup plant butter

½ cup coconut cream

½ teaspoon salt

AT HOME *(OPTIONAL)*

To make the salted caramel: In a medium pot over medium-high heat, cook the sugar and water without stirring until the sugar dissolves and turns a deep amber color. You can shake the pot a little to ensure that the mixture caramelizes evenly, but you don't want to get any sugar crystals on the side of the pot. If you do, use a wet pastry brush to dissolve the sugar crystals. Remove from the heat and stir in the butter, coconut cream, and salt with a wooden spoon. Stir well until the mixture is well combined. Store in a jar in the refrigerator or cooler until ready to serve. This will keep, refrigerated, for about 2 weeks.

CINNAMON APPLE S'MORES

2 slices of Cinnamon Apples (recipe follows)

1 roasted vegan marshmallow

1 square of vegan chocolate

2 graham cracker squares

CINNAMON APPLES

1 apple, cored and sliced

1 teaspoon vegetable oil

1 teaspoon plant butter

½ teaspoon cinnamon

Pinch of salt

1 tablespoon brown sugar

AT CAMP

To make the cinnamon apples: In a small pot over medium-low heat, cook the apple slices, oil, butter, cinnamon, and salt until the apples are softened.

Add the brown sugar, remove from the heat, and stir to coat and slightly caramelize the apples.

Store until ready for use. When ready, place a slice or two of apple on one graham cracker and build the s'more as usual.

BACKCOUNTRY RECIPES

BREAKFASTS

Citrus Poppy Seed Pancakes

Just Add Water Pancake Mix, lemon juice powder, Citrus Peel Powder

Makes 2 servings

At-camp cooking time: 15 to 20 minutes

TOOLS
Lightweight stove

Knife or small scissors

Nonstick skillet

Spatula

COOKING WATER: 1 cup, plus 3 teaspoons

1½ cups Just Add Water Pancake Mix (page 297)

2 tablespoons poppy seeds

1 teaspoon Citrus Peel Powder (page 294)

1 teaspoon vanilla powder

1 tablespoon (0.5-ounce packet) coconut oil

LEMON ICING
6 tablespoons powdered sugar

3 (0.8-gram) packets of lemon juice powder

Recently I discovered powdered lemon juice for backpacking, and now I find myself using it all the time, even just to add to my water at home. I love it almost as much as I love our Citrus Peel Powder, also used in this recipe. Here, powdered lemon juice is mixed with powdered sugar and water for a sweet and tangy icing to drizzle on top of poppy seed pancakes—a great alternative to figuring out how to pack maple syrup for a backcountry trip. You can use any type of citrus in the Citrus Peel Powder for the batter—no need to match lemon for lemon. It's a fun and special way to start the day if you have the time and fuel. —Aimee

AT HOME

Stir together the pancake mix, poppy seeds, Citrus Peel Powder, and vanilla powder in a quart-size ziplock bag.

Stir together the powdered sugar and powdered lemon juice in a ziplock bag and tuck it into the bag with the pancake mix. Tuck the coconut oil packet in the bag as well.

AT CAMP

Add 1 teaspoon of water to the bag of powdered sugar and lemon powder. Close the bag and massage it to mix everything together. Add additional water, 1 teaspoon at a time, until you have an icing you can drizzle. Set aside.

Add 1 cup of water to the bag of pancake mix. Close the bag and massage it to mix everything together.

Heat a little of the oil in the skillet, then snip off the corner of the pancake batter bag. Pour the pancake batter through the hole into the skillet, forming a 4- to 5-inch pancake.

Cook for about 2 minutes, then flip the pancake. Cook for another 2 minutes, until the pancake is cooked through, then transfer to a plate.

Repeat until all the pancake batter is used up, adding more oil as needed.

Snip off one bottom corner of the icing bag and drizzle the pancakes with icing.

> Per serving: 570 calories, 11 g fat, 104 g carbs, 14 g protein
> Weight: 11 ounces

Tip: Make sure to use a nonstick skillet, or the pancakes will likely stick.

Bacon Grits and Greens

cashew butter, cremini mushrooms, kale

Makes 2 servings

Dehydration time: 4 to 6 hours

At-camp cooking time: 5 minutes

I always struggle to find breakfast items that entice me, because most traditional savory breakfasts are full of eggs and cheese—hard to replace at breakfast. This recipe is a great alternative, and it's quick and easy to prepare. The cashew butter and nutritional yeast combination here is the secret to making a creamy, cheesy base and adding some protein for high-output days. Many of our recipes use blended cashews for a cream base, but the prepackaged nut butter has the added benefit of being nonperishable, which makes this recipe work well for backpacking. —Aimee

Lightweight stove

1-liter pot

Spork

———

COOKING WATER: 2 cups

MUSHROOM BACON

8 ounces cremini or button mush-rooms, sliced

1 tablespoon soy sauce

1 teaspoon maple syrup

1 teaspoon neutral oil

¼ teaspoon smoked paprika

¼ teaspoon garlic powder

GRITS AND GREENS

2 cups stemmed, roughly chopped kale or collard greens

½ cup quick or instant grits

1 tablespoon nutritional yeast

½ teaspoon salt

2 tablespoons unsweetened cashew butter

AT HOME

To make the mushroom bacon: Combine the sliced mushrooms with the soy sauce, maple syrup, oil, smoked paprika, and garlic powder. Mix well and arrange the mushrooms in a single layer on a dehydrator tray. Set aside.

Arrange the greens in a single layer on a dehydrator tray.

Dehydrate both the mushrooms and greens at 125° F for 4 to 6 hours. The mushrooms should be dry but still chewy; the greens should be completely dry. Pack the mushrooms in a ziplock bag.

Pack the greens (crumbling them up as necessary to fit in the bag), grits, nutritional yeast, and salt in a ziplock bag.

Pack the cashew butter in a small ziplock bag.

Tuck both the mushroom and cashew butter bags into the grits bag.

AT CAMP

Bring the water to a boil, then stir in the grits mixture. Cook, stir-ring constantly, until thickened, about 5 minutes. Remove from the heat.

Cut one bottom corner of the cashew butter bag and squeeze it all into the grits. Stir to mix.

Top with mushrooms and serve immediately.

> Per serving: 391 calories, 13 g fat, 52 g carbs, 23 g protein
> Weight: 11 ounces

Tip: If your dehydrator has stacking perforated trays, put the fruit leather insert in the lowest position tray. Stack another tray on top and start loading up the ingredients. Any smaller pieces will natu-rally fall through and land on the bottom tray; they can be captured and used in this dish. Leave no ingredient behind!

Mushroom Congee

shiitake mushrooms, scallions, soy jerky

Makes 2 servings

Dehydration time: 7 to 9 hours

At-camp cooking time: 5 minutes

TOOLS

1-quart pot

Lightweight stove

Spoon

COOKING WATER: 2 cups

6 cups vegetable broth

1 cup dried sliced mushrooms

2-inch piece of ginger, washed and sliced

⅔ cup jasmine rice, rinsed and frozen overnight in a ziplock bag

3 garlic cloves, minced

6 scallions, sliced

¼ teaspoon white pepper

Salt

TOPPING MIX

2 to 4 tablespoons soy jerky, chopped or torn into bite-size pieces

2 tablespoons roasted peanuts

1 tablespoon fried shallots or onions

1 teaspoon toasted white sesame seeds

1 teaspoon freeze-dried chives

Congee is a typical Chinese rice porridge breakfast and also the go-to meal when you're feeling a little under the weather. Each household has their own variations; my Grandma Kwan's version typically includes thousand-year-old eggs (not my favorite). I first tried our version on a backpacking trip to Little Lakes Valley with Aimee's family and our friends Amy and Kim. The only complaint I got was that I hadn't brought enough for all eight of us! —Mai-Yan

AT HOME

Fill a large pot with the broth. Add the dried mushrooms and sliced ginger, and bring to a boil over high heat.

Add the rice (straight from the freezer) and garlic to the boiling broth. Return the mixture to a boil, then lower the heat to maintain a simmer. Keep simmering the congee, stirring occasionally, until the mushrooms are soft and the texture looks like a loose oatmeal, 30 to 40 minutes.

Add the sliced scallions, white pepper, and salt and stir well.

On dehydrator trays lined with parchment or silicone mats, spread an even layer of porridge, no thicker than ⅛ inch if possible, across as many trays as needed. Any thicker and dehydration times will be significantly longer. Pull out all pieces of ginger as you find them, and discard them.

Set the dehydrator temperature to 140° F and dehydrate for 7 to 9 hours. The porridge is fully dehydrated once it looks and feels completely dry to the touch.

Working over a large baking sheet, remove the dehydrated porridge from the trays or paper, making sure to capture all the flakes.

Pack the dehydrated porridge in a ziplock bag. The flakes can be crushed into smaller bits to help reduce volume.

In a snack-size ziplock bag, combine all the topping ingredients.

AT CAMP

Bring 2 cups of water to a boil and add the dehydrated porridge. Stir until well combined and lower the heat to a simmer for a couple of minutes.

Stir well and serve with the topping mix.

Per serving: 453 calories, 9 g fat, 73 g carbs, 19 g protein
Weight: 8 ounces

Toasted Oat Muesli

rolled oats, nuts, chia seeds

Makes 2 servings

TOOLS
Bowl or mug
Spoon

_____

COOKING WATER: 1½ to 2 cups

1 cup rolled oats
¼ cup chopped almonds
¼ cup unsweetened shredded coconut
Pinch of salt
2 teaspoons maple syrup
2 teaspoons coconut oil, melted
1 teaspoon vanilla extract
¼ cup dried cherries
2 tablespoons golden raisins
4 teaspoons chia seeds
¼ cup plant milk powder

I am definitely *not* a morning person. Even the most lovely outdoor setting will not make me excited to cook before I've had two cups of coffee. So on those days when I need to get moving quickly, I look for a no-cook breakfast. At home, I buy muesli all the time and top it with whatever fresh fruit I have on hand. However, the store-bought muesli is not as satisfying when I don't have anything fresh to put on it. For backpacking, I came up with this toasted version, which makes the oats and nuts so flavorful, even without the fresh fruit. At camp, there's absolutely no cooking required. Just a 30-minute soak and it's ready to eat. —Aimee

_____

AT HOME

Preheat the oven to 350° F.

In a medium bowl, combine the oats, almonds, coconut, and salt.

Drizzle in the maple syrup, coconut oil, and vanilla extract and mix well. Spread out on a baking sheet and bake for 12 to 15 minutes or until golden brown, stirring halfway through the baking time.

Set aside to cool, then transfer to a quart-size ziplock bag. Add the cherries, raisins, chia seeds, and milk powder.

AT CAMP

Add about 1½ cups of water to the bag, seal it, and use your hands to massage the bag, mixing everything together well. Add up to an additional ½ cup of water, depending on how thick you want it. Soak for at least 30 minutes and up to overnight before serving.

> Per serving: 482 calories, 26 g fat, 53 g carbs, 12 g protein
> Weight: 10 ounces

Mochi Pancake Sandwiches

mochi flour, marmalade and nut butter filling

Makes about 2 pancake sandwiches (4 cakes)

At-camp cooking time: 10 minutes

TOOLS

Lightweight stove

Nonstick skillet

Spatula

COOKING WATER: ¾ cup

4 tablespoons marmalade and/or chocolate nut butter

½ cup all-purpose flour

½ cup sweet rice flour

2 tablespoons sugar

1 teaspoon baking powder

¼ teaspoon salt

1 tablespoon ground flaxseed

2 to 3 tablespoons neutral oil

When our kids were first placed in our care, we were told that we shouldn't expect them to eat much variety, as they were very picky. I went into the first few meals armed with mac and cheese and hot dogs. I quickly noticed, however, that when I was preparing something I thought they'd be scared of, they'd be interested and want to try it. I'd let them take mushroom stems and raw tofu and lettuce cores right off the cutting board, and they treated it like they got away with something exciting every time. I realized that saying "sure, you can have that" to things even *I* thought were odd helped them find safety and positivity in the unknown (which was most of their lives at the time). But it also helped *me* be more adventurous with my choices. They are the reason things like mochi flour are in our pantry, and why it's been so fun to cook recipes new to us. This method has proven to be a great way to discover new ingredients for camp cooking as well. —Emily

---

AT HOME

Measure the all-purpose flour, sweet rice flour, sugar, baking powder, salt, and flax into a ziplock bag. If you will be storing this longer than 1 week, store it in the refrigerator or freezer to prevent the flax from becoming rancid.

Measure your marmalade and nut butter into a small ziplock bag. If you found individual packets of these items, store those in the dry ingredient bag.

AT CAMP

Set the oil and filling bags aside, and add ³/₄ cup of water to the bag of dry ingredients. Ensure that it is closed well and massage it until it is fully mixed.

Heat the oil in your skillet over medium-high heat. Cut the corner off the pancake batter bag and squeeze out about ¹/₄ cup into the pan. Watch carefully and flip it as soon as it releases from the pan, 1 to 2 minutes. Small bubbles forming on top of the cake are also a sign it's ready to turn.

After turning, cook until the pancake fluffs up in the center and is firm to the touch on the outside, (hopefully) without burning, another minute or so. Set aside and continue the process until all of the mixture is used.

Let the cakes cool slightly, then spread about 2 tablespoons of your filling choice on half of the pancakes. Top each spread pancake with an unspread one and enjoy.

Per serving: 623 calories, 20 g fat, 99 g carbs, 8 g protein
Weight: 12 ounces

Tip: There are quite a few companies making individual packets of nut butters nowadays, so have fun experimenting with your favorite types and flavors.

Backcountry Tofu Scramble

dehydrated tofu, tomatoes, scallions

Makes 2 servings

Dehydration Time: 6 to 8 hours

At-camp cooking time: 10 minutes

TOOLS

1-quart pot with lid

Lightweight stove

Spork

COOKING WATER: 2 cups

1 pound firm tofu, frozen in its package and then defrosted

1 tablespoon olive oil

¾ cup cherry tomatoes, halved

½ cup sliced scallions

1 garlic clove, minced

¾ teaspoon salt

½ teaspoon freshly ground pepper

FOR SERVING

Tortillas

Avocado *(optional)*

Hot sauce *(optional)*

Tofu scrambles often get a bad rap. They can be flavorless and texturally far from satisfying. My biggest gripe is that there are usually far too many different veggies thrown in with the tofu, and everything cooked together ends up as a watery, bland mess. I chose to highlight only two vegetables; both are easy to dehydrate and add a burst of summery flavor to your morning meal. —Aimee

---

AT HOME

Squeeze out as much liquid from the tofu as you can, break it up into small crumbles, and set aside.

In a large skillet over medium-high heat, heat the oil. Add the crumbled tofu and cook, stirring often, until the tofu dries out and browns lightly, 3 to 4 minutes.

Stir in the cherry tomatoes, scallions, garlic, salt, and pepper. Cook for 1 or 2 more minutes, until the tomatoes break down a bit. Taste and season with additional salt and pepper if desired.

Spread the tofu scramble evenly on a dehydrator tray and dehydrate at 135° F for 6 to 8 hours, or until completely dry.

Let cool completely, then pack in a ziplock bag.

AT CAMP

Place the tofu scramble in a medium pot and add 2 cups of water, or just enough to cover it. Bring the mixture to a boil, then remove from the heat. Cover and allow the tofu to rehydrate for about 30 minutes. Return the pot to the stove and reheat it, allowing any additional water to evaporate. Alternatively, you can keep the tofu on the heat and simmer it continuously for about 20 minutes.

Serve with tortillas, avocado slices, and hot sauce.

> Per serving: 363 calories, 17 g carbs, 22 g fat, 22 g protein (without tortillas or avocado)
> Weight: 4 ounces

Tip: The trick to a successful rehydrated tofu meal is freezing the tofu before dehydrating it. This changes the texture of the tofu so that it becomes much spongier, and when you rehydrate it, the water can be much more easily absorbed.

Chai Oatmeal

rolled oats, Chai Sugar, black tea

Makes 2 servings

At-camp cooking time: 5 to 10 minutes

TOOLS

Lightweight stove

1-quart pot

Spork

———

COOKING WATER: 2 to 2½ cups

1 cup rolled oats

¼ cup soy, oat, or coconut milk powder

2 tablespoons Chai Sugar (page 295)

4 teaspoons ground flaxseed

Pinch of salt

2 black tea bags

TOPPING

¼ cup finely chopped nuts, such as almonds, pecans, or walnuts

2 tablespoons packed brown sugar

Pinch of salt

The inspiration for this oatmeal comes from my father-in-law, whose morning ritual begins every day at 4 a.m. He starts by drinking a cup of hot, sweet chai. Then for breakfast he makes a big bowl of oatmeal, but instead of cooking it with water or milk, he cooks it with two more cups of chai. The whole bowl is topped off with a crumbled-up granola bar. He's figured out how to not only drink his morning caffeine, but eat it too. —Aimee

AT HOME

Combine the oats, milk powder, Chai Sugar, flaxseed, and pinch of salt in a ziplock bag.

Add the tea bags to the ziplock bag.

Combine the nuts, brown sugar, and pinch of salt in a ziplock bag. Nest this bag inside the bag with the oat mixture.

AT CAMP

Bring 2 cups of water to a boil in a pot. Turn off the heat and add the tea bags. Brew the tea for about 5 minutes, or to your desired strength. Remove the tea bags.

Add the oat mixture to the hot tea and stir until well combined, making sure to break up any large clumps of milk powder. Allow the mixture to sit for about 5 minutes.

Turn the stove back on and cook the oatmeal for a few minutes, until it's hot and cooked through. Add additional water if needed to achieve the desired consistency.

Top with the brown sugar and nut mixture and serve.

Per serving: 345 calories, 11 g fat, 54 g carbs, 10 g protein
Weight: 5 ounces

Tip: Make it even more caffeinated, turning it into "Dirty" Chai Oatmeal, by adding ½ teaspoon of instant espresso powder.

Chai Oatmeal

Socca Tortilla (page 234)

Socca Tortilla

chickpea flour, cayenne, tortillas

Makes 2 servings

At-camp cooking time: 20 minutes

TOOLS

Lightweight stove

Nonstick skillet

Spatula

———

COOKING WATER: 1 cup

⅔ cup chickpea flour

¼ cup dried chopped scallions

2 tablespoons nutritional yeast

1 teaspoon tomato powder

½ teaspoon onion powder

½ teaspoon salt

½ teaspoon pepper

Pinch of cayenne pepper

2 tablespoons olive oil

4 6-inch flour or corn tortillas

Hot sauce, for serving *(optional)*

Socca is a crepe made with chickpea flour. It's known mostly as an Italian dish, but similar variations are made in many other parts of the world. It's extremely simple to make, as long as you use a nonstick skillet. You can eat this at any time of day, but I like it for breakfast, since it reminds me of an omelet. For backpacking, we've bulked it up a little by cooking it with a tortilla. —Emily

AT HOME

Combine the chickpea flour, scallions, nutritional yeast, tomato powder, onion powder, salt, pepper, and cayenne in a ziplock bag.

Place the bag with the chickpea flour mixture in a bag with the tortillas. If you're using packets of oil and/or hot sauce, nest those in the bag as well.

AT CAMP

Add the water to the bag with the chickpea flour mixture. Seal the bag and use your hands to massage the bag until everything is thoroughly mixed together.

Heat about ½ tablespoon of the oil in the skillet. Cut open a small corner in the bottom of the bag of chickpea flour batter and pour in about a quarter of the batter. Place a tortilla on top and gently press down to flatten the batter under the tortilla. Cook for another minute or two on medium-low heat, or until golden brown, then flip it over. Cook for another few minutes, until the tortilla side is golden brown as well.

Repeat these steps for each tortilla.

Serve immediately, with hot sauce if desired.

Per serving: 369 calories, 17 g fat, 42 g carbs, 11 g protein
Weight: 11 ounces

MAINS

Creamy Pasta e Fagioli

bean flakes, dehydrated vegetables, herb-infused olive oil

Makes 2 servings

At-camp cooking time: 15 minutes

TOOLS

Lightweight stove

1-quart pot

Spork

COOKING WATER: 2 cups

1 tablespoon olive oil

1 bay leaf

1 teaspoon dried rosemary

½ teaspoon dried minced garlic

2 ounces quick-cooking pasta like rotelle, vermicelli, or similar

½ cup bean flakes

¼ cup whole dehydrated white beans

1 tablespoon mixed dehydrated vegetables, such as bell pepper, celery, and/or carrot

1 tablespoon dehydrated arugula or spinach

1¼ teaspoon Bouillon Powder (page 286) or bouillon cube equivalent

1 teaspoon tomato powder

We have been thrilled to push the limits of our dehydrators for this cookbook, as they have greatly expanded the list of potential backcountry ingredients. But you never know when you'll be invited to join a last-minute trip that doesn't leave much time for prep. This recipe uses easy-to-find traditional backpacking ingredients that you may have stored away in an emergency bin, but the herb-infused olive oil creates a depth of flavor and creaminess that take those ingredients to the next level. —Emily

AT HOME

In one ziplock bag, pack the olive oil, bay leaf, rosemary, and garlic.

In a second ziplock bag, pack the rest of the ingredients.

AT CAMP

In a medium pot on very low heat, heat the olive oil, rosemary, garlic, and bay leaf until fragrant, about 30 seconds. Watch carefully and remove from the heat immediately if you start to see burning.

Add the water, pasta, bean flakes, whole beans, vegetables, dried greens, bouillon, and tomato powder. Stir until well combined.

Increase the heat to medium-high until the soup reaches a boil.

Lower the heat to a simmer and stir frequently, scraping the bottom, until the beans and pasta are almost done, about 5 minutes. Remove from the heat and let sit for 5 minutes to finish cooking.

> Per serving: 422 calories, 12 g fat, 67 g carbs, 14 g protein
> Weight: 7 ounces

Creamy Pasta e Fagioli (page 235)

Cacio e Pepe

Cacio e Pepe

orzo pasta, Nutty Parmesan, freshly cracked black pepper

Makes 2 servings

At-camp cooking time: 10 minutes

TOOLS

Lightweight stove

1-quart pot

Spork

———

COOKING WATER: 2 cups

⅔ cup orzo

2 teaspoons Bouillon Powder (page 286) or bouillon cube equivalent

3 tablespoons unsweetened cashew butter

3 tablespoons Nutty Parmesan (page 288)

1 teaspoon freshly ground pepper

I have spent many a mile in the backcountry mentally listing all the things I can think of that I'd be excited to eat at that very moment. Most of them are cheesy and creamy. It's difficult to bring cheesy creamy stuff into situations that require nonperishable meals, though, so I've usually had to do without.

Long ago, Aimee opened my eyes to the versatile world of nut butter and how cheesy it can become. With the use of two other veganized and nonperishable ingredients here (both located in our Staples section), you can have a cheesy and peppery pasta dish in minutes, anywhere you are, with no need to dehydrate anything ahead of time. —Emily

AT HOME

Measure the orzo and bouillon into a ziplock bag.

Measure the cashew butter into another ziplock bag and put it inside the orzo bag.

Measure the Nutty Parmesan and pepper into a third ziplock, and put this bag inside the orzo bag as well.

AT CAMP

Bring 2 cups of water to a boil.

Add the orzo bouillon mix to the water. Adjust the heat to maintain a steady simmer and stir occasionally, making sure the orzo doesn't stick to the bottom of the pot.

Boil the orzo until it is tender, about 10 minutes.

Remove the orzo from the heat but do not drain. Add the cashew butter and stir to fully mix it in.

Add about half of the Parmesan pepper mixture to the pot and stir. Divide the pasta into 2 portions, and top with the remaining Parmesan pepper mixture, to taste.

Per serving: 429 calories, 17 g fat, 54 g carbs, 18 g protein
Weight: 9 ounces

Butter Chicken

garam masala, soy curls,
tomatoes

Makes 2 servings

Dehydration time: 6 to 8 hours

At-camp cooking time: 5 minutes

Butter chicken is a rich and creamy Indian favorite, something craveable to look forward to on a high-activity day far from the comforts of home. In place of chicken, this recipe uses soy curls, a popular meat substitute that lends itself perfectly to a trip requiring lightweight, nonperishable meals. Here we make the sauce fresh and then dehydrate the whole thing. High-fat dishes don't dehydrate very well, so we minimized the oil during the at-home cooking process. To make sure it's still satisfyingly creamy, be sure to add the coconut oil at camp. —Aimee

AT HOME

To make the sauce: Heat the oil in a skillet over medium heat and add the onion, cumin, and coriander. Sauté until the onion is soft-

TOOLS

1-quart pot

Lightweight stove

Spork

COOKING WATER: 3 cups

1½ cups soy curls

½ cup freeze-dried peas

FOR THE SAUCE

1 teaspoon neutral oil

⅓ cup diced onion

½ teaspoon ground cumin

½ teaspoon ground coriander

2 garlic cloves, minced

1 teaspoon minced ginger

¼ teaspoon ground turmeric

Pinch of cayenne or other spicy chile powder

Pinch of cinnamon

1 (15-ounce) can diced tomatoes

3 tablespoons raw cashews

1 teaspoon fresh lemon juice

1 teaspoon garam masala

½ teaspoon salt

½ teaspoon sugar

FOR SERVING

Flatbread or parboiled rice

1 tablespoon coconut oil

1 teaspoon dried cilantro and/or scallions *(optional)*

ened, about 5 minutes. Add the garlic, ginger, turmeric, cayenne, and cinnamon and sauté for about 30 seconds.

Stir in the tomatoes and cook for about 10 minutes, to allow the flavors to blend and to reduce the sauce a bit. Remove from the heat and let cool slightly.

Transfer the tomato mixture to a blender and add the cashews, lemon juice, garam masala, salt, and sugar. Blend until smooth. Taste and season with additional salt. It should be fairly salty, since you'll be adding the soy curls and serving it with rice or flatbread.

Spread the sauce on dehydrator trays lined with parchment or silicone mats and dehydrate at 135° F for 6 to 8 hours, or until completely dry.

Allow the dehydrated sauce to cool fully, then transfer to a medium ziplock bag. Place the soy curls and peas in the same bag. Nest a small pouch of coconut oil inside this bag as well.

AT CAMP

In a medium pot, combine the soy curls and peas, the sauce, and water. Bring to a boil and stir well. Remove from the heat and cover. Allow to rest for about 10 minutes.

Serve with rice or flatbread.

> Per serving: 321 calories, 20 g fat, 25 g carbs, 14 g protein (without rice or bread)
> Weight: 5 ounces

Saag Tofu

spinach, Indian spices, tofu paneer

Makes 2 servings
Dehydration time: 6 to 8 hours
At-camp cooking time: 10 minutes

TOOLS
Lightweight stove
1-quart pot with lid
Spork

Kismat's mother is an exceptional Indian cook. She and I have bonded over many years as teacher and student in the kitchen. I now cook Indian food several nights a week, and I love to share it with my friends and family who may have never gotten a chance to experience it. Saag paneer is a very popular dish, but paneer is cheese, which can be difficult to bring into the backcountry when there's no refrigeration available. Tofu is actually very similar to paneer, and rehydrated tofu cubes end up being even closer to paneer texturally than fresh tofu. —Aimee

AT HOME

To prepare the tofu: In a skillet over medium heat, cook the tofu cubes with ½ cup of water and the salt, coriander, and cumin. Simmer, stirring often, until the water evaporates. Remove from the heat and allow to cool slightly. Arrange the tofu cubes in a single layer on a dehydrator tray. Put the dehydrator tray in the freezer for at least an hour.

COOKING WATER: 2 cups

TOFU

8 ounces extra-firm tofu, cut into ¼-inch cubes

½ teaspoon salt

¼ teaspoon ground coriander

¼ teaspoon ground cumin

SAAG

1 pound spinach or other leafy greens, such as collard greens or mustard greens, washed well and coarsely chopped

½ cup coarsely chopped onion

1 medium tomato, chopped

½ small green chile, such as jalapeño or serrano

2 teaspoons minced fresh ginger

2 garlic cloves, roughly chopped

1 tablespoon neutral oil

1½ teaspoons ground coriander

¼ teaspoon ground turmeric

¼ teaspoon ground cumin

¼ teaspoon salt

Pinch of cinnamon

FOR SERVING

4 flatbreads

1 tablespoon (0.5-ounce packet) coconut oil

2 small pieces preserved lemon *(optional)*

To make the saag: In a large pot, stir together the spinach, onion, tomato, chile, ginger, garlic, and ¼ cup of water. Cover and bring to a boil over high heat. Lower the heat to medium and simmer until the onions are tender, about 10 minutes. Cool slightly, then use an immersion blender, food processor, or blender to just barely puree the mixture (it should still have some texture). Set aside.

Heat the oil in a large skillet over medium heat, then add the coriander, turmeric, cumin, salt, and cinnamon. Cook just until fragrant, about 30 seconds. Add the spinach mixture and stir until well combined. Cook over medium-low heat for 5 to 10 minutes, until the mixture has thickened. Taste and adjust the seasoning.

Line a dehydrator tray with a silicone mat or parchment paper and spread the spinach mixture in a thin layer.

Transfer the spinach and the tofu trays straight from the freezer to a dehydrator set at 135° F and dehydrate for 6 to 8 hours, until completely dry.

Break up the dehydrated spinach mixture into 1-inch pieces and pack in a ziplock bag.

Pack the dehydrated tofu cubes in a ziplock bag and nest it inside the spinach bag. Nest the coconut oil packet in the bag as well.

Pack the flatbread and preserved lemon, if using.

AT CAMP

In a medium pot, bring water to a boil and add the tofu cubes. Boil for about a minute, then cover and remove from the heat. Let soak for at least 10 minutes.

Add the spinach mixture to the pot and return the mixture to a boil, stirring often. Cook until the spinach rehydrates, 5 to 10 minutes.

Stir in the coconut oil and serve with flatbread and preserved lemon.

> Per serving: 589 calories, 26 g fat, 72 g carbs, 25 g protein
> Weight: 6 ounces

Tip: This is best eaten using pieces of flatbread as a spoon.

French Dip Sandwiches

dehydrated saucy mushrooms, English muffins, au jus

Makes 2 servings

Dehydration time: 6 to 8 hours

At-camp cooking time: 5 minutes

TOOLS

1-quart pot

Lightweight stove

Spoon

COOKING WATER: 2 cups

2 tablespoons soy sauce

1 tablespoon vegan Worcestershire sauce

¼ teaspoon smoked paprika

¼ teaspoon pepper

Pinch of cayenne pepper

12 ounces mushrooms, sliced

1 small red bell pepper, thinly sliced

1½ teaspoons Bouillon Powder (page 286) or bouillon cube equivalent

1 cup soy curls

4 English muffins or similar size bread (about 2 ounces each)

FOR SERVING

Nacho Kale Chips (page 67) *(optional)*

Nutty Parmesan (page 288) *(optional)*

When my dad was going backpacking in the Los Padres National Forest, he decided to just grab some freeze-dried backpacking meals on the way out of town. He came home whiny and sick and said he couldn't get any food down the whole time he was out, because his meals all tasted the same. He had to cut his eleven-day trip short by five days. So for his next trip, I set him up with these French Dips. He came back raving about how great they tasted, and most importantly, he managed to actually eat all his food and felt much better. —Aimee

---

AT HOME

In a large bowl, whisk together the soy sauce, Worcestershire sauce, paprika, pepper, and cayenne.

Add the mushroom and bell pepper slices and toss to fully coat.

Place the coated mushrooms and pepper slices in a single layer on as many dehydrator trays as necessary, and dehydrate at 130° F for 6 to 8 hours, until fully dry.

Allow the mushrooms and peppers to cool, then pack them in a medium ziplock bag along with the bouillon and soy curls.

Pack your bread of choice, along with any of the optional toppings, just before your trip's start date.

AT CAMP

In a pot, combine the mushroom mixture and water. Bring to a boil, then simmer until the mushrooms and soy curls are tender and rehydrated, stirring occasionally, about 5 minutes.

Spoon the saucy mushroom mixture onto your bread. Top with Parmesan or kale chips, if desired.

Dip your sandwich directly into the au jus sauce in the pot as you eat it.

Per serving: 411 calories, 6 g fat, 71 g carbs, 24 g protein

Weight: 12 ounces

Enfrijoladas

pinto beans, poblano, fresh lime, hot sauce in a straw

Makes 2 servings

Dehydration time: 8 to 10 hours

At-camp cooking time: 5 minutes

TOOLS

Lightweight stove

1-quart pot with lid

Spork

———

COOKING WATER: 1¼ cups

2 poblano peppers, fire roasted (page 49) and diced

¼ cup sliced scallions

1 (16-ounce) can refried beans

½ teaspoon chili powder

¼ teaspoon ground cumin

¼ teaspoon garlic powder

¼ teaspoon onion powder

¼ teaspoon salt

10 street-style corn tortillas or 6 regular corn tortillas

TOPPINGS

2 tablespoons roasted salted pepitas

1 lime

2 packets hot sauce *(optional)*

I discovered enfrijoladas in my Rancho Gordo *Heirloom Beans* cookbook at the beginning of the pandemic when we were working through our pantry staples (I knew that hoarding lots of fancy beans would eventually pay off!). The idea is so simple: dip a tortilla in a pot of pureed beans, then top with lots of delicious things. You can make the beans ahead, it's easy to cook for a crowd, and everyone can customize the flavor profile with their toppings of choice. It is also an excellent recipe to campify for backpacking because it comes together with minimal cooking time and minimal water.

We have learned how easy it is to dehydrate your own bean flakes. Some of the other ingredients can be dehydrated and added directly to the pureed beans, but limes and roasted pepitas add texture and a hit of brightness without a lot of weight. —Emily

AT HOME

Arrange the diced poblano in a single layer on a baking sheet or dehydrator tray, along with the scallions. Set aside.

Line dehydrator trays with silicone mats or parchment paper and spread the refried beans in a thin layer.

Dehydrate both the beans and the vegetables at 135° F until fully dry. The veggies should be dry in 4 to 6 hours; the beans will take anywhere from 8 to 10 hours. Allow to cool completely before packing.

Pack the bean flakes and veggies in a ziplock bag, along with the chili powder, cumin, garlic powder, onion powder, and salt.

Pack the pepitas in a separate ziplock bag.

In a large ziplock bag, pack the corn tortillas, the bags of the bean mixture and pepitas, the lime, and the hot sauce packets.

AT CAMP

In a medium pot, bring 1¼ cup of water to a boil.

Pour in the bean mixture and boil for about 1 minute, stirring occasionally, until the consistency is smooth and the vegetables are rehydrated. Cover and set the pot aside, but keep the flame of the stove lit.

Place a tortilla directly on top of the stove flame. Carefully flip the tortilla until it's heated through, about 30 seconds.

Fold the tortilla in half or quarters and dip into the bean mixture, then transfer to a bowl. Add more beans on top if desired.

Top with pepitas, a squeeze of lime, and a few drops of hot sauce, and enjoy.

Per serving: 420 calories, 9 g fat, 72 g carbs, 18 g protein
Weight: 16 ounces (includes lime)

Korean Soft Tofu Stew

cabbage, mushrooms, gochugaru flakes

Makes 2 servings

At-camp cooking time: 10 minutes

TOOLS

Lightweight stove

Knife

Spork

1-quart pot

COOKING WATER: 2 cups or more

4 teaspoons coarse gochugaru flakes

½ teaspoon garlic powder

½ teaspoon salt

1 cup dehydrated cabbage

¼ cup sliced dried shiitake mushrooms

1 tablespoon dehydrated scallions

1¼ teaspoons Bouillon Powder (page 286) or bouillon cube equivalent

1 (11.5- to 12.3-ounce, depending on the brand) Tetra-Pak box of silken tofu

FOR SERVING

1 boil-in-a-bag rice *(optional)*

When I first moved to Los Angeles, I instantly fell in love with Korean food. This recipe is based on one of my favorite dishes, sundubu-jjigae. Typically, the dish arrives at the table in an individual-size stone pot filled with furiously bubbling stew. There are some specialty ingredients required for this dish, and the tofu box weighs 12 ounces—which will make some ultralighters gasp. But it's ready in 10 minutes and is one of the most satisfying and warming dishes I know of for a cold night out. —Mai-Yan

AT HOME

Combine the gochugaru flakes, garlic powder, salt, cabbage, mushrooms, and scallions in a ziplock bag.

Crumble the bouillon directly into the bag and seal.

AT CAMP

Carefully cut open the tofu box and drain any liquid into a medium pot. Using the box as a cutting board, cut the tofu into large cubes and set aside.

Add 2 cups of water to the pot and bring to a boil. If using, put the bag of rice directly in the water and boil until tender, according to the package directions.

If needed, add more water to compensate for evaporation. Add the contents of the ziplock bag and return to a boil. Lower the heat to a simmer and stir, making sure the bouillon is totally dissolved.

Add the tofu cubes and let simmer for another 5 minutes to heat through. Serve immediately.

> Per serving: 148 calories, 6 g fat, 10 g carbs, 15 g protein (without the rice)
> Weight: 14 ounces

Tip: If you're camping at high altitude, please note that cooking times will be longer. The stew may boil after 10 minutes, but due to a lower boiling point, a taste test will likely reveal this isn't the hot soup you're craving yet. Keep the heat on until you've reached your desired food temperature (or can't wait any longer).

Cauliflower Potato Soup

white beans, garlic, nutritional yeast

Makes 2 servings

Dehydration time: 8 to 10 hours

At-camp cooking time: 5 to 10 minutes

TOOLS

Lightweight stove

1½-quart pot

Spork

COOKING WATER: 4 cups

2 teaspoons olive oil

⅔ cup chopped onion

2 garlic cloves, minced

2 cups vegetable broth

½ pound potatoes, peeled and chopped

½ small head of cauliflower, cut into florets (about 3 cups florets)

1 (15-ounce) can white beans, drained and rinsed

2 tablespoons nutritional yeast

Salt and pepper

FOR SERVING

1 tablespoon coconut oil

4 tablespoons crumbs of Nacho Kale Chips (page 67)

This creamy soup is just the comforting meal I crave when I'm cold and tired. It tastes great and is also packed with nutrients, thanks to the cauliflower and beans. I initially tried reconstituting it straight from the dehydrator, but I ended up with chewy chunks of dried soup even after a long simmer. Powdering the soup before reconstituting it turned out to be the secret, so make sure you don't skip that step. Powdering dehydrated foods is also a great way to tell that they are fully dehydrated, as they will clump up if they are not. Adding a little coconut oil at camp makes this soup even more luscious and also boosts the calories a bit. —Aimee

AT HOME

In a medium pot set over medium heat, heat the oil. Sauté the onion until softened and translucent. Stir in the garlic and sauté for another minute.

Add the vegetable broth, potatoes, cauliflower, and white beans. Increase the heat to high and bring the mixture to a boil. Turn down the heat to low and simmer until the potatoes are softened, about 20 minutes. Remove from the heat and stir in the nutritional yeast. Allow to cool slightly.

Carefully transfer the soup to a blender or use an immersion blender. Puree the soup until it is completely smooth. Season to taste with salt and pepper.

Line dehydrator trays with silicone mats or parchment paper. Spread the soup in a layer no more than 1/4 inch thick. Dehydrate at 135° F for 8 to 10 hours, or until completely dry.

Allow to cool completely, then pull off the soup in flakes and transfer to a dry blender. Blend to a powder and pack in a ziplock bag. The yield is about 1 cup of soup powder.

AT CAMP

In a pot, combine the soup powder with 4 cups of water. Stir well to make sure all the powder is well combined. Bring the mixture to a boil, then simmer for 1 to 2 minutes. Stir again and serve.

Per serving: 482 calories, 13 g fat, 74 g carbs, 25 g protein

Weight: 6 ounces

Mac and Cheese

dehydrated vegetables, cashews, smoked paprika

Makes 2 servings

At-camp cooking time: 15 minutes

TOOLS

Lightweight stove

1-quart pot

Spoon

―――――

COOKING WATER: 2 cups

1 cup small pasta shells or elbow macaroni

¼ cup freeze-dried peas or dehydrated broccoli

CHEESE POWDER

¼ cup cashews

2 tablespoons nutritional yeast

1 tablespoon unsweetened soy or oat milk powder

¾ teaspoon salt

¼ teaspoon smoked paprika

⅛ teaspoon garlic powder

⅛ teaspoon onion powder

⅛ teaspoon ground turmeric

We had to include our take on the much loved (or hated) boxed Kraft Macaroni & Cheese. In this version, we've kept the ease of a ready-to-go cheesy powder but campified the method so no pasta draining is necessary. We initially trail-tested this gem on the High Sierra Loop in Yosemite back in 2018, and we've been holding onto it ever since. —Mai-Yan

AT HOME

Place the cashews, nutritional yeast, milk powder, salt, paprika, garlic powder, onion powder, and turmeric in a food processor or blender and pulse the mixture into a powder. If you are using something smaller (like a spice grinder), pulse in batches as needed. Pack the powder in a ziplock bag.

In a separate ziplock bag, combine the pasta and vegetables.

AT CAMP

Bring 2 cups of water to a boil. Add the pasta and vegetables and boil until the pasta is al dente, about 10 minutes.

Without draining, add the cheese powder to the pasta and mix well. Serve immediately.

> Per serving: 403 calories, 11 g fat, 50 g carbs, 18 g protein
> Weight: 8 ounces

Tip: It's hard to come by a good plant-based cheese powder, so once you've mastered this one, you'll want to experiment with other uses for it.

Matzo ~~Ball~~ Soup

noodles, dill, carrots, celery

Makes 2 servings

At-camp cooking time: 5 minutes

TOOLS

Lightweight stove

2-quart pot with lid

Spoon

COOKING WATER: 4 cups

2 matzo crackers

⅓ cup (1 ounce) short vermicelli noodles

¼ cup dehydrated carrots

7 teaspoons Bouillon Powder (page 286) or bouillon cube equivalent

2 tablespoons dehydrated celery

¼ teaspoon dried dill weed

¼ teaspoon garlic powder

I love matzo ball soup. It's something I associate with my early years in Los Angeles, staying up all night working on art projects and then stumbling into the beloved Jewish deli, Canter's. I really wanted to bring the coziness of this meal-worthy soup into the backcountry. Between Aimee and me, we probably made two hundred matzo balls trying to figure out a way to get them to stay together in the soup. Ultimately, we failed, but we kept eating the soup over and over and realized it was perfect as is. The essence of matzo is in the heart offering you the campside comfort you need. —Mai-Yan

---

AT HOME

Pulse the matzo crackers to form coarse crumbs. Pack ½ cup of the crumbs with the vermicelli, carrots, bouillon, celery, dill, and garlic powder in a ziplock bag.

If you have any extra matzo crumbs and want to have them as a topping, pack those in another ziplock bag.

AT CAMP

In a large pot, combine the soup mix with 4 cups of water and bring to a boil. Boil for 5 minutes, until the noodles and veggies are tender.

Serve with the matzo crumbs topping.

> Per serving: 246 calories, 2 g fat, 53 g carbs, 5 g protein
> Weight: 5 ounces

Backpacker's Samosas

potatoes, peas, cashews, garam masala

Makes 2 servings

Dehydration time: 2 hours

At-camp cooking time: 5 minutes

TOOLS

Lightweight stove

8-inch skillet

Spatula

Spoon

COOKING WATER: 1 cup

½ cup unseasoned instant mashed potatoes

⅓ cup roasted and salted cashew pieces

¼ cup freeze-dried peas

1 tablespoon unsweetened soy milk powder

½ teaspoon salt

¼ teaspoon garam masala

¼ teaspoon ground turmeric

⅛ teaspoon onion powder

1 tablespoon flax meal

4 soft taco-size (8-inch) flour tortillas

IF YOU HAVE A DEHYDRATOR

1 scallion, sliced

1 tablespoon chopped cilantro stems

I wanted to create a recipe that I didn't have to dehydrate ahead of time—and taking that idea one step further, I tried a soaked meal for the filling. The structure of this samosa is based on Taco Bell's Crunchwrap Supreme, which I'd never heard of before working on this book. Dehydrated cilantro stems and scallions add a nice depth of flavor; you can also try this with freeze-dried chives. —Mai-Yan

AT HOME

Dehydrate the scallions and cilantro stems at 115° F for 2 hours (optional).

Combine the instant mashed potatoes, cashew pieces, peas, soy milk powder, salt, garam masala, turmeric, onion powder, and flax meal with the dehydrated scallions and cilantro (if using) in a sandwich- or quart-size ziplock bag.

Pack the tortillas separately.

AT CAMP

Pour 1 cup water into the ziplock bag of samosa filling and seal. Stir by carefully massaging the contents of the bag together until the filling is fully rehydrated. Let sit for 5 minutes.

If your tortilla is dried out or stiff, briefly warm it in the skillet to make it more pliable. Turn off the heat and set the skillet down on a stable surface.

With a tortilla on the skillet, scoop about 6 tablespoons of samosa filling in a pile in the center of the tortilla.

To fold the samosa, lift one edge of the tortilla with your spatula and fold it up to the center of the filling. Lift the next edge and fold it to the center of the filling. Keep folding in this manner, working your way around the tortilla, keeping everything as tight as possible, until the tortilla is sealed (a small opening is fine) and resembles a hexagon.

Return the skillet to the stove and heat the samosa until the bottom is golden brown, about 30 seconds.

Flip the samosa and press down and heat for another 30 seconds.

Repeat the assembly and cooking process for each samosa.

Per serving: 460 calories, 15 g fat, 39 g carbs, 11 g protein
Weight: 10 ounces

Tip: We recommend bringing along ketchup and hot sauce packets to complement the samosas.

Japanese Curry Crunchwraps

instant potatoes, corn, soy curls, tortillas

Makes 2 servings

At-camp cooking time: 5 minutes, plus 10 minutes soaking

After the Backpacker's Samosas recipe, I couldn't stop thinking about crunchwrap fillings, kind of like Bubba in *Forrest Gump* going on and on about shrimp. This format is just so ideal for backcountry cooking, and you end up with zero dishes! Japanese curry comes in a box with packets of four to six cubes and can usually be found in the supermarket international aisle. It's one of our go-to weeknight meals, and I have yet to find something that doesn't taste good in it. At camp, the curry filling is simply rehydrated directly in the bag you packed it in, with water straight out of your hydration pack. A little origami and skillet action, and dinner is ready. —Mai-Yan

AT HOME

Chop up the curry cubes into a fine dice, then press them down with the flat side of your knife to break up any remaining chunks.

TOOLS

Lightweight stove

8-inch skillet

Spatula

Spoon

COOKING WATER: 1 cup

2 Japanese curry cubes, spice level to your preference

5 tablespoons soy curls, broken into small pieces

6 tablespoons instant mashed potatoes

¼ cup mixed vegetables, like freeze-dried corn, green beans, peas, and bell peppers

4 soft taco-size (8-inch) flour tortillas

Combine the curry cubes, soy curls, instant mashed potatoes, and vegetables in a sandwich- or quart-size ziplock bag.

Put the tortillas in a separate ziplock bag.

AT CAMP

Pour 1 cup of water into the ziplock bag of filling and seal. Carefully massage the contents together until the filling is fully rehydrated. Let sit for 10 minutes.

If your tortilla is dried out or stiff, briefly warm it in the skillet to make it more pliable. Turn off the heat and set the skillet down on a stable surface.

With a tortilla on the skillet, scoop about ¼ of the curry filling in a pile in the center of the tortilla.

To fold the crunchwrap, lift one edge of the tortilla with a spatula and fold it over to the center of the filling. Press down gently on the fold all the way to the outer edges of the tortilla. Lift the next edge and fold it to the center of the filling. Keep folding in this manner, working your way around the tortilla, keeping everything as tight as possible, until the tortilla is sealed and resembles a hexagon (a small opening is fine).

Return the skillet to the stove and heat the crunchwrap until the bottom is golden brown, about 30 seconds.

Flip the crunchwrap and press down and heat for another 30 seconds.

Repeat the assembly and cooking process for each crunchwrap.

> Per serving: 454 calories, 14 g fat, 55 g carbs, 12 g protein
> Weight: 11 ounces

Tip: Aimee's friend Miki once gave us an insider tip: she grated a bit of fresh apple into the curry we were making at home. It's a subtle move that adds a little magic to the curry. If you happen to have freeze-dried apples, try grating 1 teaspoon into the filling mix.

Southern Barbecue Feast

jackfruit pulled pork, cornbread crumbles, slaw

Makes 2 servings

Dehydration Time: 8 to 10 hours

At-camp cooking time: 10 minutes, plus 1 hour soaking

TOOLS

Lightweight stove

1-quart pot

Spoon

COOKING WATER: 1¾ cups water, divided

BBQ JACKFRUIT

2 (20-ounce) cans of jackfruit

¾ cup of your favorite barbecue sauce

1 teaspoon balsamic vinegar

½ teaspoon salt

½ teaspoon garlic powder

CORNBREAD MUFFIN CRUMBLES

2 tablespoons cornmeal

2 tablespoons all-purpose flour

5 teaspoons sugar

¼ teaspoon baking powder

Pinch of salt

3 tablespoons plant milk

1 tablespoon plant butter, melted

Aimee and Emily often talk about their Southern roots, grand-mammys, and grits (*lots* of grits talk). Over the years, I've been introduced to more of that culture and the food that comes with it. I finally got to visit North Carolina when Emily and I went to Asheville for an outdoor cooking workshop, and Emily showed me lots of local favorites, including pottery, boiled peanuts, and, of course, Carolina barbecue.

The vision for this recipe is a hearty formal meal with a main and two sides: tangy BBQ jackfruit contrasted with a sharp, vine-gary slaw and cornbread. Although there's a fair amount of prep at home, at camp the actual meal is a one-pot deal. —Mai-Yan

AT HOME

To make the BBQ jackfruit: Drain the jackfruit and rinse under cold water to help wash off any remaining brine.

Chop the jackfruit cores off of each chunk (see photo) and slice thinly by hand or pulse in a food processor.

Put the remaining jackfruit pieces (tendrils and seeds) in a large bowl along with the sliced cores. Add the barbecue sauce, vine-gar, salt, and garlic powder and stir to coat. Taste and season with additional salt if needed.

Lay out the BBQ jackfruit on as many dehydrator trays as needed in a thin, even layer.

Dehydrate at 140° F for 5 to 6 hours, until it is dry to the touch.

Pack in a ziplock bag.

To make the cornbread muffin crumbles: Preheat the oven to 350° F. Spray 2 cups of a muffin tin with cooking oil.

In a small bowl, combine the cornmeal, flour, sugar, baking pow-der, and salt. Stir in the milk and melted butter until the mixture is well combined.

Divide the batter evenly into the muffin tin cups. Bake for 20 min-utes, or until a toothpick inserted in the center comes out clean. Set aside to cool.

SLAW

½ cup apple cider vinegar

1 tablespoon sugar

1 tablespoon whole-grain Dijon mustard

½ teaspoon salt

½ teaspoon pepper

8-ounce bag of coleslaw mix

Crumble the muffins onto a dehydrator tray and dehydrate at 140° F for 1 hour.

Pack in a small ziplock bag.

To make the slaw: In a medium to large bowl, whisk together the vinegar, sugar, mustard, salt, and pepper.

Add the coleslaw mix and toss with the dressing.

Cover and let marinate for 30 minutes to 1 hour.

Toss again and distribute the marinated slaw on as many dehydrator trays as needed to keep an even, thin layer.

Dehydrate at 125° F for 8 hours. If the slaw is still moist, stir it around a bit to flip and separate pieces. Dehydrate for another 2 hours, or as long as needed for the slaw to feel dry and brittle to the touch.

Pack in a small ziplock bag.

AT CAMP

Add ¼ cup of water to the slaw and massage all the contents to mix well. Make sure the bag is sealed properly, then put in a critter-proof place to soak for 1 hour or more.

When the slaw is rehydrated, add 1½ cups of water to a pot along with the jackfruit. Stir well and heat on medium-low until it is rehydrated and hot.

Serve with cornbread crumbles and slaw.

> Per serving: 515 calories, 9 g fat, 96 g carbs, 3 g protein
> Weight: 10 ounces

Tip: If you're not much of a baker or just want to simplify the prep, buy cornbread that is already made (check the ingredients) and use that as the base for the cornbread muffin crumbles.

Southern Barbecue Feast (page 258)

Kitchadi

Kitchadi

red lentils, rice, cumin seeds

Makes 2 servings

At-camp cooking time: About 20 minutes

TOOLS

1½-quart pot with lid

Lightweight stove

COOKING WATER: 4 cups or more

½ cup instant white rice, such as Minute Rice

½ cup red lentils

2 teaspoons dried onion flakes

1 teaspoon salt

½ teaspoon cumin seeds

½ teaspoon garlic powder

½ teaspoon ground ginger

¼ teaspoon ground turmeric

1 tablespoon coconut oil

Kitchadi is an Indian dish of rice mixed with some sort of dal, cooked together into a creamy porridge, and it's absolutely comfort food. Both Kismat and our kids crave it when they're sick, or even when they're just overly tired. My mother-in-law taught me how to make it, and after seeing how simple the recipe is, I knew it would make a great backpacking meal. I've been on the fence about whether to present this as a dehydrated recipe or one that's cooked at camp. I opted to show you how to make it entirely at camp, but if you'd like to make it at home and dehydrate it, you absolutely can. —Aimee

AT HOME (OPTIONAL)

Combine the rice, lentils, onion flakes, and salt in a ziplock bag.

Combine the cumin seeds, garlic powder, ginger, and turmeric in a ziplock bag.

Nest the bagged spices and the bag or packet of coconut oil into the rice mixture bag.

AT CAMP

Heat the coconut oil in a pot and stir in the spices, cooking them until fragrant, about 30 seconds. Remove from the heat and add the rice mixture along with 3 cups of water.

Bring the mixture to a boil, stirring often. Turn the heat down to a simmer and cook for 15 minutes. Turn off the heat, cover, and let stand for another 5 minutes, until the rice and lentils are cooked through. The kitchadi will foam, so stir it often and watch it closely to keep it from boiling over. Add additional water as needed. It is done when it has reached a porridge-like consistency.

Per serving: 396 calories, 7 g fat, 67 g carbs, 15 g protein
Weight: 8 ounces

Tip: To prep as a dehydrated recipe, follow these instructions at home, then dehydrate it for 8 to 10 hours at 135° F. To rehydrate it at camp, place the dehydrated kitchadi in a pot and add enough water to cover it. Bring it to a boil and cook until it forms a creamy porridge, adding more water as needed to achieve the desired consistency.

Walnut Crumble Pasta

cashew butter, walnuts, crunchy chickpeas

Makes 2 large servings

At-camp cooking time: 10 minutes

TOOLS

Lightweight stove

1½-quart pot

Mug

Spork

COOKING WATER: 2½ cups

6 ounces angel hair pasta, broken in half

½ cup dehydrated kale or spinach

3 tablespoons raw cashew butter

2 tablespoons olive oil

½ teaspoon crushed red pepper flakes

½ teaspoon salt

¼ teaspoon garlic powder

WALNUT GARLIC CRUMBLE

3 tablespoons walnuts, finely chopped and toasted

3 tablespoons crunchy chickpeas, crushed with the flat side of a large knife

1 tablespoon nutritional yeast

½ teaspoon lemon pepper

½ teaspoon garlic powder

¼ teaspoon salt

Daniel and I tested this on a New Year's bikepacking trip on the beautiful central California coast. It was our first time on loaded bikes in a while and we had our new furry family member, Pogo, in a backpack, adding another twenty-five pounds of weight. We rolled into camp at sundown and set up quickly as the temps dropped. We were very happy to have this comforting dish to kick off the night. This is the kind of recipe that instantly becomes a go-to because of its ease and big flavors. The sauce base is simple, but the earthy nut butter flavor combined with the crunchy, lemony crumble is "mwah!" —Mai-Yan

AT HOME

Combine the pasta and kale in a ziplock bag.

Combine the cashew butter, olive oil, red pepper flakes, salt, and garlic powder in a small liquid measuring cup. Mix until well combined and pack in a leakproof container.

To make the walnut garlic crumble: Combine the walnuts, chickpeas, nutritional yeast, lemon pepper, garlic powder, and salt in a ziplock bag.

AT CAMP

Bring 2½ cups of water to a boil and add the pasta and kale. Cook until al dente, about 4 minutes, stirring the pasta to prevent everything from sticking together. Turn off the heat and scoop out about ½ cup of water with a mug and set aside. Drain the remaining water.

Stir in the the spiced cashew butter mixture. Add the reserved pasta-cooking water and mix until the sauce is creamy and well combined.

Top with the walnut garlic crumble and serve immediately.

Per serving: 678 calories, 34 g fat, 79 g carbs, 20 g protein
Weight: 12 ounces

Restorative Noodle Soup

instant miso soup packets, freeze-dried tofu, togarashi

Makes 2 servings

At-camp cooking time: 10 minutes

TOOLS

Lightweight stove

2-quart pot

Spoon

———

COOKING WATER: 4 cups

5 ounces soba noodles

4 single-serving vegan instant miso soup packets

2 to 3 sheets nori

1½ ounces freeze-dried tofu

1 tablespoon dried scallions

2 teaspoons togarashi

½ teaspoon ground turmeric

It's standard practice on a backpacking trip to pack a bunch of instant miso soup packets that you can enjoy before or after a meal, or during a little hiking break. The saltiness and hydration in such a small package are welcome friends, but it only provides a snack's worth of calories. That means you always have to cook something else, which means using more fuel and maybe cleaning out your cookware beforehand. But then we thought, *What if we just made it into a meal?* The result is a hearty soup, with added turmeric to help ease any inflammation. —Emily

AT HOME

Break the soba noodles in half so they will fit nicely in a ziplock bag and in your pot. Put them in the bag.

Open and dump the packets of miso soup directly into the bag with the noodles.

Measure out the nori, tofu, scallions, togarashi, and turmeric, and add them all to the same bag.

AT CAMP

Boil 4 cups of water.

Dump the contents of the ziplock bag into the water and turn the heat down to a simmer. Cook until the noodles and tofu are tender, about 10 minutes.

> Per serving: 478 calories, 11 g fat, 65 g carbs, 33 g protein
> Weight: 10 ounces

DRINKS

Tahini Hot Chocolate

cacao powder, tahini, toasted sesame seeds

Makes 2 servings

At-camp cooking time: 5 minutes

TOOLS

Lightweight stove

1-quart pot

2 mugs

Knife

Spork

———

COOKING WATER: 1½ to 2 cups

2 tablespoons tahini

2 tablespoons soy or oat milk powder

2 tablespoons cacao or cocoa powder

5 teaspoons sugar

2 teaspoons toasted white sesame seeds

1 teaspoon vanilla powder *(optional)*

Consuming enough calories is not just about satisfying hunger. It's about providing your body with nutrients for recovery, and it also helps warm your body up, which is especially important for chilly nights and snowy adventures. Adding a protein-rich drink to your evening camp routine can help you get more of those benefits. This is a simple, not-too-sweet homemade hot chocolate mix that will send you straight to dreamland. —Mai-Yan

AT HOME

Make sure your tahini is well stirred, so the oil and paste are well combined and the tahini looks milky and opaque before measuring into a ziplock bag, then add the remaining ingredients.

Carefully massage the hot chocolate mix inside the bag to combine everything and seal well.

AT CAMP

Bring 1½ to 2 cups of water to a boil.

If necessary, massage the hot chocolate ingredients again to mix well. Roll the bag into a log shape and cut in half through the bag.

Squeeze 1 half-log of hot chocolate mix into each mug. Divide the hot water between the 2 mugs and stir well to break up any clumps.

> Per serving: 202 calories, 14 g fat, 25 g carbs, 8 g protein
> Weight: 3 ounces

Golden Milk

turmeric, ginger, coconut oil

Makes 2 servings

Prep time: 5 minutes

At-camp cooking time: 5 minutes

TOOLS

Lightweight stove

1-quart pot

2 mugs

———————

COOKING WATER: 2 cups

6 tablespoons soy or coconut milk powder

3 tablespoons brown or maple sugar

1 teaspoon ground turmeric

½ teaspoon ground ginger

1 teaspoon coconut oil

I'm a black coffee kinda person, but once in a while I want something "fancy" and noncaffeinated to go with my meal. I've been trying a lot of golden lattes, and this is my take on them. It's a nice warming drink that blends dessert and bedtime tea into one recipe. Now we can all be fancy *and* outdoorsy! —Mai-Yan

AT HOME

Measure all of the dry ingredients into a small ziplock bag. Seal and massage to mix well.

Nest the bag or packet of coconut oil into the dry ingredients bag. Seal again tightly.

AT CAMP

Remove the coconut oil and massage the dry ingredients bag to break up any clumps.

In a pot, bring 2 cups of water to a boil.

Pour the drink mix into mugs (about 3 tablespoons per mug) and pour a little boiling water into each. Stir it around to make a slurry and break up the clumps. Add half the remaining water to each mug.

Add half of the coconut oil to each mug and enjoy.

Per serving: 163 calories, 6 g fat, 24 g carbs, 5 g protein
Weight: 3 ounces

Golden Milk

Champurrado de Café (page 270)

Champurrado de Café

masa flour, instant coffee, cinnamon

Makes 2 servings

At-camp cooking time: 5 minutes

TOOLS

Lightweight stove

1-quart pot

2 mugs

Spork

COOKING WATER: 2 cups

¼ cup brown sugar

2 tablespoons instant masa harina

2 tablespoons cocoa powder

2 teaspoons instant coffee (or 2 individual packets)

1 teaspoon cinnamon

Living in Southern California, we have access to plenty of Latin influence, and I love to take advantage of learning more about my kids' heritage with them as they grow. Food is, of course, one of the best ways to feel connected to someone's culture. I made champurrado with them at home one chilly night in place of hot chocolate because I had some pinole (roasted ground maize) on hand. We quickly realized that the drink would be perfect for backpacking: lightweight ingredients that come together quickly and pack a nutritional punch. It is thick and warming and makes adding a special drink to your menu well worth the effort. We used the more commonly available masa for the written recipe, but if you can find pinole, you can definitely substitute it for the instant masa here. —Emily

AT HOME

Measure the brown sugar, masa, cocoa, coffee, and cinnamon into a ziplock bag.

AT CAMP

In a pot, mix the cocoa mixture with 2 cups of cold water.

Heat it over medium-low heat, stirring continuously, until the drink thickens and froths on top, about 5 minutes. Watch carefully and remove it from the heat before it boils over.

Per serving: 181 calories, 1 g fat, 42 g carbs, 3 g protein
Weight: 3 ounces

Spicy Margarita Shot

spicy chile powder (not chili powder), lime, tequila

Makes 2 shots

TOOLS
2 glasses

Knife

---

2 shots (3 ounces) tequila

1 lime, quartered, or 1 teaspoon lime juice powder

SPICE MIX
1 teaspoon spicy chile powder, such as ancho or guajillo (cayenne would be extremely spicy)

2 teaspoons sugar

1 teaspoon salt

Hard liquor has many outdoor benefits over other options like wine or beer—mainly that it can be consumed at room temp and you need a very small amount for it to do its work, so it is less weight to carry. We like to figure out simple campified versions of classic cocktails that are quick to put together. This is a play on a margarita but requires only the extra weight of a lime and a few spices. Enjoy anywhere, but ideally, you create your own literal version of a margarita *frozen* or *on the rocks.* —Emily

AT HOME *(OPTIONAL)*

Measure the spice mix into a small leakproof container or ziplock bag.

AT CAMP

Rim each glass with a quarter of the lime and dip the rim into the bag of spice mix. (If using lime juice powder, you can simply sprinkle it and about $1/4$ teaspoon of the spice mix directly onto the shot of tequila.)

Pour each shot into its own glass.

If using fresh lime, squeeze $1/4$ to $1/2$ of the lime into each shot.

Chill in the snow *(optional)* and enjoy.

> **Weight: 6 ounces**

Tip: There are many types of chile powders out there, made from different types of ground chiles. These are not the same as chili powder, which is a spice mix that often includes additional spices like garlic or onion for the stew known as "chili" and should not be used for this recipe. The spicier the chile powder used, the spicier your drink will be.

Spicy Margarita Shot (page 271)

Whiskey Sour

Whiskey Sour

bourbon, citrus peel and lemonade powders, Kool-Aid

Makes 1 drink

TOOLS
Mug
Stirring spoon

COOKING WATER: ⅓ cup

1 teaspoon lemonade powder
½ teaspoon Citrus Peel Powder
⅛ teaspoon cherry Kool-Aid powder
Dried tart cherries *(optional)*
2 ounces bourbon

Not all classic cocktails can be adapted for backcountry purposes. We tried making a Bloody Mary shot, using all powdered spices like tomato and horseradish powder. The flavors were surprisingly balanced, but we couldn't handle drinking a lukewarm Bloody Mary (don't worry—we've switched it to a Car Camping Recipe so you can drink it with ice). We thought a whiskey sour would be fun, but we really wanted to figure out something backcountry-friendly to replace the *crucial* maraschino cherry. When we landed on cherry Kool-Aid as an ingredient, we knew we had hit a hilarious home run. We can see you all shopping the Kool-Aid aisle of the grocery store on the way out of town while your friends look on with confused expressions. If you're too fancy for this, though, you can use dried tart cherries instead. —Emily

---

AT HOME

Combine the lemonade powder, Citrus Peel Powder, and Kool-Aid in a small ziplock bag. Add the tart cherries to the bag as well or in place of the Kool-Aid.

AT CAMP

Pour the whiskey into a mug.

Add the water and contents of the ziplock bag to the mug. Stir to dissolve.

> **Weight: 3 ounces**

Tip: Find the coldest water you can; bonus points if you can chill your drink even further on a glacier or in a chilly body of water.

DESSERTS

Mixed Berry Crisp

homemade crumble, freeze-dried berries, vanilla powder

Makes 2 servings

At-camp cooking time: About 5 minutes

TOOLS

Lightweight stove

1-quart pot

Spork

COOKING WATER: 1 cup

¼ **cup flour**

¼ **cup rolled oats**

¼ **cup brown sugar**

Pinch of salt

2 tablespoons plant butter, softened

1½ cups freeze-dried berries, such as strawberries, blueberries, or raspberries

1 tablespoon cornstarch

1 tablespoon sugar

1 teaspoon vanilla powder *(optional)*

I have never been excited to eat most backpacking fruit crisps. They are usually just rehydrated fruit with store-bought granola thrown on top. Making your own crumble topping is so easy, and it feels like you're having a truly special dessert, rather than just that same granola you had earlier in the day for breakfast. I like to use a combination of strawberries, raspberries, and blueberries for maximum flavor and texture. —Aimee

AT HOME

Preheat the oven to 350° F.

To make the topping: In a small bowl, mix the flour, oats, brown sugar, and salt. Add the butter and use your fingers or a fork to mix it in, making sure it's evenly distributed.

Transfer the mixture to an ungreased baking sheet in a thin, even layer.

Bake for 15 to 20 minutes, or until lightly browned and fragrant.

Allow to cool completely, then transfer to a ziplock bag.

Pack the freeze-dried berries, cornstarch, sugar, and vanilla powder in a separate ziplock bag.

AT CAMP

Add the berry mixture to a pot with 1 cup water and bring to a boil.

Stir constantly until the mixture thickens, 1 to 2 minutes. Remove from the heat.

Sprinkle the crumble topping on the berry mixture and serve hot.

> Per serving: 495 calories, 12 g fat, 94 g carbs, 5 g protein
> Weight: 7 ounces

Mango Tapioca Pudding

pearl tapioca, freeze-dried mangoes, coconut milk powder

Makes 2 servings

At-camp cooking time: About 10 minutes

TOOLS
Lightweight stove
1-quart pot
Spork

COOKING WATER: 2 cups

½ cup small pearl tapioca
¼ cup sugar
¼ cup coconut milk powder
Pinch of salt
¼ cup freeze-dried mangoes

We came up with this recipe years ago; then I forgot all about it and even purchased a ready-made package of Mango Sticky Rice for a backpacking dessert on my last trip. I thought that sounded good, but when we rehydrated it at camp, it was terrible! At that moment, I remembered our recipe—and was also reminded why I decided to start making my own backpacking food rather than buying premade meals. —Aimee

AT HOME

Pack the tapioca in a ziplock bag.

Combine the sugar, coconut milk powder, and salt in a small ziplock bag, breaking up any clumps of coconut milk powder with your fingers.

Pack the freeze-dried mangoes in a separate small ziplock bag.

AT CAMP

Bring 2 cups of water to a boil in a medium pot. Remove from the heat and stir in the tapioca. Set aside to soak for about 10 minutes.

Stir the coconut milk powder mixture into the tapioca in the pot and return the mixture to a boil. Turn down the heat and simmer for about 5 minutes. Serve warm, sprinkled with freeze-dried mango pieces.

Per serving: 340 calories, 7 g fat, 71 g carbs, 1 g protein
Weight: 8 ounces

Tip: This also works well with other freeze-dried fruit, such as strawberries, raspberries, or bananas. We like the texture of the crunchy fruit on top of the chewy tapioca, but if you prefer, you can cook the fruit with the tapioca to soften it.

Chocolate Raspberry Tart

graham cracker crust,
freeze-dried raspberries

Makes 2 servings

Prep time: 5 minutes

At-camp cooking time: 5 minutes,
plus at least 20 minutes to set

TOOLS

Bowl or deep plate (about 4-inch diameter at the base)

Lightweight stove

Mug

COOKING WATER: 3 tablespoons

2 whole graham crackers, crushed into crumbs

1 tablespoon coconut oil

Pinch of salt

⅓ cup finely chopped vegan chocolate

2 tablespoons freeze-dried raspberries, crushed into a powder

1 tablespoon coconut milk powder

This dessert will make a lovely surprise if your trip coincides with anything that needs to be celebrated. It's rich and creamy and not too sweet, and it's surprisingly easy to put together. It does need some time to set, but if you're impatient and you don't mind a softer texture, it can set just enough in about 20 minutes. If it's chilly outside, the texture of the chocolate will be more firm, like a proper tart. —Aimee

---

AT HOME

Combine the graham cracker crumbs, coconut oil (if spooning out of a jar at home), and salt in a ziplock bag. Mush together so the coconut oil is evenly distributed.

Pack the chopped chocolate, freeze-dried raspberries, and coconut milk powder in a separate, smaller ziplock bag.

Nest the smaller bag inside the bag with the graham cracker crumbs. If you're using a packet of coconut oil, put that in the bag as well.

AT CAMP

Use your hands to warm the crumb mixture enough to melt the coconut oil, or submerge the unopened oil packet in some warm water.

If using a packet of coconut oil, squeeze the oil into the bag of crumb mixture and massage the bag to combine well. Press the mixture into the bottom and a little up the sides of the bowl to form a crust. Set aside.

To make the filling: Pour the chocolate raspberry mixture into a mug or another small bowl. Pull out and reserve a raspberry or 2 and set them aside to crush and sprinkle on top of the tart at the end. Stir 3 tablespoons of hot water into the mixture. Continue stirring until the chocolate melts and the filling is smooth.

Pour the filling into the graham cracker crust and spread it evenly. Crush the reserved raspberries and sprinkle them over the filling.

Put the tart in a cool place to set, protected from curious critters, for at least 20 minutes.

> **Per serving: 357 calories, 21 g fat, 39 g carbs, 4 g protein**
> **Weight: 5 ounces**

Orangesicle Chia Pudding

coconut powder, chia seeds, Citrus Peel Powder

Makes 2 servings

Our first book featured a Rocky Road Chia Pudding, and we decided to stick with the ice cream flavor theme for this dessert chia pudding. We love how simple this is to put together and also that it's packed with protein for great recovery help after a long day of hiking. It's healthy enough that I'd even eat it for breakfast. There's no cooking required, so it won't take up any precious fuel, which can sometimes be a deal breaker for dessert on a trip at all. —Aimee

TOOLS

2 mugs or bowls

2 spoons

COOKING WATER: ⅔ cup

¼ cup coconut milk powder

¼ cup chia seeds

3 tablespoons sugar

½ teaspoon Citrus Peel Powder (page 294)

½ teaspoon vanilla powder

Pinch of salt

¼ cup toasted coconut *(optional)*

AT HOME

Combine the coconut milk powder, chia seeds, sugar, Citrus Peel Powder, vanilla powder, and salt in a small ziplock bag and mix well.

If desired, pack the toasted coconut in a separate small bag.

AT CAMP

Divide the chia mixture between 2 mugs and add about ⅓ cup of water to each. Stir well and let sit for at least 15 minutes, or until the chia seeds have swelled and the pudding is thickened.

Top with toasted coconut, if using.

> **Per serving:** 410 calories, 26 g fat, 37 g carbs, 8 g protein
> **Weight:** 5 ounces

Chocolate Raspberry Tart (page 278)

Orangesicle Chia Pudding (page 279)

Speculoos Coffee Pudding Parfait (page 282)

Speculoos Coffee Pudding Parfait

speculoos cookies, instant coffee, instant pudding

Makes 2 servings

TOOLS

Bowl

Spork

COOKING WATER: ¾ cup

4 tablespoons instant vanilla pudding mix

2 tablespoons soy or oat milk powder

6 speculoos cookies

½ packet of microground coffee, such as Starbucks Via

We talk about urban foraging in the Plantry section of the book. This refers to collecting free little items, like soy sauce or jam packets, that you can conveniently add to your outdoor pantry. I'm really excited when an airline steward hands out Biscoff cookies—generically called speculoos cookies. I try to get extras and stash them to enjoy with my morning camp coffee or with a backcountry dessert. The addition of coffee really transforms the vanilla-pudding flavor profile into quite a satisfying dessert. —Mai-Yan

---

AT HOME

Combine the vanilla pudding mix and milk powder in a small ziplock bag. Nestle the coffee packet and the cookies in the bag.

AT CAMP

Remove the cookies from the bag. Transfer the pudding mixture to a bowl and add ¾ cup water. Use a spork to vigorously mix the pudding until few lumps remain.

Break up the cookies over the top of the pudding and sprinkle with the microground coffee.

> Per serving: 260 calories, 8 g fat, 43 g carbs, 8 g protein
> Weight: 6 ounces

Orange Olive Oil Cakes

Citrus Peel Powder, olive oil, easy cake mix

Makes 2 cupcakes

At-camp cooking time: 12 minutes

TOOLS

Lightweight stove

2 (1-foot) sheets of aluminum foil

1-quart pot

Spoon

Dessert can be a struggle on a trip that's focused on minimalism. When you pull it off, however, it can change the whole experience. We take the job of creating practical outdoor recipes seriously, so after a lot of testing, here's a cake(!) that can easily be included on any weight-constrained trip. It will amaze with its simplicity and elegance. The recipe is intricate and requires care to pull off seamlessly, but if anything goes wrong, the batter tastes great uncooked (always gotta have a backup plan). —Emily

AT HOME

Pack the flour, sugar, milk powder, flaxseed, Citrus Peel Powder, baking powder, and salt in a ziplock bag. If using olive oil packets, nest them in the bag.

Fold 2 foil bowls (see the tutorial in the Appendix) or use silicone cupcake forms and pack with the cupcake mix.

COOKING WATER: 1¼ cups

3 tablespoons all-purpose flour

3 tablespoons sugar

1½ tablespoons oat or soy milk powder

1 teaspoon ground flaxseed

1 teaspoon dried Citrus Peel Powder (page 294)

¼ teaspoon baking powder

Pinch of salt

1½ tablespoons olive oil

AT CAMP

Remove the olive oil packets from the bag of dry ingredients and pour into the bag.

Pour ¼ cup of water into the bag and zip the bag closed carefully.

Massage the bag well, taking care not to let it open while you work, until the ingredients are fully combined in a batter.

Ensure that the stove is well stabilized. Set a pot on the stove, then set the foil bowls or cupcake forms in the dry pot. Make sure they are level and stable. If you're having a hard time stabilizing them, crumple another small piece of foil to act as a stand.

Cut a hole in 1 bottom corner of the batter bag or simply open a corner of the ziplock. Pour about half of the batter into each cupcake form.

Carefully fill the pot with the remaining 1 cup of water around the cupcakes to make a steam bath. It should come up no higher than about halfway on the cupcake forms.

Place the lid firmly on the pot and turn the heat on high. Do not peek at the cakes for 5 minutes, or the rising batter will fall.

After 5 minutes, check on the cakes and ensure they are upright and there is still water in the base of the pot. Replace the lid, and continue to cook for about 6 more minutes, until fully cooked through. Check for doneness by pulling the cupcake apart in the center with your spoon. If it isn't fully cooked, liquid will ooze up.

Enjoy hot with a spoon.

> Per serving: 245 calories, 12 g fat, 34 g carbs, 2 g protein
> Weight: 5 ounces, including aluminum foil bowls

Tip: Try swapping out the Citrus Peel Powder for lemon or grapefruit powder. Buy individual olive oil packets to ensure a leakproof experience.

STAPLE RECIPES

Bouillon Powder

nutritional yeast, mushroom powder, turmeric

Makes 1 cup

1 cup nutritional yeast
2 tablespoons salt
1 tablespoon onion powder
1 teaspoon ground turmeric
1 teaspoon celery seed
1 teaspoon mushroom powder
½ teaspoon dried thyme
½ teaspoon dried oregano
½ teaspoon pepper

Using broth in place of water makes almost *everything* taste better. It is most commonly used as a base for soups and stews, but it also can be used with pasta, grains, and casseroles. Broth is made of water, though, so it is heavy and bulky to pack for camping and can spill. Bouillon paste is great, but it generally needs to be refrigerated and can get a bit messy. Bouillon cubes work well in situations requiring nonperishable ingredients, but sometimes one cube is a bit too much for a small recipe and can stubbornly resist dissolving fully.

Here is a powder to solve all of these problems. You can add it directly to a recipe and not worry about clumps. You can use as much or little as you want without having to figure out how to break a cube for small meals. And you can drink a cup of it as a little warm-up if you're feeling depleted. —Emily

AT HOME

Put all of the ingredients in a food processor, spice grinder, or blender and grind into a powder.

Store in an airtight container.

AT CAMP

The ratio for 1 cup of broth is 1¼ teaspoons of Bouillon Powder dissolved in 8 ounces of water.

Tip: We like to keep this in our camp bin and at home all the time, so we can always add a little something extra to a recipe when it's needed.

Bouillon Powder

Nutty Parmesan (page 288)

Nutty Parmesan

nutritional yeast, garlic

Makes about 1 cup

¾ cup almond flour or hemp seeds
¼ cup nutritional yeast
½ teaspoon salt
¼ teaspoon garlic powder

Parmesan or Parmigiano-Reggiano is a staple in many households—whether it's the familiar green can of our childhood or a beautiful wedge straight from Italy. Aged cheeses are the easiest type to carry outdoors, but they're still not nonperishable, and it's no fun to find some soggy cheese at the bottom of the cooler or moldy at the bottom of a bin. This version is shelf-stable, so it can live in a jar in your camp bin at all times. You don't need a food processor to make it, so just pull out a bowl, combine a few simple ingredients, and enjoy it as you always have. —Emily

Combine the almond flour or hemp seeds, nutritional yeast, salt, and garlic powder in a bowl, mix well, and store in a jar or other airtight container.

Cashew Dream Sauce

raw cashews, nutritional yeast, garlic

Makes 2 cups

1 cup raw cashews
1 cup hot water
2 tablespoons nutritional yeast
2 tablespoons fresh lemon juice
2 garlic cloves
1 teaspoon salt

Wes has been vegan for over twenty years; he can barely even remember the taste of real cheese. One time he ordered me a pizza and asked them to put cheddar on it, because he didn't know what was typical. We've done vegan-cheese taste tests, and he always likes the ones that taste least like real cheese. *Not me.* I'm a cheese lover, and that's my explanation (as it is for many others), for why I struggle to fully commit to a dairy-free life. I couldn't stand vegan cheese substitutes and thought there was no hope for me, until I discovered cashew cream. It is the perfect base for so many cheesy things that I now never have to stress if I want nachos or mac and cheese or broccoli cheese soup or . . . also, it's really easy to make! —Emily

AT HOME

Put the cashews, hot water, nutritional yeast, lemon juice, garlic, and salt in a blender and let sit for about 5 minutes.

Blend on high for at least 1 minute, until silky smooth and creamy.

Keep refrigerated until ready to transport in the cooler.

Tip: Do not substitute roasted cashews for this; it won't be as creamy.

Cashew Dream Sauce

Sichuan Chili Oil

Sichuan peppercorns, crushed red pepper flakes, star anise

Makes 2 cups

Cooking time: 15 minutes

6 tablespoons crushed red pepper flakes, divided

½ teaspoon crushed Sichuan peppercorns, divided

¼ cup *whole* Sichuan peppercorns

2 cups neutral oil

4 whole star anise

2 cinnamon sticks

I discovered this versatile chili oil on my quest to create the ultimate plant-based dan dan noodle recipe. It's adapted from a site called *The Woks of Life,* an excellent source for Chinese home cooking recipes. Sichuan peppercorns (also called prickly ash) are known for their tingling or numbing sensation but are not actually spicy in any way. The addition of crushed red pepper flakes in the recipe does add a little heat, but the standout quality of this chili oil is how deeply flavorful it is from the aromatic infusion. I've been making this as a holiday present and constantly get requests (demands?) for refills. I suggest you gift this to yourself and make sure you always have a jar in the fridge. —Mai-Yan

Put 3 tablespoons of the crushed red pepper flakes and ¼ teaspoon of the crushed Sichuan peppercorns into each of 2 (8-ounce) Mason jars.

Put the oil and the whole Sichuan peppercorns, star anise, and cinnamon sticks in a medium pot and heat over medium heat. Let the oil temperature slowly come to 325° F—measure with a candy thermometer. When the temperature is close, you'll see small bubbles starting to form in the oil, typically around the 10-minute mark.

Turn off the heat and let the oil cool slightly for 5 to 7 minutes.

Set a liquid measuring cup on a heatproof surface and strain the oil into it, discarding the aromatics left in the strainer.

Pour the oil into the jars with the crushed red pepper flake mixture and let them cool until the jars can be handled with bare hands. Screw the lids on tightly and keep them refrigerated (up to a year) until ready to use.

Tip: Have this on hand for (Almost) Instant Saucy Noodles (page 175) and Chili Crisp Roasted Nuts (page 135).

Seitan

*vital wheat gluten,
nutritional yeast,
vegetable broth*

Makes 2 (12-ounce) loaves, about 8
servings

Cooking time: 40 minutes

1¼ cups vital wheat gluten
¼ cup nutritional yeast
2 garlic cloves, minced
½ teaspoon salt
½ teaspoon pepper
7 cups vegetable broth, divided
2 tablespoons soy sauce
1 tablespoon olive oil

This recipe is adapted from Wes's delicious homemade Italian-style vegan sausages, which we made for Emily and Wes's camping wedding. Although seitan is not pretty in its dough form, it is extremely versatile and a great source of protein. It easily adapts to different flavor profiles, and it can be sliced thin straight from the pot or pan-fried to get a satisfying crispy texture. Try a hot, hearty sandwich like our Smothered Seitan Sandwich (page 179) or use it to make your own Cracked Pepper Seitan Jerky (page 72). —Mai-Yan

In a large bowl, combine the wheat gluten, nutritional yeast, garlic, salt, and pepper. Mix well.

Add and stir in 1 cup of the vegetable broth along with the soy sauce and olive oil and mix until well combined.

Gently knead the dough in the bowl for 1 minute to help develop the gluten. Set aside.

In a pot over high heat, bring the remaining 6 cups of vegetable broth to a boil.

Divide the dough in half and submerge both halves in the broth. The broth should cover the dough, and there should be enough room for it to move around, as it will expand as it cooks. If the broth isn't covering the dough, add a little water.

Return the broth to a boil, then turn the heat down to low and cover. Simmer for 40 minutes, flipping the seitan over about halfway through. Remove from the heat and let the dough cool in the broth before handling.

Refrigerate up to 5 days (or freeze up to 2 months) in a leakproof container with the vegetable broth it was cooked in until ready to use.

Tip: If you have a pressure cooker, you can steam your seitan in just 1 cup of broth instead of 6. Follow the recipe to make the seitan dough, then add 1 cup of broth to the pressure cooker with the steamer basket in place. Pressure cook for 40 minutes, and naturally release it for 15. Just be aware that if you thought your seitan looked like brains before, it's even more the case when it takes on the shape of the steamer grate.

Seitan

Citrus Peel Powder (page 294)

Citrus Peel Powder

citrus zest and nothing else

Makes 1½ tablespoons

Dehydration time: 3 hours

1 pound citrus fruit (orange, grapefruit, lemon, lime, tangerine, tangelo, mandarin . . .)

When you are blessed with a neighborhood of citrus trees and the fruit ripens, you want to take full advantage. Luckily my kids are great juicers, so my family gets a serious boost of vitamin C for a few months. But that doesn't fully use all of the fruit or satisfy our needs for the rest of the year. This year, I've discovered drying and powdering citrus zest. I got an air fryer/toaster oven/dehydrator machine during quarantine because my oven broke. At first I didn't expect much from the dehydration function, but it really has been delightful to have it available on the countertop. This recipe takes less time than other dehydration recipes and will set you up for citrus happiness year-round. —Emily

AT HOME

Using a vegetable peeler, carefully peel the citrus zest (mainly the colored part, not the white pith) from each piece of fruit.

Lay the pieces on a dehydrator tray or trays in a single layer.

Dehydrate at 135° F for about 3 hours, or until the peels are dry and crackly when you crush them.

Use a spice grinder or blender to grind the citrus peel into a fine powder. Store it in an airtight container.

Chai Sugar

ginger, pepper, cinnamon, cardamom

Makes about 1¼ cups

1 cup coconut sugar
1½ tablespoons ground cardamom
1 tablespoon ground ginger
2 teaspoons ground cinnamon
1 teaspoon pepper
1 teaspoon ground fennel

I had the best chai of my life at a London tea shop a few years ago. The sweetener was coconut sugar, and I think that's the secret. Along with the usual chai spices, it makes for a deeply flavored but not too sweet cup of chai. I've been playing with this recipe for a couple of years, tweaking the proportions of spices to get them just right. Now I use it in everything from the obvious cup of chai, to sprinkling it on buttered toast, to an amazing tahini and chai spiced date shake that Mai-Yan showed me how to make. It's the main ingredient in our Chai Oatmeal (page 232) and Iced Oat Chai Latte (page 199), and a good thing to keep around for any other great ideas you may come up with. —Aimee

Add the coconut sugar, cardamom, ginger, cinnamon, pepper, and fennel to a mixing bowl or Mason jar. Stir until well combined.

Store tightly covered for up to a month.

Tip: To make a big cup of chai, brew 1 to 2 black tea bags (I use 2 because I like my chai strong) in 1 cup water. Stir in 2 to 3 teaspoons of Chai Sugar and about ⅓ cup hot oat milk.

Just Add Water Pancake Mix

soy milk powder, vanilla powder, potato starch

Makes 6 cups pancake mix, about 24 (5-inch) pancakes

At-camp cooking time: 4 to 5 minutes per pancake

PANCAKE MIX

4 cups all-purpose flour

¾ cup soy milk powder

½ cup potato starch

½ cup sugar

3 tablespoons baking powder

2 teaspoons vanilla powder (*optional*)

1½ teaspoons salt

TO MAKE ABOUT 6 5-INCH PANCAKES

1½ cups pancake mix

1-1¼ cups water

Cooking spray, neutral oil, or plant butter

Finding a plant-based pancake mix at the grocery store seems to be pretty hit or miss, and they don't always taste the best. Here's a simple mix that you can keep in your pantry at home or in your camping bin. To make it at camp, you just need to add water, and it's super versatile. Pack a small portion for a backpacking trip, or bring the whole batch with all the toppings for a large crowd on a car camping trip. This is the mix we used to create the Caramelized Banana Pancakes (page 123) and the Citrus Poppy Seed Pancakes (page 220). —Aimee

AT HOME

Combine the flour, soy milk powder, potato starch, sugar, baking powder, vanilla powder, and salt in a large resealable container or ziplock bag. Mix everything together well.

AT CAMP

In a medium bowl, stir together 1½ cups of the pancake mix with 1 to 1¼ cups of water, depending on how thick you like your pancakes. Mix well, but don't worry if there are some lumps.

Heat a griddle or skillet over medium heat. Spray with cooking spray or melt a little butter in the skillet.

Pour about ⅓ cup of pancake batter onto the hot skillet. Cook until bubbles form on the pancake and the bottom is golden brown. Flip the pancake and continue cooking until the second side is golden brown.

APPENDIX

SAMPLE MENUS

It can feel a little daunting to figure out a whole meal with so many appealing recipes at your fingertips. Here are some pairings we hope will inspire you for your trip-planning endeavors. In some cases, you will notice menus are created from multiple sections of the book and even use store-bought elements to help round out a meal. Customize these menus to suit your unique outdoor experiences.

Campfire Birthday Bash

Camping trips are a great opportunity to celebrate special occasions. Do most of the cooking around the campfire while catching up with friends, and surprise everyone with a delicious cake straight out of the cooler.

- Campfire Party Chickpeas (page 146)
- Orange Mojitos (page 204)
- Butter with a Side of Vegetables (page 163)
- Mushroom Pilaf (page 160)
- Grilled veggie sausages
- S'mores Cooler Cake (page 209)

Get-Up-and-Go Breakfast

Sometimes there's only time to make a cup of coffee before heading out for your day trip. Planning ahead and preparing a few things for breakfast that can be eaten when you get there makes this no big deal—you just have to remember to grab them on your way out!

- Coffee
- Tropical Yogurt Bowls (page 113)
- Almond Butter Granola Brittle (page 75)

Leisurely Last Day Breakfast

The last day of a camping trip is all about getting ready to head back home. Make the most of the morning at camp and linger over breakfast. Use up any leftover pieces of firewood to toast bread and make plans for your next trip.

- Autumn-Spiced Fig Jam Toast (page 121)
- Smoky SoCal Hash (page 124)
- Fresh fruit salad

Picnic Social

Sometimes the best way to get together with friends is a simple picnic at a local park. Ideally,

you can schedule it for after you've baked one hundred mini chocolate chip cookies you're looking to share (or save yourself from). Have your friends bring blankets and accompaniments to complete the picnic.

- Winter Vegetable Platter (page 71)
- Herby Red Lentil Spread with crackers (page 74)
- Crunchy Chocolate Chip Cookies (page 79)
- Iced Oat Chai Latte (page 199)

Hike-a-Lunch

It's Day 1 of a five-day backpacking trip and it's time to stop at the first waterfall for lunch. You have your last fresh, bulky meal in the brain of your backpack since it doesn't need to fit in the bear canister. Enjoy every last bite before transitioning to dehydrated fare for the rest of the trip.

- Lemony Dill Chickpea Salad Sandwiches (page 88)
- Nacho Kale Chips (page 67)
- Pistachio Date Balls (page 78)

Backcountry Breakfast

It's sometimes hard to justify the time needed for a hot breakfast on a backpacking trip, but if you're setting the stove up to boil water anyway, throwing a skillet over the flame for a "hot minute" isn't much more effort.

- Golden Milk (page 268)
- Power Biscotti (page 86)
- Socca Tortilla (page 234)

Southern Feast

You're planning to spend a lot of days off the grid this season in your adventure vehicle. You've packed some meals in your camp bin and just spotted some great produce at a roadside stand. This menu mixes nonperishables with fresh seasonal fare, allowing you to feast wherever your adventure takes you.

- Fried Pickles (page 149)
- Dirty Rice and Beans (page 173)
- Mac and Cheese (page 250)
- Sautéed greens
- Mixed Berry Crisp (page 274)

FUROSHIKI WRAPPING TUTORIAL

Reducing disposable waste is an important step in lessening our environmental impact. It can be tempting to try out all of the new reusable products on the market, but they aren't always satisfying replacements. This furoshiki method is inexpensive, practical, *and* beautiful, using commonly found household items. We're providing directions for sandwich wrapping here, but the technique can be used to wrap anything, from burritos to holiday gifts.

Directions:

STEP 1. PREWRAP YOUR SANDWICH IN A PIECE OF PARCHMENT PAPER

1. Lay out an approximately 1-foot-by-1-foot sheet of parchment paper diagonally on a flat surface. Place the sandwich in the center, with the top and bottom edges parallel to the surface edge rather than the parchment paper.
2. Pull the bottom corner up and over the sandwich.
3. Fold both sides of the parchment over the sandwich, following the straight edge across the bottom. You should now have what looks like an open envelope.
4. Fold the top corner down past the bottom edge of the sandwich and tuck the point into the fold that was created by folding over the sides.

Step 1

Step 2

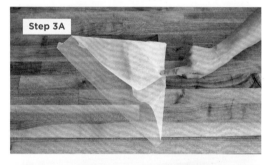

Step 3A

Step 3B

Step 4

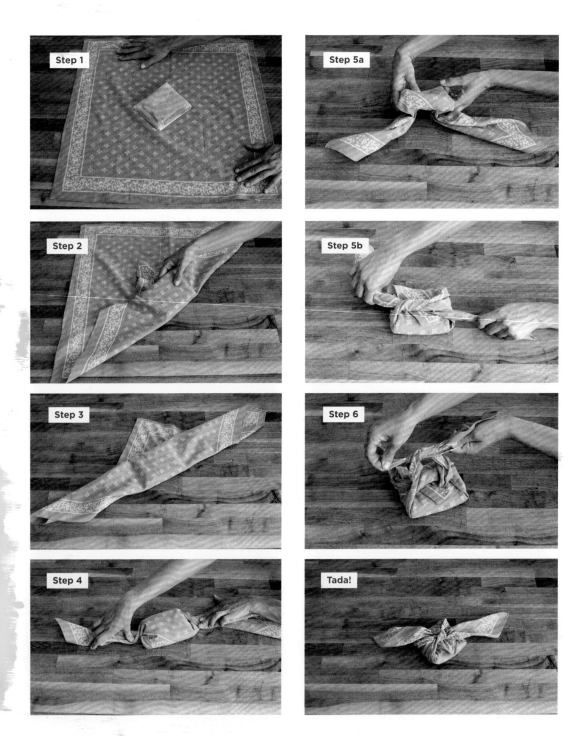

1. Place a bandana with the pattern side face down diagonally on a flat surface. Place the parchment-wrapped sandwich in the center of the bandana, with the bottom edge parallel to the surface edge rather than the bandana, just as you did with the parchment paper.
2. Fold the bottom corner of the bandana up over the sandwich and tuck it down around the top edge of the sandwich.
3. Roll the sandwich toward the top corner of the bandana until it is fully rolled up, leaving the top corner pointing up and lying flat on the surface.
4. Pinch the edges of each long side in toward the center of each side of the sandwich to narrow the width and close them up, similar to a paper-rolled candy.
5. Tuck the long ends under the sandwich, flip it over, and tie with an overhand knot. The knot will now be the top of the package.
6. Tie another knot in the opposite direction as the first (creating a square knot) and pack in your backpack.

LOG CABIN CAMPFIRE TUTORIAL

There are many ways to build a fire, but we love the log cabin campfire structure for campfire cooking. It is easy to build the same way each time and it allows enough airflow to keep the fire growing without much finagling. The key is to spend time setting up your structure before lighting it and having a back stock of kindling nearby just in case. Remember to use only downed wood (if permitted) or locally purchased wood.

Directions:

1. Start by gathering a nest of tinder in the center of your campfire. This should be rather large, so you don't have to keep adding to it after the fire is lit.
2. Place two pieces of kindling parallel to one another on either end of the tinder pile. Place two more pieces of kindling across those two, forming a square around the tinder pile.

Step 1

Step 2

Step 3

Step 4

3. Continue in this pattern, adding to the top/bottom sides and then to the left/right sides with kindling pieces, forming a log cabin structure that has air gaps between all of the pieces of kindling. The pile should measure 6 to 8 inches tall when it's finished.

4. To light the fire, stick a long lighter or match into the tinder pile through a gap in the log cabin or straight down from the top. If done correctly with dry wood, your log cabin should light evenly and without any manipulation.

5. Once the kindling is sufficiently burning, carefully place one or two fuel logs across the top. If you're concerned about collapse, angle them tepee style to allow the log cabin to remain intact.

6. Add more fuel logs as needed after the first have firmly caught on fire.

CAMPFIRE COMPONENTS

Tinder: Tinder is the spark that will get the fire going. Good examples of tinder include dry pine needles, cardboard, paper towels, and tiny sticks. These pieces should catch on fire with ease, but won't hold a flame for very long. Their purpose is to light the kindling.

Kindling: Kindling is made up of thin sticks that range in thickness from the size of a pencil to a small forearm. Start with the smaller pieces at the bottom for a log cabin structure. Kindling should hold onto the flame long enough to get the fuel logs to catch on fire.

Fuel: Time for the big logs! Any type of wood works as fuel as long as it has been dried out (seasoned) sufficiently. Soft wood catches more quickly than hard wood and so builds embers faster. As a result, soft wood won't last as long, so you'll need more of it. Hard wood takes longer to start, but produces better coals and less smoke. If you have the choice, use a mix of both soft and hard woods.

DUTCH OVEN BAKING CHART

Dutch Oven Size		BAKING TEMPERATURE (°F)					
		325°	350°	375°	400°	425°	450°
		Number of Charcoals Needed*					
8"	TOTAL	15	16	17	18	19	20
	On Lid	10	11	11	12	13	14
	Bottom	5	5	6	6	6	6
10"	TOTAL	19	21	23	25	27	29
	On Lid	13	14	16	17	18	19
	Bottom	6	7	7	8	9	10
12"	TOTAL	23	25	27	29	31	33
	On Lid	16	17	18	19	21	22
	Bottom	7	8	9	10	10	11
14"	TOTAL	30	32	34	36	38	40
	On Lid	20	21	22	24	25	26
	Bottom	10	11	12	12	13	14

Based on standard-size charcoal briquettes.

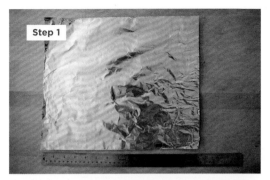

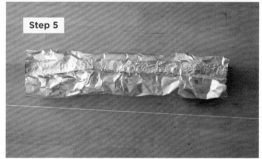

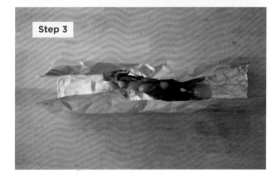

FOIL POUCH TUTORIAL

Many of our campfire recipes require cooking in an aluminum foil pouch. It's simple, and there are no dishes to deal with after the meal. The key to making a good foil pouch is to have plenty of foil—more than you think you will need. Make sure there is ample room around the contents of the pouch so heat can build up inside the pouch, creating a mini-oven. If you skimp, the worst can happen: an overfilled foil pouch bursting open as you are handling it. Don't be responsible for ruining dinner!

Basics:

- You'll need a minimum length of 12 inches of foil to make a proper foil pouch

- Splurge on the heavy-duty aluminum foil. It's worth it!
- Use long-handled tongs to transfer foil pouches in and out of the fire.

Directions:

1. Find a flat surface to work on and pull out a sheet of foil at least 12 inches long.
2. Place the food right in the center of the foil. Add oil and seasonings if you haven't already done so.
3. Grasp the two long edges of foil and bring them together in the center above the food. (If your piece of foil is more like a square, choose the side that is facing you, to keep things simple.)
4. Fold the edges down, creating a small overlap, about ½ inch, along the entire length of the foil. Make sure there is room between the food and the foil (1½ to 2 inches) so heat can build up inside the packet.
5. Fold the joined edges over so the seam lies flat on top of the foil pouch. The top of the foil pouch should now be sealed, leaving two open short edges.
6. At each end, press the short edges together and fold over once to create another ½-inch overlap. Again, make sure there is plenty of room between the food and the edge of the foil.
7. Fold the end with the overlap over so it lies flat on top of the foil pouch. The foil packet should now be tightly sealed on all sides and stay closed when you handle it.
8. Handle the foil pouch along the folded edges (where there are several layers of foil) rather than the middle (where the foil can easily tear with a jab from your tongs).

Tips for adding food to the pouch: Plan to add all of your contents at once, since it is not easy to open the pouch multiple times during the cooking process. Choose items that don't require a lot of stirring. Also, expect a little char. Since this material is one of the thinnest options, the food will cook quickly and probably a little unevenly unless you move it around consistently. That's OK, and adds a lot of flavor to foods like roasted peppers or chicken. Enjoy the campfire flavor!

FOIL BOWL TUTORIAL

Origami craft time! It is really easy to make a foil bowl and should take you five minutes, tops. This is used in making our delicious Orange Olive Oil Cakes (page 283), and it's a handy trick to have in your back pocket when you need a bowl in a pinch (say, when you're enjoying trail mix but don't want to spill, or when sharing your water with the dog).

Directions:

1. Cut a length of foil roughly equal to the height of the sheet, aiming for as close to a square as possible.
2. Fold the foil in half, corner to corner, to make a triangle.
3. Fold the top corner of the triangle down so the right edges meet the bottom edge. Press down to crease, then unfold.
4. Fold the bottom-right corner up so its tip meets the left edge of the foil at the creased line.
5. Next, fold the bottom-left corner up so it meets the corner you just created.
6. Fold the top flap down toward you. Fold the other flap down to the back side.

If you're prepping this at home, leave the bowl flat until you're ready to use it, and make sure to pack it in a spot where it won't get ripped.

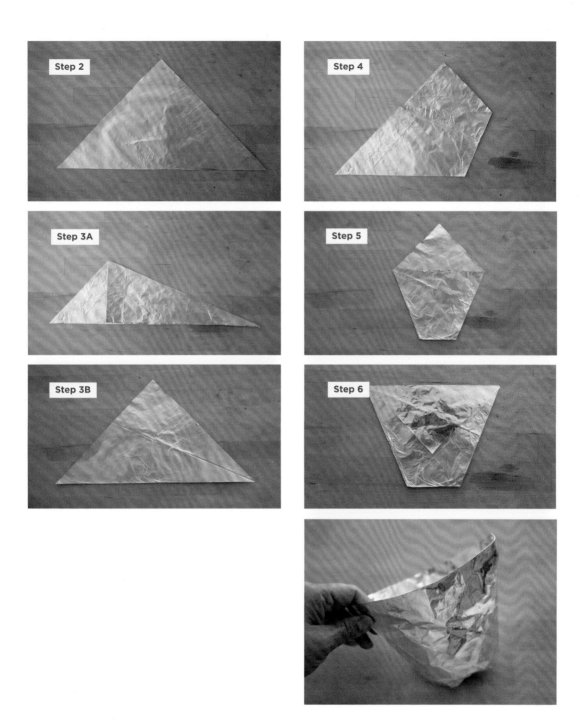

BACKCOUNTRY RECIPE INFORMATION GUIDE

BACKCOUNTRY RECIPES	TYPE	CALORIES*	FAT (g)	CARBS (g)	PROTEIN (g)	WEIGHT**	DEHYDRATE***
Backcountry Tofu Scramble	Breakfast	363	22	17	22	4 oz	•
Bacon Grits and Greens	Breakfast	391	13	52	23	11 oz	•
Chai Oatmeal	Breakfast	345	11	54	10	5 oz	
Citrus Poppy Seed Pancakes	Breakfast	570	11	104	14	11 oz	
Mochi Pancake Sandwiches	Breakfast	623	20	99	8	12 oz	
Mushroom Congee	Breakfast	453	9	73	19	8 oz	•
Socca Tortilla	Breakfast	369	17	42	11	11 oz	
Toasted Oat Muesli	Breakfast	482	26	53	12	10 oz	
Backpacker's Samosas	Main	460	15	39	11	10 oz	
Butter Chicken	Main	321	20	25	14	5 oz	•
Cacio e Pepe	Main	429	17	54	18	9 oz	
Cauliflower Potato Soup	Main	482	13	74	25	6 oz	•
Creamy Pasta e Fagioli	Main	422	12	67	14	7 oz	
Enfrijoladas	Main	420	9	72	18	16 oz	•
French Dip Sandwiches	Main	411	6	71	24	12 oz	•
Japanese Curry Crunchwraps	Main	454	14	55	12	11 oz	
Kitchadi	Main	396	7	67	15	8 oz	
Korean Soft Tofu Stew	Main	148	6	10	15	14 oz	

BACKCOUNTRY RECIPES	TYPE	CALORIES*	FAT (g)	CARBS (g)	PROTEIN (g)	WEIGHT**	DEHYDRATE***
Mac and Cheese	Main	403	11	50	18	8 oz	
Matzo Ball Soup	Main	246	2	53	5	5 oz	
Restorative Noodle Soup	Main	478	11	65	33	10 oz	
Saag Tofu	Main	589	26	72	25	6 oz	•
Southern Barbecue Feast	Main	515	9	96	3	10 oz	•
Walnut Crumble Pasta	Main	678	34	79	20	12 oz	
Champurrado de Café	Drink	181	1	42	3	3 oz	
Golden Milk	Drink	163	6	24	5	3 oz	
Spicy Margarita Shot	Drink	n/a	n/a	n/a	n/a	6 oz	
Tahini Hot Chocolate	Drink	202	14	25	8	3 oz	
Whiskey Sour	Drink	n/a	n/a	n/a	n/a	3 oz	
Chocolate Raspberry Tart	Dessert	357	21	39	4	5 oz	
Mango Tapioca Pudding	Dessert	340	7	71	1	8 oz	
Mixed Berry Crisp	Dessert	495	12	94	5	7 oz	
Orange Olive Oil Cakes	Dessert	245	12	34	2	5 oz	
Orangesicle Chia Pudding	Dessert	410	26	37	8	5 oz	
Speculoos Coffee Pudding Parfait	Dessert	260	8	43	8	6 oz	

* Calorie information is per serving. Recipes are designed for 2 servings.
** Weight includes packaging using typical ziplock bags. Quantity of bags used per recipe varies.
*** For instances where the recipe is designed to be dehydrated as an entire meal and no store-bought equivalents exist.

INDEX

ABOUT *dirty* GOURMET

Aimee, Emily, and Mai-Yan started *Dirty Gourmet* in 2010 as a blog to document years of outdoor cooking created from their past experiences. The blog's success led to a colorful array of projects with outdoor industry leaders like REI and *Sunset* magazine, including catered camping trips, product testing, modeling, and outdoor cooking workshops. We have taken vans full of camp-kitchen gear and food all over the United States, to the tops of mountains, deep into backcountry valleys, and even out to remote islands. We've cooked for groups of hundreds of people, taking care to accommodate the nutritional needs of all, no matter the weather or lack of amenities available. These experiences have shaped who we've become as cooks and outdoorists, and we continue to love every minute of learning and growing with fellow explorers.

We have always aimed to encourage new and experienced outdoor enthusiasts to make food an inspirational part of their trips rather than an afterthought. We *still* believe that every adventure should include food that is nourishing and comforting, no matter the trip or the nutritional requirements. Food can seem like a wall too high to climb when planning an adventure, and our goal is to be a trusted resource to get everyone over that wall and out into nature.

We are excited to see more and more people taking up outdoor recreation as a regular pastime. Though this creates new concerns for the health of the environment, it has always been our stance that motivation to protect

the natural world starts mainly with people who are personally attached to it. The more people cramming themselves together at campgrounds and on trails, the more likely it is that the need to preserve the holistic well-being of those spaces will become a mainstream cause. We're all on this journey together, and jumping in to "get dirty" is the best way to learn.

Learn more at dirtygourmet .com and find us on Instagram: @dirtygourmet.

ABOUT THE AUTHORS

EMILY NIELSON

My first real experience in the outdoor industry was an Outward Bound trip in North Carolina when I was fifteen. Though I'd been camping with my family my whole life, this trip taught me that firsthand experience with the outdoors was a big part of why anyone would be interested in protecting it. I was an extremely shy kid, and I gained a sense of self-confidence and self-reliance that I didn't think I had in me.

I have worked in the outdoor industry my entire working life because of that trip, including outdoor experiential education, retail gear sales, and fieldwork. My favorite outdoor activities are rock climbing, hiking, and skiing, and I'm always finding tricks to make cooking for these activities quick and delicious. This has been an especially important talent since 2019, when Wes and I adopted three little adventurers (Anastasia, Aisla, and Mojave) to come on all our trips with us. Their journey from daily fast-food hamburgers when we met them to living in our vegetarian household was tough at first, but they are now an inspiration to picky eaters and vegetable haters everywhere. Reach Emily at emily@dirtygourmet.com

AIMEE TRUDEAU

I started cooking when I was a young teenager. I used to read my mom's *Bon Appetit* magazines after school and then cook elaborate meals for dinner while my folks were still at work. My obses-

sion with food continued into college, where I studied Family and Consumer Sciences (Home Ec!), with a specialization in Food Science.

Our family went camping nearly every weekend when I was growing up, and some of my earliest memories involve watching coffee percolate on a camp stove. We always ate well on our family camping trips, even though the meals were simple and familiar. Once I started camping as an adult, I began to experiment with more interesting food. Four months of bike touring really made my cooking creative, and it opened my eyes to how different the food I was making was compared to other campers I met.

My husband, Kismat, and our kids, Asha and Ravi, have been vegan for about seven years. We are a homeschooling family, and I enjoy sharing my interests in dehydrating, baking, and fermenting with my kids as part of our school days. Reach Aimee at aimee@dirtygourmet.com

MAI-YAN KATHERINE KWAN

I grew up in Quebec City, Canada, the product of Chinese and French Canadian parents. Both cultures are very food-centric, which helped develop my palate early on. My first experiences outdoors were at my grandparents' house in the countryside. The nearby forest and river became my personal sanctuary, fostering a great sense of play and adventure.

When I moved to California, more than twenty years ago, to attend art school, the climate and cuisine were a revelation. The freshness and year-round availability of produce expanded my cooking arena, and my thinking about food turned more serious. I became more intimate with my Chinese culture while cooking meals alongside my grandma and dad. At the same time, I started formalizing my love for the outdoors. I rediscovered camping and became an avid backpacker and cyclist.

Recent adventures include walking all fifty-two secret stair walks in Los Angeles, kayak camping on Catalina Island, and bike touring with my husband, Daniel, and fur baby, Pogo. Reach Mai-Yan at mai-yan@dirtygourmet.com

ABOUT SKIPSTONE

Skipstone is an imprint of independent, nonprofit publisher Mountaineers Books. It features thematically related titles that promote a deeper connection to our natural world through sustainable practice and backyard activism. Our readers live smart, play well, and typically engage with the community around them. Skipstone guides explore healthy lifestyles and how an outdoor life relates to the well-being of our planet, as well as of our own neighborhoods. Sustainable foods and gardens; healthful living; realistic and doable conservation at home; modern aspirations for community—Skipstone tries to address such topics in ways that emphasize active living, local and grassroots practices, and a small footprint.

Our hope is that Skipstone books will inspire you to effect change without losing your sense of humor, to celebrate the freedom and generosity of a life outdoors, and to move forward with gentle leaps or breathtaking bounds.

All of our publications, as part of our 501(c)(3) nonprofit program, are made possible through the generosity of donors and through sales of 700 titles on outdoor recreation, sustainable lifestyle, and conservation. To donate, purchase books, or learn more, visit us online:

SKIPSTONE
LIVE LIFE
MAKE RIPPLES

www.skipstonebooks.org
www.mountaineersbooks.org

YOU MAY ALSO LIKE

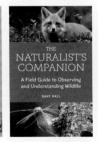